PRISONER OF INFINITY

PRISONER OF INFINITY
UFOs, Social Engineering, and the Psychology of Fragmentation

Jasun Horsley

AEON

First published in 2018 by
Aeon Books Ltd
12 New College Parade
Finchley Road
London NW3 5EP

British Library Cataloguing in Publication Data

A C.I.P. for this book is available from the British Library

ISBN-13: 978-1-91159-705-6

Typeset by Medlar Publishing Solutions Pvt Ltd, India

www.aeonbooks.co.uk

"What we see enacted on the stage of world history happens also to the individual. The child is guided by the power of the parents as by a higher destiny. But as he grows up, the struggle between his infantile attitude and his increasing consciousness begins. The parental influence, dating from the early infantile period, is repressed and sinks into the unconscious, but is not eliminated; by invisible threads it directs the apparently individual workings of the maturing mind. Like everything that has fallen into the unconscious, the infantile situation still sends up dim, premonitory feelings, feelings of being secretly guided by otherworldly influences."

—Carl Jung, *Aspects of the Masculine*

"I can see the claustrophobia that would attend to the realization that one was trapped in an infinity that could never be escaped. In fact, I can feel it. It's a little like being in a room you can never leave, or a prison."

—Whitley Strieber, *Solving the Communion Enigma*

"So long as the overwhelming event is at least slightly larger than the soul's capacity to absorb it, it will be construed as infinite."

—Greg Mogenson, *A Most Accursed Religion: When a Trauma Becomes God*

For W., the canary in the coal mine.

With thanks to M*, the Eurydice of my Underworld.

CONTENTS

Trigger Warning: This book includes an ongoing investigation into my own past, specifically the "lost years" between birth and (roughly) the age of seven. It's possible this entails suppressed memories of sexual abuse, as well as what has been termed "alien abduction." If so, some of this material might prove disturbing for readers who have had, or may have had, similar experiences.

ACKNOWLEDGEMENTS

This book, though one work with a single voice, is largely the result of dialogues. It has come about through exchanges with *other parties*, exchanges that intensified my interest in, and deepened my commitment to, getting to grips with this material. These exchanges began long before I started the book. They began when I first read Whitley Strieber's *Communion* and found his accounts "dialoguing" with my own beliefs, dreams, and memories. Strieber was the original snowflake that started the ball rolling, and since there would be no exploration without that initial impetus, my first thanks must go to him.

Strieber has resisted my attempts at having an actual dialogue with him, and what little he has communicated to me over the years suggests he does not support this present work. Interestingly, much of my inspiration for this book has been ostensibly *adversarial*. I first wrote about Strieber in 2008, and again in 2010, and it was an online attack on me by the (now defunct) "Mother-strangled" website (that was also analyzing Strieber's work) that first prompted me to take another, closer look at Strieber, in 2013.

My contact with Jeffrey J. Kripal sparked the thesis (and first chapter) of this book, and once again I found myself in opposition to Kripal's views. Ditto, to a lesser extent, with the feedback of Peter Levenda, whose attempts to refute my arguments about alien abduction, annoying as they were, helped me to fine-tune them.

The main dialoguer-contributor was my wife. She read each installment as I wrote it and invariably sent numerous articles and book citations to deepen, expand, or explode points I was addressing. More than any other single factor, her *musings* led to the size and scope of the present work.

Thanks also to those who read early drafts of the book and participated in dialogues for the *Crucial Fictions* podcast: Phil Snyder, Keith Zavatski, Sleepy Tim, Doug Lain, Julian West, and, later on, Louis Proud and Mark Ehrman. Also thanks to Ty Brown for his groundbreaking research, and to LilyPat for her inside view of "the Honey Pot." There are others whose attention and interest helped keep this snowball rolling, and I offer both thanks and apologies to all those I have not named.

Lastly, my thanks to Gary Heidt, an anomaly among agents, and to Rod Tweedy and Aeon for having the courage of conviction to midwife this strange hybrid life-form into literary (and literal) existence, and risk the wrath of our overlords.

Jasun Horsley, 2017

Quotes from the following works are reproduced by permission:
Communion: A True Story, by Whitley Strieber, 1987 from Souvenir Press.

Psychic Research: A Challenge to Science, by Edgar Mitchell, from Cosimo Books, 2011.

Aspects of the Masculine (2015) by C. G. Jung, and *The Inner World of Trauma* (1996), by Donald Kalsched, both from Routledge, reproduced by permission of Taylor & Francis Books UK.

US rights for *Aspects of the Masculine*, 1989, Princeton University Press.

Excerpt from pp. 80–81 from *The True Believer* by Eric Hoffer. Copyright 1951 by Eric Hoffer, copyright renewed 1979. Reprinted by permission of HarperCollins Publishers.

Excerpts from *The Super Natural: A New Vision of the Unexplained* by Whitley Strieber and Jeffrey J. Kripal, copyright © 2016 by Walker & Collier, Inc. and Jeffrey J. Kripal. Used by permission of Tarcher, an imprint of Penguin Publishing Group, a division of Penguin Random House LLC. All rights reserved.

Conditioned to believe

"Is it possible for us to actually disappear into our own imagination?"

—Whitley Strieber, 1988

First up, for the unfamiliar reader, a few words about the principal (human) subject of this book. Whitley Strieber was born in San Antonio in 1945, of German descent. He went to Catholic school. He studied at the University of Texas, London Film School, and London School of Economics. He somehow managed to graduate from all three in 1968 (an especially mysterious year in Strieber's life, as we will see). He studied at the Gurdjieff Foundation and entered the world of New York advertising in the early 1970s. A press kit for his 1990 novel *Majestic* said: "Before he became a writer Strieber worked first in the newspaper business, then in the film business and finally in the advertising industry, leaving in 1978 as a vice president." 1978 was the year he published his first novel, *The Wolfen*, which became a best-seller and was turned into a Hollywood movie in 1981, the year he published *The Hunger* (which also became a Hollywood movie). Both books were about a hidden, supernatural, highly intelligent predator that sees humans as its rightful prey.

Strieber's younger brother, Richard, had by then become a lawyer, like their father Karl. Though Strieber was successful, he turned his back on his worldly career to dedicate himself to (what I can only assume was) his passion, and returned to the world of the imagination. (I say returned because, according to Strieber, he wrote his first story when he was six—it was about the Moon.) By 1983, with the release of *The Hunger* film (with David Bowie), he was at the top of his game as an author of horror fiction. His follow-up novels, *Black Magic* (about government attempts to harness psychic energy) and *The Night Church* (about a satanic cult), were less successful, and in 1984 he entered into quasi-nonfiction terrain with *Warday* (written with James Kunetka), about the aftermath of nuclear war. In an article he wrote for MUFON in 1986, "My Experience with the Visitors," Strieber drew a clear line between his two types of writing: "Before *Warday* I published four entertainment novels ... While these were horror novels, I have certainly never been a believer in the occult. My important books concern problems of the real world and are based on carefully researched fact."

The reason Strieber was writing for MUFON was this: In 1986, he released his most famous and successful book, *Communion: A True Story*. The book recounts Strieber's alleged experiences of alien abduction that began (consciously) in late 1985, though in the book and its many sequels he claims to have experienced alien contact throughout his life, starting in his early childhood, but to have suppressed all memory of it until the breakthrough event of 1985. As a result of this breakthrough event, Strieber-the-writer was propelled headlong (literally screaming) into the chapel perilous of fantastic nonfiction, a rarified domain he shared with Carlos Castaneda but precious few others. At this time, the line he had drawn between his "entertainment [horror] novels" and his "important, carefully researched" books was effectively erased. Strieber's horror fiction spilled over into his life, and his life turned into a nonfiction horror novel—literally.

While *Communion* turned out to be his most financially successful work ever (Strieber allegedly received a million dollar advance for it), it came at a considerable cost to his reputation. A popular horror writer whose sales are flagging and who comes out with an incredible, horrifying account of alien contact—insisting it is a *true* story—is inevitably going to be met with a degree of skepticism, even hostility. But Strieber's dilemma went even deeper than that of a writer's potential ostracization. He was (by his own account at least) presented with the most disturbing dilemma a writer can face: the possibility that, by writing about these experiences, he was unleashing a terrifying reality into the world, and into his own life.

In 1988, he asked an interviewer:

> What have I done? Have I conjured something, in effect by occult means, by writing these books or …? I mean sometimes I have the feeling they're like breaking through—that I've opened a door that is supposed to remain closed, that they're just sort of coming through it like a bunch of, you know, like they're hungry little monsters; and at other times I feel like it's an absolutely wonderful thing that's happened. I just don't know what exactly [sic] the direction to go. (Blackmore & Curtis, 1988)

Like Robert Louis Stevenson and his Brownies—who brought him not just nightmares but the tale of *Dr. Jekyll and Mr. Hyde* to keep the bankers at bay[1]—Strieber seems to have felt torn down the middle, as the same force that provided him with his livelihood also threatened to devour him. Whether that force is that of his own imagination or of something greater and more autonomous—and to what extent there is a measurable difference—is one of the primary questions this present work will explore. Strieber, in any event, seems to have reconciled this tension by embracing the role of spokesperson for another world (and its apparent inhabitants), and to have successfully created a ministry by which to spread his own gospel of contact.

In his introduction to *Solving the Communion Enigma*, Strieber complains about being "absurdly … labeled as an advocate of alien contact" (2011a, p. 2). Later, he writes, "Had I known what I know now, I would never have allowed [*Communion*] to have been published with a cover that telegraphed the idea that it was about alien contact. My life is not about alien contact. It is about contact with a greater humanity" (2011a, p. 201). Yet despite his insistences, he devotes almost 100 pages (from chapters 5 to 11, including Part Two, "The Extreme Strangeness of the Evidence") to discussing UFO phenomena *in the context of a "hypothetical model" of an extraterrestrial species interacting with our planet*. Admittedly, he is only using it as a framing device; he never states that he *believes* the visitors are extraterrestrial (he actually states the opposite several times, elsewhere in the book). But why choose a hypothesis that can only reinforce the idea of alien contact in readers' minds, and then complain about being associated with such an idea?

*

In *Modern Man in Search of a Soul*, C. G. Jung writes, "It should be said in passing that unconscious contents are by no means exclusively such as were once conscious and, by being repressed, have later grown into unconscious complexes. Quite otherwise, the unconscious has contents peculiar to itself which, slowly growing upward from the depths, at last come into consciousness."

It has often been noted how specific elements of UFO experiences frequently appear first in fiction, only later to emerge as (alleged) fact. I think this relates to the UFO as a *crucial* fiction, that is, a way for the collective psyche to deal with the unknown, by turning it into something familiar, using familiar images, words, concepts, and beliefs. These fictions then become "real," in a partial sense, because *they generate their own evidence.*

UFO lore as we know it began at least as far back as the 1940s, meaning there are almost no researchers or experiencers today who didn't grow up in a cultural milieu suffused with such lore, via movies, comic books, TV shows, coffee mugs, stuffed toys, pop songs, etc., etc. We belong to those generations which have been conditioned to believe (or at the very least, to *want* to believe) in the UFO; even those who disbelieve in it disbelieve in something they once believed in, as kids—i.e., the idea that UFOs are physical craft from elsewhere, etc., etc.

Insofar as it acts as a surrogate for real knowledge and understanding, belief in anything at all is an obstacle to truth.

I was first drawn all the way into UFO-land by Whitley Strieber's 1987 book *Communion*. That led me to John Keel and Jacques Vallee and eventually to my own apparent quasi-memories of alien contact. There was even a period in which I may have believed, or at least suspected, that the "beings" in question were of extraterrestrial origin. It's hard to say what I believed because, as I say, belief doesn't take hold of us consciously, by choice, but through conditioning and as a response to deep (unconscious) psychological needs. We might even deduce that the only reason we believe anything is out of a need to do so. If so, then the degree to which we are unconscious of that need determines the degree to which we are enslaved to our beliefs, in other words, the degree to which we take them as certainty, as "fact."

At one time in my life I needed to believe in UFOs and aliens as having some sort of "out there" existence that would someday transform my own existence from the mundane into something more magical—and which, to that extent, was already doing so (by promising to do so). In later life, probably around the time I turned forty (which Jung marks as the time in which our attention should naturally move from the outer world to the inner), I became less and less interested in UFOs and aliens as an "out there" thing, without losing interest in the psychological implications of my belief in them, and even the (I think irrefutable) psychic reality of people's experiences. That was the time, not coincidentally, that I wrote my first study of Whitley Strieber, in 2008.

You might say that, ever since I first let the UFO into my life (into my imagination), I have been struggling to come to terms with it, to find common ground where the alien and I could meet and make peace. I believe I have finally found this ground, and, perhaps no surprise, it's the ground that was always there: the ground of the psyche and of my own body.

My position is now both complicated (many-faceted) and very simple: The UFO, in all its manifestations, emerges from the human psyche itself, and, in secondary but no less significant ways, in and through the body. This is not to dismiss the UFO or alien abductions as mere fantasy, however (or even phantasy), because my understanding more and more is that the psyche and the body are the twin poles of human existence, and that, to a certain extent, *everything* emerges through them. C. G. Jung makes this point emphatically in *Modern Man in Search of the Soul*:

> Does there exist for the psyche anything which we may call "illusion"? What we are pleased to call such may be for the psyche a most important factor of life—something as indispensable as oxygen for the organism—a psychic actuality of prime importance. Presumably the psyche does not trouble itself about our categories of reality, and it would therefore be the better part of wisdom for us to say: everything that acts is actual. (1933, pp. 72–73)

The UFO, by its nature, is a riddle that, like the existence of God, has driven men and women to the edges of sanity to find an answer. This is why I think it's worth giving our special attention—not as a scientific question so much as *a psychological and philosophic one.*

Elsewhere in the same work, Jung makes the point that it's impossible to understand dream content without being familiar with the daily circumstances of the dreamer. While the symbols that emerge from the unconscious have some degree of universal meaning, they also adapt themselves to fit the conscious awareness of the dreamer. In other words, *consciousness is the context—the only one we have—for interpreting the unconscious.* I'd suggest the same of the UFO: that it can't be approached separately from the circumstances and personality of the experiencer whose life it has entered into and/or emerged from. Generally, UFO researchers assume that the UFO represents a cosmic, universal phenomenon that is wholly external, rather than allowing it to (also) be an individual and *internal* event, one that can't be separated from the inner and outer life of the experiencer—any more than an animal can truly be studied outside of *its* natural environment.

This idea, though it might seem radical, doesn't actually go against even a more conventional view of the "alien" as an actual other, "out there," because many abduction reports (and the nature of the phenomenon itself) are highly personal and individual. There are few "White House lawn landings" in UFO lore, mostly a series of intimate, often one-to-one, encounters. If you are at all interested in UFOs, and unless you are a confirmed experiencer, you have probably got most of your "information" from books and from other people's testimonies: in other words, from narratives. Yet since the UFO is an *unknown*, any narrative created around it must, to some degree, strip it of its most essential and primary quality: that of being *unidentified*. It's an unremarked irony of ufology that the term "UFO"—being a means of *identification*—is a misnomer, an oxymoron, a self-cancelling description. What does it mean to identify something *as* unidentified?

*

> "If what I was dealing with amounted to some sort of deep and
> instinctive attempt to create a new deity for myself, to remain
> agnostic was to put the conscious me in the interesting position
> of opposing my own unconscious aim."
> —Whitley Strieber, *Communion*

Although *Prisoner of Infinity* is not meant to be a book for the UFO field, I've obviously considered how readers in that field might receive it.

I imagine they might receive it with some frustration, impatience, and exasperation, because, for most of the first part at least, the book doesn't really look at UFOs much at all. The principal subject of this book is not UFOs, or even socioreligious engineering. The subject of this book is narratives and how (and why) they are generated. This is the subject of every book, but it's a subject that's usually carefully concealed. Most books try to communicate their narratives directly to the reader so the reader's awareness *of reading* won't interfere with their experience of being absorbed into the narrative. Disbelief must be suspended so the reader's *belief* can co-generate the narrative. In a similar way, we generate an internal narrative: By unconsciously erasing the line between what's being thought and what is doing the thinking, we come to believe that we *are* our thoughts.

There's a teaching that, if we go deeply enough into any field of knowledge at all, we will reach an understanding of the total nature of existence. This may go double for the UFO. The UFO acts like a strange attractor or black hole that all-but compels a researcher to go *all the way in* and out the other side. It's not possible to really investigate the UFO without winding up knee-deep in epistemological and psychological waters. The alternative—which means to drop the "really" and do it by halves—is simply to build upon preexisting narratives. This is what almost all the UFO books on the market have done—and if they didn't, they probably wouldn't be on the market. How would we even identify them?

This book is for the *serious* UFO investigator, and for the experiencer who recognizes that there is something ultimately unresolved about their experiences, who is willing to question the interpretations passed down to them by the "experts," by other experiencers, and by their own beliefs. It is also for anyone interested in how beliefs are created, how they influence our perceptions and shape the narratives that engender our beliefs, and so on. It delves into the experience and the psychology of one, high-profile "experiencer," not in order to undermine his work but in order to reach a proper understanding of the phenomena being observed—*by observing closely the observer himself*. Yet, as the author of this exploration, I am also the observer who must be observed—hence the seemingly incongruous amount of autobiographical material that seeps into this narrative, since it is only fair to place my own psychology under the same microscope as I am placing Strieber.

Prisoner of Infinity takes a psychological approach to the UFO and to abduction phenomena, and even offers a psychological (partial) explanation *for* them; but my goal is not to reduce this mystery to mundane terms or to pathologize it. On the contrary, it is to expand and deepen that mystery by presenting a new, more nuanced context for it. It is not only that the UFO mystery can be better understood by applying psychology to it, but that psychology can be seen in a new and more truthful light by introducing it to the mystery of the UFO.

Above all, *Prisoner of Infinity* attempts to offer an explanation for the UFO mystery that is *as fantastic and as challenging to our ideas about reality as the phenomenon itself.*

Simply stated, to understand the UFO, it is necessary to understand ourselves. This means understanding how the narrative of a "self" is created. To think we might be able to understand a phenomenon as protean, mercurial, and resistant to identification as the UFO without exploring in new ways the nature of our own perceptions is like expecting to learn to swim without getting wet.

On the other hand, to seek a deeper understanding of the UFO—and of paranormal, spiritual, and parapolitical realities—is to *invite* a process of inner-outer discovery. It is a process that won't be over until it's over: until we have identified the most unidentified "object" of all, the human soul. For the soul to be something more than a generality requires focusing on a specific example. I chose Whitley Strieber not by any conscious process but because of an affinity I felt for his work that went deep, all the way into unconscious levels of my own being.

PART I

PASSPORT TO MANCHURIA

"Few tasks are as appealing as inquiring into the laws that govern the psyche of exceptionally endowed individuals."
—Sigmund Freud

CHAPTER I

Heaven Stormers

"And from the days of John the Baptist until now the kingdom
of heaven suffereth violence, and the violent take it by force."
— Matthew 11:12

This book began in early 2013. I was looking into the work of the popular writer, mystic, and "alien abductee" Whitley Strieber for the umpteenth time. I was approaching his work with a new focus, that of socio-spiritual engineering. I had been looking into a report issued by Stanford Research Institute (SRI) in 1973, commissioned by the US Department of Education several years earlier. It was called *Changing Images of Man*. The researcher Ty Brown ("Dream's End"), wrote a series of thought-provoking pieces about Strieber in 2007. In "10,000 Heroes: SRI and the Manufacturing of the New Age," he called the book "a conspiracy theorist's wet dream" and "nothing less than a blueprint for a vast social engineering project undertaken by the very highest levels of the military/industrial complex." According to Brown and other researchers, "SRI was at the hub of just about every major development in the evolving 'New Age' community." From the report:

Of special interest to the Western world is that Freemasonry tradition which played such a significant role in the birth of the United States of America, attested to by the symbolism of the Great Seal (on the back of the dollar bill). In this version of the transcendental image, the central emphasis is on the role of creative work in the life of the individual. (In "true Freemasonry" there is one lodge, the universe, and one brotherhood, everything that exists. Each person has the "privilege of labor," of joining with the "Great Architect" in building more noble structures and thus serving in the divine plan.) Thus this version of the "new transcendentalism" (perhaps more than other versions imported from the East more recently) has the potentiality of reactivating the American symbols, *reinterpreting the work ethic, supporting the basic concepts of a free-enterprise democratic society, and providing new meanings for the technological-industrial thrust.* (Markley & Harman, 1982, pp. 184–185, emphasis added)

What this quote suggested to me was that organized spirituality (or "new transcendentalism") had been coopted (or even created) as a means to prop up and inject new life into the Western capitalist system. While it referred specifically to Freemasonry, what were the chances that other spiritual and/or magical doctrines had been similarly "seeded" as carriers for an anything-but spiritual movement?

I had always read Strieber's work with great interest. Now I was looking at a (perhaps unwitting) part of a larger program of social engineering, I reached out to a couple of individuals associated with Strieber. One of them was Jeffrey Kripal. Kripal wrote the foreword to Strieber's 2011 book, *Solving the Communion Enigma: What Is to Come* (as well as other books, most recently *The Super Natural*, written with Strieber). The next day, Kripal responded with a warm email, to which he attached his forthcoming article, "The Traumatic Secret." Though ostensibly about George Bataille, the French intellectual who died in 1962, the article uses Strieber as an example of Kripal's focal interest, which is the relationship between early trauma (often sexual in nature) and mystical states of realization. It begins with a quote from *Solving the Communion Enigma*: "Had I not as a child been brutalized by whoever this was, I don't think that I ever would have been able to perceive the visitors" (the nonhuman beings Strieber came into contact with as a child).

I knew from previous research that Strieber was referring to memories of abuse, from around the age of four to nine, as part of a government secret program carried out at the Randolph Air Force base, under the direction of someone he named "Dr. Antonio Krause" (unsubstantiated). Strieber first began to write publicly about these disturbing incidents at his website, Unknown Country:

> I went to classes at Randolph, and they were terrible, terrible experiences. Fear was everywhere, fear was my life. I believe that it is why my immune system shut down when I was seven. It was just the sheer stress of it all, stress so great that my little body literally tried to die. But I did not die. Instead, I went on to become quite at ease with close encounter experiences and to do what I have done with my life. (Strieber, 2000)

Before reading Kripal's article, I responded to him by email that, while I agreed with his premise, I thought there was a distinct danger that trauma-induced spirituality would be *informed by* the trauma, in other words, that it would be compensatory. I suggested there might be an authentic enlightenment in contrast to a form of dissociation, or fragmentation, which might feel, and even look, like enlightenment, but was not. Learning to recognize the signs of this latter, I said, might be one of the fruits of studying a case like Strieber's.

Kripal replied that this was the case for almost any saint, mystic, guru, or visionary that he had studied in the history of religion. He said that he placed Strieber in this history because his case so closely resembled every other case he had studied in depth. He mentioned that there is nothing about enlightenment in South Asia that makes it incompatible with psychopathology or emotional trauma, and that what we might call madness is often seen as a sign of transcendence in that context. Likewise, numerous Hindu and Buddhist saints show signs of trauma side by side with enlightenment experiences, making it not a matter of either-or but both-and. In retrospect, I realized that, perhaps unconsciously, Kripal appeared to have sidestepped my point. As it happened, his article provided me with ample opportunity to clarify my argument.

The first thing that struck me in the piece was the following passage:

> The terror of the erotic and its subsequent concealment and censorship. The "cohesion of the human spirit" and its "potentialities." The deeper unity of the ascetic and the erotic. The refusal to collapse these spiritual and sexual potentialities into one another and

a move beyond both into a deeper, more fundamental Ground. The mirroring, coordinated structures of the sacred and sexual arousal around the social and psychological dynamics of taboo and transgression. These are the leitmotifs of both my work, and I dare say my life-experience, from the very first pages of *Kali's Child* (1995), a heavily censored, now tabooed book, to my most recent work on the paranormal in books like *Authors of the Impossible* (2010), where this both/and is reframed now via the bizarre mind-over-matter events of psychical and paranormal phenomena and the history of parapsychology in both elite theory and popular culture. In effect, the "cohesion" and "coordination" of the mystical and the erotic have morphed into the "cohesion" and "coordination" of the mental and the material. (Kripal, 2015, pp. 154–155)

The key point for me in this passage was the correlation of a mystical-erotic dichotomy with that of a *mind-body* one. The first question that occurred to me was this: Is the "spiritual engineering" currently underway in Western society contingent on *a de-eroticization of the spiritual?* Just to clarify this point, the word erotic shouldn't be seen as synonymous for sexual. Just as the erotic includes the sexual but is not limited to it, so sexuality can be uncoupled from eroticism, which is very much the point. *Eros* is both what stirs the life force into motion and a full body expression of it (though it can be expressed through language as well as movement). A dancer, painter, or writer may be expressing *eros* or life force, while someone having sex with a shoe (and almost all pornography) does not.

De-eroticization would be perceivable not only in trends (such as the New Age movement) but also in individuals. If so, is it possible that the sort of sexual trauma which someone like Strieber appears to have undergone might be a requirement to be deemed eligible for seeding the memes of a de-eroticized spirituality? In other words, *are sexually traumatized individuals sought (or even created) as spokespeople for the propagation of a mind-based spirituality designed to serve sociopolitical agendas?*

To clarify one point: De-eroticized spirituality entails a much subtler and more nuanced subterfuge than simply rejecting the body as "sinful." In fact many "mind-based" spiritual systems pay lip service to the body and reject the idea of a mind-body duality. But despite this, they still betray a subtle bias towards mind, as evident in the use of language. It is very clear what we mean when we say body, but what do we mean when we say "mind"? Even the idea of mind as existing independently of the body, as a *concept*, betrays a certain anti-body bias—as does the equation of mind with consciousness. Logically, the body is conscious before mind even exists; yet the mind somehow imagines it can exist beyond the confines of the body, as "consciousness." But consciousness of what?

Catholicism, and Christianity in general, has always skirted a similar trap, albeit with the mind-concept of a "soul" in place of mind *per se*. (There is not much eroticism in the Bible besides the Song of Solomon. There are also few jokes, at least in the translated version.) One result of de-eroticizing religion (equating celibacy with piety) is that sexuality comes out in secret, deviated forms, such as the much-documented sexual abuse of children by Catholic clergy, or, more obvious still but less commented on, the *fetishism* of Catholic paraphernalia and rituals. Deviated *eros* is not only rife in the Catholic Church, however. As the recent revelations in the UK around Jimmy Savile make clear, such de-eroticized expressions of libido may be far from exceptional inside the upper echelons of corporate and political power structures. In fact, the evidence indicates that psychopathic individuals like Savile are essential to the functioning of these structures.

British television celebrity Jimmy Savile's long career in sexual abuse included not only children and teens but convalescents and even (possibly) corpses. This was only made public after his death. A joint report by the NSPCC and Metropolitan Police, "Giving Victims a Voice," stated that 450 people had made complaints against Savile, with the period of alleged abuse stretching from 1955 to 2009 and the ages of the complainants at the time of the assaults ranging from eight to forty-seven (Gray & Watt, 2013). The suspected victims included twenty-eight children aged under ten, including ten boys aged as young as eight. A further sixty-three were girls aged between thirteen and sixteen and nearly three-quarters of his victims were under eighteen. Some 214 criminal offences were recorded, with thirty-four rapes having been reported across twenty-eight police forces (*Sky News*, 2013).

More striking even than Savile's sexual appetites was the fact that his activities continued for as long as they did, despite countless reports and at least six investigations (the first in 1958). As Chris Hastings wrote for the UK *Daily Telegraph* in 2006, the BBC (where Savile worked) was extremely thorough about vetting its employees and worked in tandem with MI5 (British intelligence) to do so. Those implicated in the conspiracy of silence include not just police but childcare homes, medical establishments, the BBC, intelligence agencies (MI5, MI6), even the royal family. With the Savile case, so-called "conspiracy theory" went mainstream in the blink of an eye, as national TV networks in Britain reported bare facts (including personal testimonies) that seemed more at home in a David Icke presentation. At least one witness stated that the sexual abuse he had suffered as a child was part of ritual enactments, and that all of his abusers were Freemasons. The claim was taken seriously enough for there to be a call for child abuse investigators to declare whether or not they were Freemasons.

Jimmy Savile was a Catholic and belonged to the religious order of the Knights of Malta. Of the many honors he received, only some were removed after the truth came out. Savile was given an OBE (Officer of the Most Excellent Order of the British Empire) in 1972, a Knight Bachelor "for charitable services," and a Papal knighthood (Knight Commander of the Pontifical Equestrian Order of Saint Gregory the Great (KCSG)) from Pope John Paul II, in 1990. He held an honorary doctorate of law (LLD) from the University of Leeds, was an honorary fellow of the Royal College of Radiologists (FRCR), had the Cross of Merit of the Order pro merito Melitensi, an honorary green beret from the Royal Marines, an honorary doctorate from the University of Bedfordshire, and he was a Freeman of the Borough of Scarborough. In short, he was a national institution, albeit one that has been torn down since the truth came out.

I mention all this in passing as an extreme (but *institutionalized*) example of how the libido looks and acts once it's uncoupled from authentic erotic impulse. Deny the divine access to our natural urges, and the devil will gladly take them over.

Kripal's essay offered me still more to chew on. For example:

> Bataille observes that transgression derives its power from the taboo, that the transgression does not remove the taboo but suspends, completes, and transcends it, and that taboos were put in place very early in the development of human society *in order to enable work and the construction of a social order*. (2015, p. 159, emphasis added)

This intersects neatly with the *Changing Images of Man* quote about using Masonic symbolism to strengthen the work ethic. Willis W.

Harman, senior social scientist at SRI who coedited *Changing Images*, was reputed to have been a key influence on Marilyn Ferguson's best-selling book, *The Aquarian Conspiracy*, published in 1980. Harman was also president of the Institute of Noetic Sciences; cofounder, fellow and trustee of the World Business Academy; former consultant to the White House's National Goals Research Staff; on the board of directors of the Albert Hoffman Foundation; among many more honors (the list is a long one).[1] Ferguson's book reiterates many of the ideas found in *Changing Images*, including this one: *"In the new paradigm, work is a vehicle for transformation."*

Bataille believed that the primary function of taboos was to shape and maintain a social order, with a particular focus on *work*. The implementation of taboos gave rise to the idea of transgression, and the effect of transgression is not to remove taboo but to complete it (just as crime consolidates the force of law through opposing it).

Taboos are primarily sexual taboos. De-eroticized spirituality is, like Christianity at its worst, a means to internalize taboos so they become intrinsic parts of philosophic belief, rather than being socially imposed (which only creates resistance to them). Nietzsche denounced Christianity for its "slave morality." He also wrote: "Christianity gave Eros poison to drink; he did not die of it but degenerated to vice" (2003, p. 105). The most effective worker is either one who is devoid of erotic impulses or who channels those impulses into work itself (for example, by turning work into a game of "making out," bringing the excitement of competition to what would otherwise be dull and soulless activity). For individuals to be incorporated into the social body, they have to first be cut off from their own bodies, and from the natural world.

This ties into what has been called "the Singularity," the spiritualized or religionist goal of technology to leave the planet via space travel (reach heaven) and achieve eternal life via consciousness-to-machine interface, that is, through creating a nonbiological vehicle for the personality to exist through. This is an example of what *Changing Images of Man* calls "new meaning for the technological-industrial thrust"—a spiritual or quasi-spiritual incentive for both industrialization (and labor) and scientific progress. (In "10,000 Heroes," Ty Brown writes that "In the introduction [to *Changing Images*], the authors complain that Judaism and Christianity are no longer filling their proper function"—hence the need to supplant Christianity with a New Age scientific-mysticism, a.k.a. "scientism.")

So where does trauma come in? Kripal cites Bataille on how "human beings generally hedge their bets when it comes to their desire for the continuity of being." While they desire some contact with the sacred, they also want to survive and exist as discontinuous beings outside of that totality. There is a fundamental conflict, in other words, between the religious urge to surrender and be absorbed into the infinite (the underlying unity of existence), and the desire to separate from it and pursue happiness through individual existence. "Basically, they want it both ways, and ritual violence allows them to do this"—that is, allows for congress with the divine without being totally absorbed into it, by offering up a *surrogate sacrifice*. Bataille suggests there is a deep connection between sacrifice and mystical experience, "as both attempt to reveal the sacred realm of the continuity of being."

> "Although clearly distinct from it, mystical experience seems to me to stem from the universal experience of religious sacrifice" [Bataille]. It should be observed that, in this model, "divine continuity is linked with the transgression of the law on which the order of discontinuous beings is built," hence *the sacred is accessed ritually and mystically primarily through the violation of taboo*, otherwise known as "sin" in Christian theology. Little wonder, then, that in Christianity the sacred is so "readily associated with Evil." (Kripal, 2015, p. 161, emphasis added)

Kripal's paragraph contains a pile of powerful ideas packed together into a few lines. What Bataille (and Kripal) appear to be saying is this: Ordinary social, communal order is constructed around the idea—the tangible reality—of the existence of discontinuous beings and it requires certain codes to maintain that order (thou shalt not kill, steal, or lust after your neighbor's wife, for example). Conversely, mystical experience and religious doctrine pertains to the opposite idea, that of a continuity of being in which everyone is equally subservient to (and inseparable from) the divine order (God). So, while social order is maintained largely through the implementation of religious *taboos*, the mystical and religious imperative is to *transcend the social order* and discover the underlying continuity of being. This inevitably entails the breaking of socioreligious taboos.

The work ethic necessary to maintaining a community, for example, depends on a social agreement about what is permissible and what is not. But there also exists an opposing desire to access the sacred and return to "oneness"; since this requires the breaking of these taboos, it inevitably threatens to upset the social order. The way to square this circle (so far as I can see) is for the social order (community) to be seen as equivalent to the divine order (Church and state as one): This allows the individuals within it to "sacrifice" themselves (their individual desires) to the community and experience "continuity of being" as part of a social body. This only works up to a point, however, because, when all is said and done, the community is a poor substitute for the infinite and cannot absorb the individual into its body in a lasting or meaningful way. While human beings have a powerful communal instinct (preservation of the species), they are equally driven by more selfish instincts for procreation and self-preservation, which as often as not pit them against others in the community. The solution is to redirect those more selfish instincts (which paradoxically include the antisocial drive for a mystical experience of continuity of being) into collective, religious activity.

While I was unfamiliar with Bataille's work before reading Kripal's essay, it closely echoes the work of the French philosopher René Girard, specifically his theory of mimetic desire and the "scapegoat mechanism." Mimetic desire is a kind of infectious desire that results from wanting what other people want simply *because* they want it. Desiring what someone else wants leads to rivalry (unless there is a surplus), and eventually to violence. Hence, "Thou shalt not covet thy neighbor's wife." The example Girard gives, in fact, is that of two friends who become enemies because of their desire for the same woman. Girard describes the necessity of ritual sacrifice (of a party everyone agrees is guilty) to prevent internal violence from breaking out within a community. This may be an *apropos* example here, since sexual desire is the desire for union, that is, for continuity of being. Yet within the context of the community and of mimetic desire, the result of sexual desire is often violence, which is the inverse: the desire to separate, for *dis*continuity of being. The scapegoat mechanism of sacrificial violence is a way to maintain community cohesion, because it is a way of directing mimetic desire into a community-bonding ritual, sublimating the (sexual) desire for continuity of being into a religious practice.

A community requires religious taboos (especially around sexuality) in order to prevent rivalry and violence from breaking out. Yet, as Kripal makes explicit, the spiritual urge to experience continuity of being is itself a sexual drive, at least in part. So the separation of spirituality from the erotic is an act of violence—splitting what was one into two—and it creates a gulf in the human psyche. When the erotic drive for oneness is not allowed to express itself through the religious rituals meant to answer that drive, some sort of surrogate ritual enactment is required, to allow the libido an alternate form of release and bridge that gulf. The dark solution that presents itself is that of sacrificial violence. This is why the predatory psychopath type (popularly "the serial killer," in reality someone closer to Jimmy Savile) could be seen as the most extreme form of debased "spiritual" expression, both individual and collective, which arises once the desire for transcendence is uncoupled from the body, and from true eroticism. Where Eros cannot go, Thanatos reigns supreme.

As Freud saw it, the human ego's function is to mediate between external reality and the id. However, the ego that is not strong enough to accept the reality of death can only do so by "developing a certain opacity protecting the organism from reality" (Brown, 1985, p. 160). This is known as negation, and negation is "a more active form of dying" (ibid.). Negating the reality of separation from the mother's body develops into negation of self, which is repression, and negation of the environment, which is aggression. All "evil" or psychosis is the result of unconscious, and hence delusional, attempts to access and integrate past memory-fantasy material; but it is in fact serving an even deeper and more primordial agenda, that of maintaining a state of blindness and dissociation by which to keep the reality of our oneness with divine reality at bay. Since oneness amounts to the loss of a separate identity, it is equated by the narcissistic ego with death. And so what consciousness is actively seeking, the conscious self—trapped within its narcissistic dream world—is hardwired to avoid at all costs.

Kripal goes on to describe how Bataille's *Eroticism* has influenced his own thinking, even thirty years after last reading the work. He describes Bataille as "a constant companion" throughout his writing career, citing examples. Kripal's first book, *Kali's Child* (his dissertation), a study of the nineteenth-century Hindu saint Ramakrishna, related to the question of how "the sexual and spiritual systems can activate one another." His later works, *Roads of Excess, Palaces of Wisdom,* and *The Serpent's Gift,* discussed how suicide attempts due to "psychosexual" confusion can overlap with spiritual "conversion." Thirdly, he mentions his 2007 work, *Esalen: America and the Religion of No Religion*, and cites the English author Aldous Huxley, whom he describes as probably having had "more influence on the human potential movement as a whole than any other single person." It was at this point I realized that Kripal's essay overlapped, not just indirectly but *directly*, with the subject of socio-spiritual engineering.

I knew Huxley's work well. It had been twenty years since I'd read his most famous text, *The Doors of Perception*, but I had recently quoted it in my article "Autism and the Other" (which I'd sent to Kripal after finishing his piece). I had taken note at the time of Huxley's use of the term "Mind at Large," and wished he'd chosen a better one to describe the overarching and underlying intelligence of existence. In his article, Kripal attributed Huxley with coining the expression "human potentialities" and being "instrumental in bringing a new word into the English language (psychedelic or 'mind-manifesting')." He then referred to Huxley's "little Blakean tract, *The Doors of Perception*." While it was true Huxley got his title from Blake's *The Marriage of Heaven and Hell*, it's hard to imagine anything *less* Blakean than the idea of God as a great big Mind. Blake despised philosophers like John Locke and René Descartes, and would probably have derided Huxley's phrase for its obvious head-o-centricity. It was at this point, perhaps not coincidentally, that I began to question some of Kripal's assumptions.

But I am getting ahead of myself. Here's the next passage that caught my eye in the piece:

> Nothing in our everyday experience gives us any reason to suppose that matter is not material, that it is made up of bizarre forms of energy that violate, very much like spirit, all of our normal notions of space, time, and causality. Yet when we subject matter to certain drastic treatments, like CERN's Hadron Collider near Geneva, Switzerland, then we can see quite clearly that matter is not material at all. But—and this is the key—we can only get there through a great deal of physical violence, a violence so extreme and so precise that it cost us billions of dollars and decades of preparation to inflict it. (Kripal, 2015, p. 165)

Kripal's provocative statement leads into the last section of his essay, titled "The Alien Abduction Literature." Before I get to *that* can of ectoplasm, let's look at the idea of violence as the necessary means to discover that "matter is not material"—and how it may be the "scientistic" equivalent of "taking the Kingdom of Heaven by storm."[2]

*

"What worries me is finding fifty years from now those books have created some kind of grim religion."
—Whitley Strieber, 1988

In my twenties and thirties, I was something of a Nietzsche-reading anti-Christian. My spiritual path entailed psychedelic-ingestion, occult rituals, shamanizing, voluntary hardship and poverty, and extremely *in*voluntary celibacy. I believed that Heaven was only for those with the balls to storm it (an idea suggested in Whitley Strieber's *The Key* with these words, "Your place will not be given you. You must be strong enough to take it" (2001, p. 47). After Castaneda's books, *The Key* was probably the greatest literary influence on me during this period). Now I am in my late forties, with at least some of the sobriety that middle age brings, I would see this outlook (along with Blake's "road of excess") as the privileged folly of youth—if it weren't for the mounting evidence that I was *conditioned and misdirected* into my folly *as part of a larger social agenda*. If "heaven" is largely synonymous for the harmony of consciousness with the body, then today I would argue that violence is the surest way to keep us out of Heaven, because violence can only ever strike a discordant note in the body.

In *Life Against Death: The Psychoanalytical Meaning of History*, Norman O. Brown, developing the ideas of Freud, describes how the consciousness of every individual is seeking a return to oneness, doing so not through the senses but through fantasy of the mind. It could be argued that loss of union with the mother is the sole source of the desire for oneness, and that "spirituality" is nothing but the sublimation of unmet infant desire. I'm not going to argue that, because I think there *is* an *authentic spiritual drive of consciousness to rediscover oneness*. But I also think that both the scientific and spiritual quest to "dematerialize/spiritualize matter" (and so merge with it), even if it can't be reduced to it, conceals that infant drive to be reunited with the mother, and that scientists with their Hadron Collider, covert intelligence programs trying to forge the key to the human psyche, psycho-spiritual think tanks bidding to engineer evolution, space programs attempting to colonize outer space, and traumatized seekers and mystics plundering their nervous systems with hallucinogens, spiritual practices, or sexual excess, can all be placed in the same category—that of stormers of heaven.

If I read his article correctly, Kripal is comparing the process of shattering matter to the means by which an individual can access higher or deeper (mystic) realms of perception as a result of physical and psychological trauma. While I can allow this to be true, my question to Kripal, regarding his piece, is: At what cost? Writing about Strieber, Kripal states that he "… does not reduce the later mystical events to the earlier trauma. Rather, he suggests that physical and sexual trauma can 'crack open the cosmic egg' and so reveal a 'hidden reality' of unimaginable scope. In short, he offers us another version of the 'traumatic secret.'"

Kripal sees this as "a both-and, not an either-or" question. To some extent I would agree. I'm not arguing, as others might, that mystical states or visions which result from trauma are merely hallucinations resulting from a form of dissociation. I am in agreement with Kripal that Strieber and other mystics can and do enter into authentic experiences of imaginal or archetypal reality (i.e., the collective psyche). The problem is that genuine trauma that leads to authentic mystical states may inevitably lead to an equally real *misuse* of those experiences *as a means to protect the person from re-experiencing the past trauma*. This misuse of the mystical trance state would not only preclude a proper understanding of the visions undergone, but also prevent the opportunity of fully integrating and embodying the trauma. My sense is that it is not only mystical vision that must be embodied, but also the trauma that allowed for it. Otherwise, the mystical vision will not become a full body experience, but only be possessed by the mind, that is, become the stuff of thoughts and not direct, sensory experience. The mind (thought) can then use the experience to maintain its separation from the body—that is, to keep in place the gap between the erotic and the spiritual, by sacrificing the body to the "sacred."

While this kind of psychological subterfuge (which I will discuss in more detail in the next chapter) may be all too obviously at work in exoteric religions such as Catholicism, it proceeds in a more discreet and covert fashion in the more esoteric philosophies of spirituality, mysticism, occultism, and "ufology." Here, instead of an outright demonization and rejection of Eros as "the work of the devil," what happens is a sort of mystical reframing and rechanneling of the libido into something "spiritual" or otherworldly. This is roughly what's known as sublimation, which Freud defined as "an especially conspicuous feature of cultural development; it is what makes it possible for higher psychical activities, scientific, artistic or ideological, to play such an important part in civilized life" (1961, p. 97). For Freud, sublimation allowed people to act out socially unacceptable impulses (taboos) by converting them into more acceptable forms of behavior. One example of this might be redirecting erotic urges into a communal/spiritual work ethic so as to create a willing slave class as the body-vehicle for technological progress, and to keep the dominant capitalist paradigm intact. Whereas Freud saw sublimation as a sign of maturity, however, the author Norman O. Brown, who developed Freud's ideas in surprising new ways in the 1970s, saw it differently.

> Sublimation negates the body of childhood and *seeks to construct the lost body of childhood in the external world* …. Sublimation is the search for lost life; it presupposes and perpetuates the loss of life and cannot be the mode in which life itself is lived. Sublimation is the mode of an organism which must discover life rather than live, must know rather than be. (1985, pp. 170–171, emphasis added)

When I reread this phrase while working on the present chapter, I think at once of Strieber. Strieber, with his grand cosmic vision of otherworldly contact, his tales of trauma and transformation, and his continuous probing into a past filled with secret schools, hidden agendas, and suppressed memories, making his entire opus an attempt to "construct the lost body of childhood in the external world." Or in the stars.

CHAPTER II

An archetypal traumatogenic agency

"The resistance thrown up by the self-care system in the treatment of trauma victims is legendary .... Most contemporary analytic writers are inclined to see this attacking figure as an internalized version of the actual perpetrator of the trauma, who has 'possessed' the inner world of the trauma victim. But this popularized view is only half correct. The diabolical inner figure is often far more sadistic and brutal than any outer perpetrator, indicating that we are dealing here with a psychological factor set loose in the inner world by trauma—*an archetypal traumatogenic agency within the psyche itself.* [T]he traumatized psyche is self-traumatizing."

—Donald Kalsched, *The Inner World of Trauma: Archetypal Defenses of the Personal Spirit*

In 2010, after reading Norman O. Brown's *Life Against Death*, I threw together a bunch of notes to try to sum up Brown's insights. Brown's work reinterprets certain of Freud's ideas and places them in a larger, more metaphysical context. I have some reservations about drawing on Freud's psychological models at all, partially because of Freud's dismissal of child sexual abuse as harmless.[1] On the other hand, I consider

Freud's work to be invaluable (however out of fashion), and no one is without their blind spots (a fact that this present exploration is about). There is compelling evidence (see *Sigmund Freud's Christian Unconscious* by Paul C. Vitz) that Freud was himself a victim of sexual interference as a child (that he was seduced by his nanny).

In *Life Against Death*, Brown describes culture as the collective product of repression, negation, and sublimation, a kind of external matrix created and maintained by infantile drives to recover the lost object of the mother's body. According to Brown, both culture and the ego-identity that arises from it (or in tandem with it) are empty of substance, because both belong to *a fantasy-generated reality* and are images of the past, superimposed onto the present. Brown writes of how death anxiety "is relative to the repression of the human body; the horror of death is the horror of dying with what Rilke called unlived lines in our bodies." He presents the "... construction of a human consciousness strong enough to accept death [as] a task in which philosophy and psychoanalysis can join hands—and also art .... Only if Eros—the life instinct—can affirm the life of the body can the death instinct affirm death, and in affirming death magnify life" (1985, p. 109).

When a child's life force or libido desires the love-object of the mother and is separated from it, the child withdraws into fantasy by identifying *with* the love-object and having a fantasy relationship with an internally generated image–like Norman Bates in Hitchcock's Psycho, inspired by real-life "mother's boy" and prototypical serial killer, Ed Gein. (After his mother's death in 1973, Jimmy Savile "sequestered himself with her body for five days, which he subsequently claimed [to Louis Theroux] were the 'best five days of my life.'"[2]) The life force is hijacked by the still-forming ego and used *as an energy source* to create a fantasy-based relationship with reality, and with the body. Eventually, this develops into both sublimation and *desexualization*, intellectual, abstract beliefs through which to interact with reality—or rather, *not* to interact with reality. "The transformation of object-libido into narcissistic libido [i.e., through creating an internal image of the love-object] obviously implies an abandonment of sexual aims, [hence it is] a process of desexualization" (Brown, quoting Freud, 1985, p. 162).

For Brown, the religious idea of "soul" (i.e., life force separate from the body) is "the shadowy substitute for a bodily relation to other bodies" (1985, p. 162). Narcissistic fantasy caused by traumatic separation creates a "spiritualized ego," via the idea of a self separate from the body, that is, a "soul-self," though, personally, I prefer the term "mind-self," albeit a mind with a religious bent to it. When the original sensual-sensory experiences prove too painful for the infant's psyche, the child's senses *close down*. One result of this closing down is what Freud called "genital organization,"[3] when the life force becomes trapped inside, and limited to, the genitals. In a larger sense, the erotic, sensual, bodily awareness is imprisoned in a matrix made up of early patterns of trauma and loss, patterns which have been woven together into *a de-eroticized ego identity*. "Primal fantasies" occur during this formative stage when the life force is being redirected away from the body; being primal, these fantasies occur in *a qualitatively different state of awareness to our present state*, hence they cannot be remembered, only *reenacted*, consciously or unconsciously. Mostly, they are reenacted unconsciously, throughout our lives, *as neurotic, delusional behavior*. They exist only as "hallucinations in the present which serve to negate the present" (Brown, 1985, p. 166).

While this psychoanalytical model can (and if true must) be applied to everyone, to one degree or another, it seems especially relevant when trying to understand more mystical or otherworldly experiences, such as those reported by Strieber (and interpreted by Kripal): Strieber, with his seemingly endless reenactments of trauma at the hands of apparent "aliens," and his countless "screen memories." In the final section of his article dealing with alien abduction, Kripal quotes near-death-experience (NDE) author Kenneth Ring, who contends that "a history of child abuse and trauma plays a central etiological role in promoting sensitivity to UFOEs and NDEs." Ring agrees that "such conditions tend to stimulate the development of a dissociative response style as a means of psychological defense," and links this dissociative response to an ability to "'tune into' other realities where by virtue of his dissociated state, he can temporarily feel safe *regardless of what is happening to his body*. In this way … dissociation would directly foster relatively easy access to alternate, non-ordinary realities."

Ring is careful to suggest that such "attunement" is "not a gift of dissociation itself, which only makes it possible, but of a correlated capacity, that for what is called psychological absorption."

> Hence "it is the ability to dissociate that governs access to alternate realities," but these alternate realities cannot be explained by the psychological mechanism of dissociation. And there is more. Such "encounter-prone personalities" and "psychological sensitives"

come to develop *"an extended range of human perception beyond nor-mally recognized limits."* ... Ring concludes, in a bold but extremely common move in the alien abduction literature, that such traumati-cally transformed individuals may well represent *"the next stage in evolution."* (Kripal, quoting Ring, 1992, p. 144, emphases added)

After he began to remember his "abduction" experiences in late 1985, Strieber underwent intense physical and psychological symptoms. In *Communion*, he writes:

> I had a feeling of being separated from myself, as if either I was unreal or the world around me was unreal .... In the ensuing days, I experienced more bouts of fatigue. I would be working and suddenly would get cold and start to shake. Then I would feel so exhausted that I could not go on, and crawl into bed quivering and miserable, sure that I was coming down with the flu .... Nights I would sleep, but wake up in the morning feeling as if I had been tossing and turning the whole time .... My disposition got worse. I became mercurial, frantic with excitement about some idea one moment, in despair the next. (1987, p. 35)

What Strieber describes here overlaps with symptoms I've suffered throughout my adult life. On top of these physical and psychological ailments, I also had night terrors as a child, usually precipitated by ill-ness and fever and accompanied by extreme despair. On many occa-sions, I would wake from a profound dream, possessed by the visceral and overwhelming certainty that something terrible had happened, either to me or to reality itself. Something had been altered in some fundamental way, and everything was now terribly and irrevocably *wrong*. The change I perceived was tiny, infinitesimal, yet it had left me adrift on a dark, indescribably vast sea of confusion and despair. What-ever had happened, my reaction to this incomprehensible awareness, like Strieber's, was primal: I literally fled the scene of the "violation," desperate to get as far away from my bed, room, and house, as pos-sible. On more than one occasion I ended up in the street in my pajamas before coming to my senses. Whatever I was fleeing followed me.

*

"[T]his was an unusual experience, to say the least, and I can assure you that it is just as amazing as it sounds. There is no elegant way to dismiss it as an illusion or some sort of 'imaginal' experience. It was real."

—Whitley Strieber, *Solving the Communion Enigma*

I had no explanation for these experiences, at least until my early twenties when I read Strieber's *Communion*. After that, I began to believe my nightmares related to nonhuman intervention and that the "change" I'd undergone was more than the product of my imagination. Among the literature I consumed, I read accounts of abductees who experienced molecular transformation at the hands of "the visitors." I was twenty-five or twenty-six when I experienced what I took, at the time, to be my first conscious memories of "alien interaction." I was staying at a Buddhist community in France during the winter, planting trees in exchange for food and board.

As the dream-memory began, I found myself among a group of young people, possibly schoolchildren. We were in "the firm and relentless hands of government" (here and elsewhere I am quoting my journal from the time), waiting to go underground. Very few of us knew what was about to happen. I seemed to know more than most, but even so I had little idea of what to expect. There was something about "watches"—possibly we were asked to remove them. Then we were ordered, compelled, to be enclosed in a dark space for a period of hours, by way of preparation, perhaps as a kind of quarantine or acclimatization process. I was aware, already, that we were going to encounter the unknown, and that it might involve other life forms. There followed then our delivery into the underworld, by what means was unclear, but at the end of which we arrived at a well-lit complex which I knew was under the ground. All I remembered of this area upon waking was a sort of bar or buffet, a counter with seating that seemed to go round in a circle. There were some receiver-transmitter apparatuses, like TV sets, mounted well above our heads at regular intervals. From this salon, secret bar, or waiting room, presently, we were moved to another place. This second space was curiously insulated: no air seemed to get in there, yet we were breathing.

We were amidst the other beings. Upon waking I couldn't remember the actual contact with these mysterious figures, only that, little by little, we realized where we were and what was happening. The experience was incredible beyond belief, strange beyond my wildest imaginings, terrifying with an intensity I would not have dreamed possible. No words could do it justice. Yet at no time were we in any danger, of harm or even of physical-mental abuse. So far as I remembered, we were not subjected to any of the "ordinary" abduction procedures, but this might have been due to gaps in my recall. The only thing I clearly remembered was a small black child, the very first amongst us to see one of them, turning to me and saying, "Jesus!" I looked at what he was seeing and said the same. This one word—"Jesus"—seemed to sum up all the vastness of the new world before us, all of the horror, wonder, and awe that possessed me and annihilated all that was left of my reason, on seeing this incredible, unacceptable sight.

The beings were blue. There was something about their eyes, not black, but somehow hollow, as if I could see right through them. The beings themselves, their skin or their form, seemed fluid; not like ordinary solid matter but more alive, more *livid*. Yet the beings were partly human, I knew this instinctively. I also knew that this was a memory of the past, I was almost sure of it; because, if it were only a dream, there would be no reason for the intensity of my emotions. Yet I brought to it my present level of awareness, including knowledge of other people's accounts of similar experiences, so I was curious as to just what these beings were. They seemed to be neither like the "grays" nor like the "cobalts," but rather somewhere in between.

At one point, I said to someone: "They're a hybrid?" A military figure, old, immensely dignified, and known to me, affirmed my question curtly, without explanation. I was aware that we were being kept from interfacing with the higher order of beings (I referred to them as the "thin ones" in my original account) by this human, military presence—not for our (or their) protection, but to keep us from the truth and to deny us the uplifting and illuminating soul experience of contact with the "pure breed." I was in no position to lament this, however. The most prominent feeling in the dream, being face to face with this incredible life form, was one of wonder. I knew that it was not human, and I could find no way around this realization. My whole being, including physical, was shaken in a kind of apocalypse of the soul. I felt my world being torn apart just to look at them. Yet at the same time, I was aware of somehow forgetting the experience even as I was having it. My everyday reason would not allow me to carry the burden of this revelation, and even as it was being forced to acknowledge the reality of what it was seeing, it was busy denying its existence. It would do so as continually and as thoroughly as it could, until no trace remained.

I was aware that the forgetting, which was inevitable, was less a result of deliberate maneuvers on their (human or alien agencies) part, more the result of my own self-protective instincts. It seemed like it would be a relief to forget, and that I would surrender the memory willingly if only the boundless terror would go with it. Yet what I was so afraid of was hard to explain. Then I blacked out. There was a hole in the plot, a hole so large as to render the plot incoherent. I couldn't remember the interface, or even if there was one, nor the exact form or features of the beings. Nor do I recall the return to the surface, if we were indeed under the earth.

One thing I remembered clearly on waking was the phrase INTEL-LIGENT LIMBS. The phrase occurred and recurred throughout the experience. The concept was of an intelligence that spreads out and takes hold from many (maybe infinite) different points at once, like the roots of a tree, while remaining at the same time hidden, hence protected. I interpreted this as a description of the hive-like activities of the "visitors." Each one of them moves about as a limb, neither separate nor independent, because guided by the intelligence of the head. Yet at the same time they were expendable, because when you cut off a limb, another immediately takes its place. Like the heads of the Hydra, the beings were mere extensions of a central force, or "head"; should the "limb" be injured or captured, the intelligence could simply be withdrawn and redirected, leaving only an empty and useless shell, and possibly not even that.

After this, the dream descended into nightmare. I was in a car and the light went out. I was waiting for someone or something when an eerie sound began to engulf me. I was afraid, confused. I climbed out of the car to try to ascertain what the sound was and only then realized that it was coming from inside the car. I climbed back inside and realized that it was the radio, which had been turned off before. It was tuned to no particular station, emitting a sort of high insistent hum or whine, with an underlying buzz or crackle that could easily be mistaken for distant voices. I had candles on the dashboard, like an altar, and they burned down in a matter of seconds. Something was not right. An unknown influence was changing all the laws of physics, and of nature.

I was paralyzed. I felt as though contained in a powerful field of energy, one that caused both an internal tension and an external paralysis in me. It was like I was exploding, but contained, with no way to let it out. There was a sound in my ears like a plane crashing and taking off at once: the high ascending roar/whine which I had by then come to associate with astral projection. I was in my bed now, I realized, as well as inside the car, yet the new awareness brought no relief. I was mortally afraid, because I had already come to associate the paralysis with *them*. I felt their presence all around me and yet I was helpless to act: all I could do to protect myself was to keep my eyes closed. The feeling was hideous, unbearable. How could I have ever wished for this? No one could endure such an encounter, these beings were *inhuman*. The mere fact of their existence filled me with a horror bordering on nausea.

It occurred to me that the force that trapped me and seemed to crush me and to tear me apart at the same time was the force of my own fear. I lay in my bed, curled up in terror, the only thing between me and the vast unknowable darkness that wanted to devour me the thin layer of bedding which I had wrapped around me and covered my head with. Even as I did so, I knew it was hopeless, but the alternative—to draw back the covers and gaze into that abyss—was unthinkable. This happened again and again, while in the dream, it was as if nothing changed. I was in the car, waiting for their arrival, for disaster, and I continued returning to my bed and going through the same sensations, the same terror. By this time I didn't even know if I was awake or asleep, whether the beings were present or if they were about to arrive. And the moment I started to doubt it and they began to recede, I began to call them back. As soon as they responded, and I knew it was real again, I would have done anything, *anything*, to escape them. It was as if my desire was too terrible for me to endure.

Finally, after countless repetitions of this process, the dream was released, all the way into nightmare. I climbed out of the car and went down towards the forest, knowing I would encounter them but compelled to go, as if by an external force. I saw a patch of red ahead of me, a small figure in the darkness. They were not human: they were waiting for me. Then, as I looked at them, they faded away. "Ordinary" people took their place, several of them around a sort of table in the forest. I was laid down on the table to be treated. For some inexplicable reason, I trusted these "people." I kept looking at the one in charge, the doctor. There was something about him: he was disturbingly real, nothing like dream faces that change and blend myriad features together. His face was fixed, I could still see it clearly when I woke. He was fleshy around the neck, with fat cheeks, sweaty, slightly unshaven, with curly dark hair that receded extremely, bald on top. He was wearing thick lens spectacles with a dark plastic rim. As I lay there, he leaned forward and inserted a large needle into the back of my neck. I knew that the treatment was not for any disorder but more for immunity, some kind of acclimatization. As I lay there I began to realize that the whole purpose of my trip underground was just this: acclimatization, to get us used to these beings.

The other people held me down, although I wasn't struggling. The doctor injected me again in the same place. I grew slightly afraid and began to want to get away. The doctor told me then that he would need to inject me many, many times. I think he may even have said "thousands" of times! I cried out, "Not tonight!" He shook his head, "No, no," and I experienced relief. Something changed then in my point-of-view, and I began to grow suspicious of these "people." They weren't quite right, there was something about them. A scene ensued: Two of the "people" (all of them were wearing bright anoraks and track-suit type clothing), were struggling with a child who was refusing to go with them. They were supposed to be the boy's parents, but he sensed that something was wrong. The father grabbed the boy and slapped him. He said, "Fran! Be a good girl Fran!" The boy shouted in horror, "I'm not a girl! I'm a boy!"

It was obvious now: the cat was out the bag. The "people" were not his parents at all—they didn't even know what sex he was! They were some kind of synthetic beings, robots. The "father" slapped the child over and over again, then dragged him towards a house. I watched in impotent horror. I was beginning to suspect malevolence on the part of these beings where I had so fervently prayed for benevolence. There was a big ditch in the middle of the field, full of real people. I prayed that they were sleeping and not dead. At that moment one of the robots who was holding me earlier—and who also had very distinct features— staggered over to the ditch and keeled over. Another robot, an exact replica, stepped out to replace him. I realized then that these "robots," whatever they were, had a very limited life span and were for temporary use only. The "visitors" used them to get the situation arranged according to their needs, then stepped in without encountering any resistance. I was trapped in a plot I could never hope to understand.

The alien robots looked like humans and they had been among us for a long time; now they had received a new program and were to begin the executions. They killed with a single shot between the eyes. At times, they even killed on a whim, being licensed (or programmed) to do so, and this was the only sign they gave of spontaneous action. The only single human emotion they seemed to have picked up was that of sadism! For half the dream, I was even identifying with one of these killing machines.

As I awoke from this experience, I recalled an earlier dream I'd had: just before waking, still in darkness, I had felt, physically felt (without any corresponding dream to account for the sensation), a needle entering into the back of my neck and liquid flowing into my body. I was deeply afraid. I was a pawn in the hands of something I did not even know existed; or rather, something I could not admit existed.

The sense of foreboding, of some intrusive presence, some alien "other" lurking in the shadows of my sleep and at the edges of my consciousness, had been palpable throughout my life, as palpable as a strange figure in the room that did not belong there. In *Communion*, Strieber describes a similar sense of foreboding before his memories of "contact" first begin to surface. It may even have been an affinity for that lurking paranoia—a shared sense of foreboding—that drew me to his work in the first place, which caused it to resonate so deeply for me.

The "easy" answer to that sense of foreboding was that, like Strieber, I had been abducted by aliens. But that kind of answer raised a thousand other questions.

*

"The familial metaphor is called into play as a basic model of propitiating *any* overwhelming event whatsoever."
—Greg Mogenson, *A Most Accursed Religion*

In the beginning, my predominant feelings for Strieber were a mix of fascination, sympathy, and affection laced with envy. Increasingly, over the years, I began to feel less and less envy and more bewilderment, exasperation, and frustration. Strieber always impressed me as a man wrestling with gigantic questions, haunted, driven, dedicated, and painfully earnest in his quest for understanding. A searching mind, full-bodied and big-hearted, he also struck me as a "straight-up sort of guy."

Probably what appealed to me most about him was his combination of sincerity and intelligence, being qualities I value highly in others. There was also something touching about him: For all his knowledge, eloquence, and insight, he came across as a simple, conventional family man from Texas with traditional values—a square.

On the surface, and despite his outré tales of courting and loving the alien, Strieber seemed to uphold basic human values. His combination of simple humanness with the startling nature of his experiences held a very basic appeal for me over the years (as I suspect it has for many others). At the same time, from what I have gleaned of his personality outside of his writings, he and I never seemed all that compatible. Where Strieber comes across as extroverted and brash, assertive and impatient, I am withdrawn, reserved and tentative, especially with strangers. We were worlds apart as individuals—as far apart as Yorkshire and Texas. Yet his experiences, and most of all his evocative writing skills, drew me into his world, both inner and outer, and made me feel intimately involved with it—almost like a family member.

I grew up in a middle-to-upper class family in Yorkshire, England, the same district where Jimmy Savile was born and lived, and where Peter Sutcliffe, the notorious Yorkshire Ripper (whom Savile met), stalked his victims during my teen years. (Yorkshire has also been described as a hotbed of UFO-activity.) Savile was a television "icon" of the period (roughly the equivalent of Dick Clark in the US), and everyone my age knew who he was. I grew up watching him on TV (the kids program *Jim'll Fix It* and *Top of the Pops*), and my sister even had his autograph. (Apparently my father gave it to her after he met Savile on an airplane, presumably a public flight.) As the head of Northern Foods, my father was a highly respected businessman with political connections. Without going any further into this material (which I have explored elsewhere), the point is that, just as with Strieber, there is at least as much evidence in my past for some sort of *human* interference as there is for "aliens." Yet it wasn't till my forties that I started to see this fact. Until then, it had been aliens all down the line.

Finding Strieber's accounts may have given me a suitably cosmic lens through which to look at my early trauma; at the same time, part of what made that lens helpful may have been the degree to which it *obscured* the truth and made it more palatable to me. It was only as I drew closer to integrating those early experiences that I became willing to put down the cosmic lens and see what things looked like *with my own eyes*.

Through writing—exploring the subject in a literary form—I began to see the traumatogenic agencies at work, and at play, in my own life: a recurring, in fact continuous, relationship with some unseen "other," in the form of a visceral sense of foreboding, childhood nightmares, and *apparent* alien encounters as an adult.

Through the act of writing this nonfictional narrative, I have begun to see what an archetypal agency looks like, *feels* like, and *does*, at the level of personal experience. I have begun to see why I always felt "possessed by some diabolical power or pursued by a malignant fate," and why Strieber's tales of power, which look more and more like part of a psycho-cosmic *cover-up*, have held such a deep and lasting fascination for me: because they provided indispensable ingredients for the assembling of my own crucial fiction.

CHAPTER III

A life full of holes: daimonic defense and national security

"This inner [guardian] figure was such a powerful 'force' that the term daimonic seemed an apt characterization ... It could play a protective or a persecutory role—sometimes alternating back and forth between them."

—Donald Kalsched, *The Inner World of Trauma: Archetypal Defenses of the Personal Spirit*

In the second chapter of Strieber's 2011 release, *Solving the Communion Enigma*, titled "The Mirror Shattered," Strieber describes a psychological phenomenon which he calls "shattering the mirror of expectation":

I was very young when these things happened. Whatever they were, they certainly shattered the mirror of expectation for me, leaving me, like my wife and so many other people whose understanding of reality has been upended in childhood, open from then on to noticing what most people assume to be impossible and therefore do not see. Once the mirror of expectation is shattered, the door of perception is open, and there is something there, something alive, looking back at us from where the mirror once stood. (2011a, p. 24)

In 2007, a Jungian therapist recommended a book to me called *The Inner World of Trauma: Archetypal Defenses of the Personal Spirit*, by a clinical psychologist named Donald Kalsched. In it, Kalsched writes about a similar phenomenon as that described by Strieber, but reaches a somewhat different conclusion. Based on his psychotherapeutic work with abuse sufferers, Kalsched describes how early experiences of trauma "destroy outer meaning"—in reaction to which, "patterns of unconscious fantasy provide an inner meaning to the trauma victim." He relates these "inner images and fantasy structures" to "the miraculous life-saving *defenses* that assure the survival of the human spirit when it is threatened by the annihilating blow of trauma" (1996, p. 1). Kalsched's description precisely echoes Strieber's accounts of being rescued by the visitors from abuse at the hands of unethical government agencies, as a child. In Kalsched's model, the visitors are equivalent to *psychic agents of daimonic intervention.*

> The word "daimonic" comes from *daiomai,* which means to divide, and originally referred to moments of divided consciousness such as occur in slips of the tongue, failures in attention, or other breakthroughs from another realm of existence which we would call "the unconscious." Indeed, dividing up the inner world seems to be the intention of [the daimonic] figure. Jung's word for this was "dissociation," and our *daimon appears to personify the psyche's dissociative defenses in those cases where early trauma has made psychic integration impossible.* (1996, p. 11)

Intense anxiety in early childhood threatens to annihilate the child's personality, causing "the destruction of the personal spirit." When severe trauma occurs in early infancy (i.e., before a coherent ego and its defenses have formed), "*a second line of defenses* comes into play to prevent the 'unthinkable' from being *experienced*" (Kalsched, 1996, p. 11). This allows the child to survive psychologically and physically, but in later life the psychic defense system becomes a prison, preventing "unguarded spontaneous expressions of the self in the world. The person survives but cannot live creatively" (1996, p. 4).

> When trauma strikes the developing psyche of the child, a fragmentation of consciousness occurs in which the different "pieces" (Jung called them splinter-psyches or complexes) organize themselves

according to certain archaic and typical (archetypal) patterns, most commonly dyads or syzygies made up of personified "beings." Typically, one part of the ego *regresses* to the infantile period, and another part *progresses*, i.e., grows up too fast and becomes precociously adapted to the outer world, often as a "false self." The *progressed part* of the personality then caretakes the *regressed part*. (1996, p. 3)

A person suffering from trauma may experience what appears to be an authentic spiritual awakening. Yet the "awakening" is really a form of (necessary) dissociation to escape the effects of trauma, and entails a splitting of the psyche into a progressed ("enlightened") part and a correspondingly *regressed* part. This latter is in constant need of the protection and care of the "higher self." The progressed part then acts as a "guardian," whose function is not just to prevent further trauma, but also to prevent *psychic integration*.

While dissociation protects the psyche from being overwhelmed by trauma, it also prevents the experience from being fully "integrated," or processed. This forces the person to *continuously reenact the trauma* because he is unconsciously seeking "closure." Such an unconscious process is two-fold: The individual "relives" the trauma in the form of flashbacks, dreams, compulsive self-judgments or self-harming practices, and even via physical encounters that echo or shadow the original event (such as a series of abusive relationships). At the same time, the compulsive retraumatization entails a further splitting within the psyche that allows for continued dissociation. This can be seen in how a traumatized person cuts herself to release dopamine in the body: the compulsive traumatic reenactment being an unconscious means to bring about the relief of dissociation.

To this end, the "daimonic" or archetypal guardian will go to any length to protect the traumatized child-part of the psyche—even to the point of killing the "host" personality (suicide). Kalsched notes how the "progressed part of the personality" (the caregiver-guardian) is "represented in dreams by a powerful *benevolent or malevolent great being* who protects or persecutes" the regressed part, keeping it "safe," but also "imprisoned within." The progressed part has two faces and is "a 'duplex' figure, a protector and persecutor in one" (1996, p. 3). The picture this paints is an almost perfect match for Strieber's "visitors," whom he continues to perceive alternately as "angelic" and "demonic."

Kalsched's description of how archetypal defenses prevent personality development closely mirrors both Strieber's experience and his personality. Archetypal defenses, Kalsched writes,

> ... keep the personal spirit "safe" but disembodied, encapsulated, or otherwise driven out of the body/mind unity—*foreclosed from entering time and space reality*. Instead of slowly and painfully incarnating in a cohesive self, the volcanic opposing dynamisms of the inner world become organized around defensive purposes, constituting a "self-care system" for the individual. Instead of individuation and integration of mental life, the archaic defense engineers dis-incarnation (disembodiment) and dis-integration in order to help a weakened anxiety-ridden ego to survive, albeit as a partially "false" self. (1996, p. 38, emphasis added)

Early trauma may be an effective means of predisposing a person towards individuation and eventual enlightenment. But at the same time, and far more frequently, it can be crippling. Clearly not all sufferers of early trauma go on to become spiritual seekers, much less enlightened; nor does it seem likely that early trauma is essential to a spiritual outlook. (Kripal makes the same point in his article.) This may be a somewhat moot point, however, because trauma *has always been something of the norm in human society*, including (if we take into account the effects of modern medical birthing procedures, not to mention the continuing preponderance of child abuse) in the last century. If we allow that mysticism, spirituality, etc., are among the healthier and more natural responses to trauma, they are still far less common reactions than drug addiction, alcoholism, prostitution, depression, suicide, and so on.[1] In comparing all of these responses, however—specifically in comparing Strieber's and my own experiences—I would say that *dissociation from the body* is very much the key to understanding them.

Kalsched describes how dissociation allows life to continue "by dividing up the unbearable experience and *distributing it to different compartments of the mind and body, especially the 'unconscious' aspects of the mind and body*" (1996, p. 13, emphasis added). Kalsched's ensuing description reads like a blueprint for Strieber's fragmented accounts:

> Flashbacks of sensation seemingly disconnected from a behavioral context occur. The memory of one's life has holes in it—*a full*

narrative history cannot be told by the person whose life has been inter-rupted by trauma. For the person who has experienced unbearable pain, the psychological defense of dissociation allows external life to go on but at great internal cost. The outer trauma and its effects may be largely "forgotten," but the psychological sequelae of the trauma continue to haunt the inner world, and they do this, Jung discovered, in the form of certain images which cluster around a strong affect—what Jung called "the feeling-toned complexes." These complexes *tend to behave autonomously as frightening inner "beings"* … (1996, pp. 12–13, emphasis added)

Paraphrasing, if early trauma cannot be assimilated by the conscious mind and is pushed down into the unconscious, *into the body*, the individual's inner world is "haunted" by personified agents of trauma. The task of these psychosomatic "beings" is to bring the dissociated ego's awareness *back* to wholeness, back to the body. As we'll see, Strieber's encounters with the visitors entailed extreme physical inter-actions, including violations of his body. To this day, Strieber says he was raped by the visitors, even while professing love for them (a typical response of the abused). Strieber also experienced somatic symptoms after the memories first began to resurface, even possibly to the point of stigmata, and it was these symptoms that fully alerted him to the past traumatic events.

While Strieber insists that his experiences with the visitors are real, and that the visitors exist independently of his own imagination, Kalsched would almost certainly reject the need to differentiate the real (physical) from the imaginary (psychic). When we hear the word "psyche," we tend to associate it with "mind," hence with something that is unreal. Yet psyche means "soul," and the only way for soul to come all the way into mind-awareness is for it to be experienced through, and *as*, body. Psychic integration (bringing the elements of our unconscious being into consciousness) happens not in the mind, but *in and through the body*. This is because psychic fragmentation (disintegration) takes place in the body. What we think of as mind (or at least the way we experience the thing we call "mind") is merely the *result* of psychic fragmentation.

Spiritual experiences can accompany a soul-body (psychosomatic) integration; but they are more commonly used as a surrogate for it. Like sex and drugs, they can allow us to "bliss out" and further dissociate from body awareness and into mental fantasies that provide some scant bodily relief. This would be especially so if dissociation was a "trick" which the psyche learned early on, because dissociation then becomes unconscious, automatic behavior. If dissociation involves numbing our awareness of the somatic affects of trauma, it follows that genuine spiritual awakening—becoming fully embodied—would entail allowing awareness to awaken to those early affects. This is far more likely to be painful than blissful. Bliss states might *appear* to be leading to fuller embodiment when they are really the result of the mind using spiritual fantasies (dissociation) to release anesthetizing chemicals in the body *to stave off integration* (just as heroin or morphine can be used to create pleasing physical sensations). The very sort of techniques we learned as infants to protect ourselves from trauma, we then adapt as adults under the guise of "spiritual practices." This is a very apparent danger of "spiritual awakenings" that result from trauma.

The later trauma (Strieber's abduction in 1985, say) is almost certainly a reenactment of an original trauma that caused early dissociation, making it an attempt of the psychosomatic system to reintegrate the experience into awareness. Turning it into a "spiritual awakening" or shamanic initiation may be the means by which the "guardian" (the self-care system) tricks the individual into escaping the terrifying impact of a full bodily awakening. "Repressed material can only resurface into consciousness in an atmosphere of denial and negation, so a fuller awakening means an ever greater distortion of consciousness and increase in neurosis" (Brown, 1985, p. 232).

In "The Traumatic Secret," Kripal references Aldous Huxley's *The Doors of Perception* (a book I first read in my very early twenties, in the same period I discovered Carlos Castaneda), specifically Huxley's idea of a "Mind at Large" and how the brain works as a reducing valve. Kripal writes about how we can't access this universal "mind" because we lack a "safe way to shut down the filter. Because of this, the conflation of consciousness and brain states or cultural conditions is more or less … unassailable." He laments this conflation and chalks it down to the desire to "study what we have easy and reliable access to, not what we do not have access to and can only know once or twice in a life-time, if at all" (Kripal, 2015, pp. 167–168).

An interest in uncoupling consciousness from brain states and gaining repeat access to "Mind at Large" appears to be a primary, driving interest of intelligence communities (from MKULTRA to remote viewing) as well as for both Strieber and Kripal. It is in fact what has hitched their starships together, as seen in their latest offering in 2016, a full-blown collaboration called *The Super Natural: A New Vision of the Unexplained*, by which Kripal appears to be working to legitimize Strieber's until now marginal (if best-selling) accounts. Both Kripal and Strieber represent themselves as literary outliers doing groundbreaking research into generally overlooked, even maligned, subject matter; on the surface this appears to be true. On the other hand, there's a substantial area of overlap between the margin which Kripal and Strieber appear to be occupying, and the hidden mainstream represented by decades-long intelligence and governmental research into consciousness and matter. There also seems to be a shared disregard for how the means of accessing the unconscious might influence the end. This was my main argument with Kripal, and it was one which I never felt he addressed, namely, that observing how dissociation of the psyche in response to trauma allows access to "transpersonal," disembodied realms of consciousness leaves unanswered the question of how reliable the experiences will be once we get there. Ignoring this question—which both Kripal and Strieber do—seems to lead inexorably—and prematurely—to the idea of applying the equivalent of a Hadron collider to the human psyche.

If, through the intervention of technology—and perhaps more ordinary modes of interference such as sexual abuse—it is possible to access the hidden realm of matter by attacking children's psyches, can there be any doubt that such attempts are being made? Is there any difference between Kripal's "safe way to shut down the filter" in the brain, and Strieber's shattering the mirror of expectation? And how safe is this process really? Kripal asserts that "the sacred is accessed ritually and mystically primarily through the violation of taboo," and compares this age-old tradition to the Hadron collider. The key, he argues, is that "we can only get there"—there being the realization that "matter is not material at all"—"through a great deal of physical violence, a violence so extreme and so precise that it cost us billions of dollars and decades of preparation to inflict it."

*

"There is the possibility, as I have discussed, that conscious life extends into an energetic level that is completely detached from the physical."
—Whitley Strieber, *Solving the Communion Enigma*

In the third chapter of *Solving the Communion Enigma*, Strieber discusses a shadowy organization called "the Finders," whose activities first came to light when reported by *The Washington Post* in February 1987. Two white males were arrested in Tallahassee Park, with six disheveled children, all under the age of seven. From the Customs report from February 12, 1987:

> The children were covered with insect bites, were very dirty, most of the children were not wearing underpants and all of the children had not been bathed in many days. ... The men were somewhat evasive in their answers to police and stated only that they were the children's teachers and that all were en route to Mexico to establish a school for brilliant children. The children were unaware of the functions of telephones, television and toilets, and stated that they were not allowed to live indoors and were only given food as a reward. (*Educate Yourself*, 2005)

A warehouse purportedly in use by the organization was discovered and evidence of its activities found. The Finders were described in a court document as a cult that conducted "brainwashing" and used children "in rituals." Photographs allegedly showed naked children involved in bloodletting ceremonies of animals and sexual orgies, including a photograph of a child in chains. Evidence was found for an international network of child trafficking for sexual and other purposes.[2] The investigation was abruptly ended, however, when the US Justice Department named it a matter of "national security." It was turned over to the CIA as an "internal security matter." The evidence was suppressed (there's no Wikipedia page for the case), and the children were released back to the same adults who had been arrested for abusing them.[3]

Why, in a book about alien contact, does Strieber have a chapter about this group? The answer is that he has ample reason to suspect that he was also inducted, as a child, into whatever murky operation was being carried out under the cloak of national security. In "The Boy in the Box" (Unknown Country, March 14, 2003), Strieber remembers being taken to a school for "brilliant children" in Monterrey, Mexico, though he is left with "very little recollection of what happened there."

> There is one flash of memory of seeing another child holding a bloody saw. I was told that this child had killed somebody with it.

The child appeared absolutely terrified. While this person, whom I still know well, seems to have no memory of this incident, she has lived a ruined, disturbed life. She has never been healthy, either physically or mentally. My wife tells me that I have mentioned seeing Jewish babies there, and that I once said that the school was located in a villa owned by somebody connected with the Pan American Sulphur Company. I have no recollection of saying either of these things. The Pan American Sulphur Company did indeed exist, and was once a powerful influence in Mexico. (2003a)

Strieber first wrote about this period of his life (growing up in San Antonio, Texas, in the 1940s and 1950s) in 1997, in *The Secret School*. The book recounts a "hidden life" in which Strieber and other children belonged to a secret school run by "the visitors" (curiously, he remembers them mostly as *nuns*, called "Sisters of Mercy"). It was six years later, at his website in 2003, that he first shared memories of a secret government program that involved systemized traumatization of children, for ends never fully explained.

Strieber's psychic odyssey presents two very different narratives playing side by side: a terrifying human program of psychological and physical interference, and a "sublime," transcendental apprenticeship to nonhuman beings. The two narratives overlap, invisibly, in Strieber's writings, and we can only assume they do so in his mind. Strieber bridges this apparent gulf by suggesting (in "The Boy in the Box") that "… the close encounters were real, and that they involved literally breaking through into another level of reality in order to escape the hell I was enduring in this one." Yet what Strieber is describing is classic dissociation. Even if the encounters were psychically real, it ignores the fact that his body was being submitted to equally real physical abuse while the supposedly "transcendental" lessons were taking place. Unless, that is, he believes he was *physically* taken away by these beings?

At this point, it may be wise to state my position more clearly. I am not arguing that nonhuman and intelligent beings, similar to those described by Strieber, do not exist, or even that they don't interact with us. And while this might seem to some readers to be *the* crucial question here, I consider it beyond my capacity—and possibly anyone's—to ascertain. I am not even arguing that some of Strieber's impressions and memories may not relate to genuine encounters with divine-infernal beings, outside of (though undoubtedly working in tandem with) his own "archetypal defenses." This is all uncharted territory, and such hypothetical beings may very well be involved. What I *am* suggesting, or at least wondering, is how he, and others in similar positions, are putting together the pieces to assemble a seemingly coherent narrative that, quite frankly, *does not add up?*

There are two areas which I have been drawn to focus on to answer this question: the missing pieces that have been excluded—the "holes" in Strieber's narrative created by a dissociated psyche. And, in direct response to that omission, any elements that have been added to, or superimposed *onto*, the picture, in order to take advantage of the dissociation and "fill in" those holes. The first question—locating missing pieces—is almost wholly psychological; the second—identifying any spurious elements which have been added—while also psychological (everything is), overlaps with the parapolitical question of social and religious engineering, namely this:

To what degree have the narratives which Strieber and other "contactees" (and mystic commentators such as Huxley and Kripal) report, and which they may well sincerely believe, been discreetly shaped by *outside agencies* to exploit deeper, archetypal associations in the collective psyche, thereby giving a richness of meaning to a *manufactured* narrative, fueling a political agenda with "the stuff of dreams"?

In other words, is there an actual, ongoing sociopolitical agenda using a combination of "traditional" beliefs with newly created ones, or new arrangements and interpretations of old ones, for the creation of a "scientistic religion"? The evidence for such an agenda is compelling, and it strongly suggests the psychological manipulation of individuals (possibly from an early age) in an attempt to access and harness the human potential for psychism. In the process, leaders, teachers, and spokespeople for the new paradigm (such as Strieber) are being created, from childhood on. Most disturbing of all, the basis of this (hypothetical) sociopolitical agenda, or at least one primary aspect of it, appears to be the appliance of *trauma* as the means to activate the psychic centers of the human brain, ushering in a "new evolutionary stage" for the species that (it is hoped) will act as a socially acceptable (i.e., manipulable) surrogate for authentic (full body) spiritual enlightenment.

Whatever agendas *might* be at work in society, however, is less my concern than undoing my own psychic conditioning by mapping the state of *Strieber's* psyche. In both cases (my own and Strieber's), what I am starting to see is how much early trauma has caused fragmentation and left "holes", or cracks, in our psyches and our pasts. *"The memory of one's life has holes in it—a full narrative history cannot be told by the person whose life has been interrupted by trauma."* These holes are inevitably filled by *other energies*. Whether such energies come from the environment or from our own unconscious—or, as is generally the case, both at once—they appear to have their own agendas. Identifying what kind of energies have filled the holes and what their agendas might be is only part of the process. The next step is finding out what lies *behind* those energies. This entails locating the holes in the plot—the cracks in the mirror—and uncovering the cover story which Strieber, or I, or all of us, have been telling ourselves, throughout our adult lives.

It means not only finding the holes, but going all the way *into* them.

CHAPTER IV

The infinite infant: the singularity & the resurrection of the body

"To rise above the body is to equate the body with excrement."
—Norman O. Brown, *Life Against Death*

When I started out this written exploration, it was meant as a knock-off response to Kripal's thought-provoking article, "The Traumatic Secret." Several days and 8,000 words later, the end seemed to be receding ever further into the distance. I hardly expected to be recounting a history of the Finders, for example, much less delving into satanic ritual abuse conspiracy lore. Now I am embarked on a much larger project, my aim becomes to report the facts as well as I can, to follow the connections wherever they lead me, and to present a reasonably coherent picture of the leviathan-like morass which we call "civilization." Jimmy Savile, the BBC, MI5, the CIA, the British monarchy, the Catholic Church, SRI, MKULTRA, the Finders, Strieber's "visitors"—all of these strands *appear* to be inextricably interwoven; so, they must surely all belong here? (There's another that does too, the persistently recurring (in so-called "conspiracy" research) group known as The Process Church. This peculiar psycho-spiritual organization has been connected to Scientology, the Manson family, and the Son of Sam murders. I shouldn't have been surprised, perhaps, to discover that Strieber was making a documentary about them, in London in 1968, at precisely the time he started to have (non-alien related) "missing time" experiences. But more on this later.)

One connection I made (in my own mind at least) early on was to the transhumanist movement, something I'd been researching while looking into autism (a project that got steamrollered by this one). I had looked briefly into Ray Kurzweil and "the Singularity," and planned to cite it in passing in the larger context of SRI and spiritual engineering. Then I rediscovered the Norman O. Brown/Freud material and that gave the material a more complex, psychological dimension. (I added the Kalsched material later still.) Most of the Brown material I used referred to the mother (tying in nicely with Jimmy Savile as the archetypal "national-institution-as-psychopath" guy). The question naturally arose: Where was the father in all this? It was a question both little and large: Where *was* "the Father"?

To try to answer this question, I am going to look a little at Ray Kurzweil. I do this with some reluctance, because, unlike Strieber, I have zero affinity for Kurzweil. What Strieber is to the aliens, Kurzweil is to the Singularity: probably the leading spokes-prophet of his time. The word "singularity" originally meant "singleness of aim or purpose" but the mathematical sense of singularity, a "point at which a function takes an infinite value," was coined in 1893. In the context of technology, the term was popularized by the science-fiction writer Vernor Vinge, who argued that artificial intelligence, human biological enhancement, or brain-computer interfaces could be possible causes of the singularity. The specific term "singularity"—as a description for technological acceleration causing an unpredictable outcome in society—was coined by the mathematician, John von Neumann, who in the mid-1950s spoke of "ever accelerating progress of technology and changes in the mode of human life, which gives the appearance of approaching some essential singularity in the history of the race beyond which human affairs, as we know them, could not continue" (Ulam, 1958). The concept has also been popularized by futurists such as Kurzweil, who cited von Neumann's use of the term in a foreword to von Neumann's classic *The Computer and the Brain*.

Curiously enough, in 1997, Whitley Strieber wrote a short story called "The Open Doors" about John von Neumann—*in relation to the visitors*. Von Neumann's theory is apparently the basis of Strieber's on-again, off-again theory that the visitors *need our belief in them to enter into our reality*—a startling and unexpected connection between supposed alien contact and the technological "singularity" event.

Rolling Stone magazine called Kurzweil "the most radical futurist on earth" (Kushner, 2009). According to the same article, he has also been called "the rightful heir to Thomas Edison" and received White House honors from three presidents, "including the highest prize in his field, the National Medal of Technology." Kurzweil was a child prodigy who turned eighteen in 1967; his interest was less in psychedelics than cybernetics, however. "LSD was a pretty imperfect technology because you couldn't control it," he told *Rolling Stone*. "That wasn't my idea of transcendence." He went on to design the first program that allowed computers to read text, and subsequently the first program to translate text into speech. His interest is primarily in *the merging of the human organism with technology*. By 2045, Kurzweil predicts, human beings and machines will belong to a single species. Apparently he's no slouch in the prediction department either:

> During the 1980s, Kurzweil correctly predicted the fall of the Soviet Union due to decentralized technologies, the rise of the Internet and the ubiquity of wireless networks. He announced that a computer would be a world chess champion by 1998—a reality that occurred in May 1992 when Deep Blue defeated Gary Kasparov .... "There's something inexorable about these progressions," Kurzweil says. "We really can predict—not exactly what's going to happen, but the power of these technologies .... We won't experience 100 years of progress in the 21st century—it will be more like 20,000 years of progress .... Nanobots in our physical bodies will destroy pathogens, remove debris, repair DNA and reverse aging," Kurzweil predicts. "We will be able to redesign all the systems in our bodies and brains to be far more capable and durable." By scanning the contents of your brain, nanobots will be able to transfer everything you know, everything you have ever experienced, into a robot or a virtual reality program. If something happens to your physical body, no problem. Your mind will live on—forever. (Kushner, 2009)

Kurzweil's dream is the oldest dream of all, but there's an additional wrinkle. His first goal isn't eternal life but, in good "Christian" spirit (though Kurzweil is anything but conventionally religious), *the resurrection of the body:*

Death represents the loss of knowledge and information .... A person is a mind file. A person is a software program—a very profound one, and we have no backup. So when our hardware dies, our software dies with it .... I've made an issue of overcoming death. And the strongest experience I've had with death is as a tragedy. (Quoted by Kushner, 2009)

Kurzweil plans to resurrect not his own body but *his father's*, and he has stored boxes of his dad's possessions, *external objects* onto which he projects his longing, including "his letters and music and bills and doctoral thesis."

We can find some of his DNA around his grave site, that's a lot of information right there ... The AI will send down some nanobots and get some bone or teeth and extract some DNA and put it all together. Then they'll get some information from my brain and anyone else who still remembers him .... Just send nanobots into my brain and reconstruct my recollections and memories .... If you can do it right, it's worthwhile .... If you bring back life that was valuable in the past, it should be valuable in the future. (Quoted by Kushner, 2009)

Kurzweil is an interesting case study (almost as interesting as Strieber). On the one hand, like Colonel Kurtz ruling over his savages in *Apocalypse Now*, he *appears* to be barking mad. Yet he is also well-attuned to the *zeitgeist*, and, at least as far as technology is concerned, he seems to know what he is talking about. So what he's saying can't simply be dismissed as insanity, any more than Strieber's works can. It represents the precise point at which science and mysticism meet and the dream-nightmare of the illumineers begins to creep over into waking reality. And what is this vision? To conquer Nature and replace the absent father—God—with our own self-generated image. Lucifer's dream is Oedipus' nightmare. As Norman O. Brown writes:

The child has to make a choice between love of self and love of the other: according to Freud, the boy's self-love or narcissism turns him away from his mother. But the self so loved is fraudulent: self-love replaces parental love, but ... only at the cost of splitting the ego into parent and child. Through the institution of the super-ego the parents are internalized and *man finally succeeds in becoming father of himself, but at the cost of becoming his own child and keeping his ego infantile.* (1985, p. 129, emphasis added)

Kurzweil appears to be suffering from the same psychic schism as Strieber. This suggests that it may be a collective condition in the Western world (for men at least)—not to say a universal one. Perhaps the best summation of Kurzweil's cosmic goal would be: "The universe is not conscious—yet. But it will be." While Kurzweil means the statement as a promise, somehow it comes out sounding more like a threat.

In "Uploading Life: Send Your Personality to Space" (featured at Kurzweil's Accelerating Intelligence site), "Senior Space Writer" Leonard David quotes sociologist William Sims Bainbridge (we'll be hearing more from him later) describing "the gradual merging of human beings with their computers over the next century." Bainbridge provides fuel for Kurzweil's (literally infantile) dreams when he predicts this will lead to "interstellar immortality." The article sums up Bainbridge's vision of employing cognitive neural science, genetic engineering, nanotechnology, and information systems to found "a cosmic civilization." This need not require transporting "living human bodies and all the necessities of life to other planets." Instead, computer technology will allow these transhumanist hopefuls to archive personalities, "albeit at low fidelity." Making "digital, audio/visual copies of a person's perceptions, speech and behavior" is already possible, Bainbridge claims. Eventually, "the ability to reanimate human personalities at ever-higher fidelity is a sure bet."

"Only a goal as valuable as eternal life can motivate investment in substantial scientific infrastructure on the Moon or Mars," says Bainbridge, an interesting choice of words that suggests that eternal life, as the motivational factor, is *a means rather than an end.* The idea of eternal life is as deeply seated as any religious belief, and hence more or less guaranteed to get people's attention. Since most people are religiously rather than scientifically oriented, and since the desire to colonize space is far less on their minds than the question of what happens to them when they die, it makes perfect sense to use the religious impulse to fuel the engine of scientific progress. Bainbridge's grand galactic plan is to turn human beings into pure information and send them (it?) into outer space; to spread the cultural virus of traumatized, mother-bonded, father-abandoned egos across the galaxy, dragging God down *into* the machine—*Deus in ipsam machinam?*—and in His absence create a brave new universe of "Mind at Large." Possibly the transhumanist illumineers really believe this fever dream of technological transcendence, but it may be more likely they have come up with a suitably *religiose* narrative to inspire the masses to support their sociopolitical agenda and allow it to move forward unimpeded.

> By offering the stars to people living today, the second wave of the spaceflight movement would be spurred into being ... The future demands a powerful, motivational force to create interplanetary and interstellar civilizations [Bainbridge said], and a new spaceflight social movement can get us moving again. (David, 2001)

But moving towards what?

*

> "The implant also enables me to travel almost anywhere in space and time, or even outside of space time. It acts as a sort of accellerator [sic] of being, intensifying my ability to move out of my body and into many remarkable realms."
> —Whitley Strieber, 2005[1]

Kurzweil and Strieber share a common preoccupation with extending their existence beyond the physical, even to the point of completely detaching themselves (their ego-minds) from their bodies. There may be a psychological explanation for this preoccupation, besides simply fear of death.

During the first years of the infant's life, there is a fundamental need to fully separate from the mother's body, to "disenmesh" from her psyche and develop an autonomous, authentic sense of self. For this to happen a strong paternal presence is required to "fish" the child out of the mother's psyche and provide an environment for the child to gradually shift his focus, *away* from the mother and onto the world at large. The father's task is to preside over this transition from mother-dependency to autonomy, to help the child to develop his awareness as a separate body and a correspondingly healthy ego. When—as is so often the case in the Western world—the father is absent and/or indifferent (or, possibly worse, abusive), there is no way for this process to happen. As a result, the child remains hopelessly lost in what Margaret Mahler called "symbiotic psychosis," a "delirious state of undifferentiation between the ego and the object" (Thomson, 2005).[2]

The mother-bonded adult experiences himself as somehow trapped, confined, restricted. He feels prevented (often by some hidden, sinister force) from experiencing reality and himself as they truly are. Without awareness of the underlying cause of this "bondage," there is a natural tendency to place the focus outside of the self, onto the universe at large. At the same time, the feeling of imprisonment is projected *onto the body itself*. A very real, deeply felt need to complete the separation from the mother's body is experienced as *a need to escape from the body*. Such a "complex" could give rise to a preoccupation with "exteriorization" from the body, whether by converting consciousness into digital data and sending it across space-time, or (as in alleged "remote viewing" programs of the US military) accessing a "subtle," "astral," or energy body and projecting it outward, through space and time, to become, like Strieber with his implant, a major Mental Traveler.

The creation of a "mental body"—an image of the body which can be used as a vehicle for self-consciousness to leave the body—is a common feature of occult writing about psychism and "sorcery," and something I've been familiar with at least since my early twenties, when I first read Carlos Castaneda—including this passage from *The Eagle's Gift*:

> [T]he *dreaming body* is sometimes called the "double" or the "other," because it is a perfect replica of the dreamer's body. It is inherently the energy of a luminous being, a whitish, phantomlike emanation, which is projected by the fixation of the second attention into *a three-dimensional image of the body* [emphasis added]. [T]he *dreaming body* is not a ghost, but as real as anything we deal with in the world. [T]he second attention is unavoidably drawn to focus on our total being as a field of energy, and transforms that energy into anything suitable. The easiest thing is of course the image of the physical body, with which we are already thoroughly familiar from our daily lives and the use of our first attention. (1981, p. 23)

In *The Ego and the Id*, written in 1923, Freud describes the ego as being "ultimately derived from bodily sensations, chiefly from those springing from the surface of the body. It may thus be regarded as *a mental projection of the surface of the body*" (Tiemersma, 1989, p. 83).[3]

The psychoanalyst Jacques Lacan developed this idea further in his critical reinterpretation of the work of Freud in the 1930s, '40s, and '50s. He called it "the mirror stage" of infant development. Lacan drew on work in physiology and animal psychology and noticed how the human infant passes through a stage in which *"an external image of the body"* produces a *"psychic response"* that gives rise to "the mental representation of an 'I.'"' This external image can be its body *reflected in a mirror*, or it can be represented to the infant through the mother or primary caregiver—that is, the infant as he sees himself *through the mother's eyes*. Either way, the infant identifies with the image, which "serves as a gestalt of the infant's emerging perceptions of selfhood." Since the image of a unified body does not correspond with the underdeveloped infant's physical vulnerability and weakness, however, this "imago" is established as an "Ideal-I" toward which "the subject *will perpetually strive throughout his or her life*" (*CriticaLink*, 1998).

A perpetual striving towards an "Ideal-I," a perfected *mental* image of the body: This sounds like a fairly universal condition, in the West at least, where we seem to be stuck in the "mirror stage" of infant development. It may also be the condition that sorcerers, transhumanists, and alien-abducted mystics have all picked up and run with, in effect, magnified to cosmic proportions.

As a perpetual striver after an Ideal-I, I have had my share of "astral projection" experiences, including "transhuman" (and/or alien) states of perception and being. One thing I eventually came to notice was how often I returned from such excursions to an unusually poor state of health, so much so that it would sometimes take me an hour or more to feel strong enough to get out of bed. Eventually, a Jungian therapist I was seeing informally (the one who recommended Kalsched) suggested that all of my out-of-body journeys and dreams of space flight were, at base, an attempt to escape the reality of my body. She advised me to turn my focus around, to the inside of my body and the ordinary, mundane aspects of life. I have been following this advice ever since, and my astral journeys and/or visionary dreams have mostly tapered off. Do I miss them? Yes. Am I more grounded in (and accepting of) my everyday self and reality? Yes. Ironically, or perhaps not, the less I experience what I was perpetually striving to experience, the less perpetual my striving has become. I also find it a lot easier to get out of bed in the morning.

Trauma leads to dissociation; dissociation is when a part of the individual's psyche withdraws from an intolerable situation because it is impossible to withdraw physically. Strieber, and countless others in the fields of religion, psychism, and ufology, are arguing that dissociation and/or out-of-body experiences that result from trauma are ways to access realms of experience otherwise unavailable to us. While (based on my own experiences) trauma can and does lead to authentic "soul journeys," what is not being discussed, so far as I can tell, is the assumption that, because they are genuine—or to the degree which they *are* genuine—these visionary states are desirable and beneficent to us.

My own position is that these non-corporeal excursions not only depend on a disconnection from the body but *exacerbate* it. I would even suggest (again based on direct experience) that this is the sole imagined "benefit" of such experiences, namely, that they allow for *a surrogate form of individuation* and a "pseudo-enlightenment," one which I suspect is not only no substitute for the real thing but which may severely reduce the chances of it ever happening. If we find a convincing counterfeit for what, at the very deepest level, we are striving for, we may suppress our knowing that something isn't right, in order to settle for the more easily available substitute. Yet the substitute cannot ever satisfy. And meanwhile, there is also nothing quite as addictive as the cure that *almost* works.

The attempt to escape psychological bondage to the mother by leaving the body (or the planet) behind is the attempt to extend the infantile into the infinite. It's like the star child at the end of *2001: A Space Odyssey*—the favorite "trip" movie of the counterculture. The floating fetus or the infinite infant is the final goal of both science and fantasy: Man creating God in his own image. But the star child projected onto the screen, like the body in the mirror (or in our mother's eyes), is not a real flesh and blood body; it's only an image. Its perfection is the result of perfecting an illusion.

CHAPTER V

The secret guardian

"When innocence has been deprived of its entitlement, it becomes a diabolic spirit."

—J. Grotstein, "Forgery of the Soul"

A life full of holes. A cluster of fragments, swirling, roving, seeking a place to fit, seeking coherence, seeking meaning. A wound in the soul; a psyche in mortal peril. What *is* Whitley's secret? And why have I felt compelled to probe his work again and again throughout my adult life, like a tongue returning to an infected tooth? Whatever Whitley's secret wound, finding it would mean—would *depend* on—finding my own. So how do you seek a secret you are keeping from yourself?

"The visitors appeared to be using our distorted perception as a vehicle."
"You're chained to the ground."
"There was a strange darkness. I did not want to look; I didn't even want to be near it."
"You may be irretrievably lost."
"An energetic level that is completely detached from the physical."

"I can imagine no greater honor than to be called human."
"This is the trigger for intervention, the destruction of a living
world."
"He would say only that something had gone wrong."
"I acquired an effective coping tool: The more frightening they
got, the stronger I became."
"I do not now find the small, gray beings terrible. I find them
useful."

In *Solving the Communion Enigma*, published twenty-five years after
Communion, Strieber recounts a strange memory which also occurred
when he was twelve, when he found a photograph of his father lying
in a coffin, eyes closed and arms crossed. Young Whitley showed the
picture to his father, who tore it up, flushed it down the toilet, and
never spoke of it again (Strieber, 2011a, p. 25). As Strieber recounts the
incident, the desk in which he finds the photograph had recently been
given to him by his father, suggesting Whitley was *meant* to find the
photograph at that precise time. For a boy on the brink of adolescence,
seeing his father as a corpse would have had a profound impact on his
psyche, an impact that would only have been deepened by his father's
demonstration of the *forbidden* nature of the image. Totem and taboo.

Among the countless fragments that stand out in the Strieber material are several other descriptions of his father. When Whitley is being
subjected to strange procedures as a child—whether at the hands of
alien beings or human ones or both—his father appears only as a powerless and frightened figure. It's logical enough, since for Whitley to
have been subjected to such traumatic treatments in his childhood, his
father must have been remiss, ineffective, or simply absent.

In *Communion*, Strieber describes a memory of being on a train, surrounded by soldiers lying unconscious in beds. He is twelve and his
father is there, afraid, and the young Whitley is reassuring him. He tells
his father that it's all right, and his father replies, "Whitty, it's not all
right! It's not all right!" (1987, p. 62). The picture of a twelve-year-old
boy trying to comfort his father puts the son in the role of the father,
and vice versa. Later in the book, Strieber mentions a "confused recollection" of his father crouched at the back of an upper berth on the train,
"his eyes bulging, his lips twisted back from his teeth." He later attributed the memory to a nightmare brought on by violent illness, during
which he "... vomited until I thought I would die, and for no apparent

reason. Nothing came up but bile, but the spasms simply would not stop" (1987, p. 118). Elsewhere in the same work, another fragment from Strieber's childhood describes his father in a similarly terrified (and terrifying) light:

> Almost in slow motion [my father's] face simply broke up. He threw his head back and something like an electric shock seemed to go through him, making him spread his fingers and shake his arms. His eyes bulged and his mouth flew open. Then he was screaming, but I could hear it only faintly, a muffled shrieking, full of terror and despair. (1987, p. 126)

In *The Secret School*, Strieber describes the effect of seeing his father's terror in starkly visceral terms: *"his fear just seemed to pour into me like a freezing torrent"* (1997, p. 206). In *Transformation*, Strieber's follow-up to *Communion*, he describes being in a moment of terror and despair, wanting to give up, "to sink down and just scream," knowing his young son "might wake and he mustn't see his dad like this" (1988, p. 232). Here, Strieber is speaking from painful experience.

The earliest memory I have of my father—the only one I have of him while he was still living with us—is when I was around six or seven: he was half naked and unconscious—dead drunk—on the bedroom floor. No doubt the shocking nature of the scene seared itself onto my consciousness, and forever after I associated my father with unconsciousness, powerlessness, and incapacitation (maybe even death, if I didn't understand what had happened to him). My clearest impression of him, then, was as *an absence*.

That Strieber was impacted in a similar way, specifically by the photograph, would seem to be confirmed by repeat mentions of coffins, boxes, and confined spaces throughout his writings. He first went public about his traumatic "schooling" experiences at his website with "The Boy in the Box," describing memories of being confined in a small space for long periods of time.

> Among my worst memories, one that has come back to me again and again and again over the course of my life, is of waking up and finding that I am in a coffin. A box. I wake up when I try to move, and my head bounces against the top of the thing. I cannot get out. I'm trapped. The silence is absolute. The air is heavy. Soon, my

> breathing is agonizing. I'm in torment. But it doesn't end. It keeps
> on and on and on. I remain for what seems like hours at the edge
> of suffocation. I scream, I see demons staring at me, I see angels,
> I see my grandfather Strieber there, then I see a long horizon, the
> sun either rising or setting. (Strieber, 2003a)

In *Solving the Communion Enigma*, the coffin image recurs in a more
cosmic context, when Strieber mentally asks one of the visitors, "What
does the universe mean to you?"

> Instantly, there appeared in my mind a bright, clear image of a
> closed coffin .... I wondered how anyone could think of our mys-
> terious universe that way? But then I realized that, of course, they
> have probably reached its limits, or worse, discovered that reality
> has no limits. I can see the claustrophobia that would attend to the
> realization that one was trapped in an infinity that could never be
> escaped. In fact, I can feel it. It's a little like being in a room you can
> never leave, or a prison. (2011a, p. 71)

By what strange logic can infinity be compared to a closed coffin? The
logic of trauma, perhaps? It is as if Whitley's whole universe has become
the casket in which his absent father is concealed, and matter the tomb
in which the divine is forever buried. Like Kurzweil, Strieber seems to
have projected his unhealed trauma onto infinity.

At seven, Strieber's immune system broke down and he fell ill, after
which he was apparently taken out of the secret school (the non-alien
one). Strieber's father was upset and paced the room, but "would say
only that something had gone wrong" (2011a, p. 23). If, as this seems
to imply, Strieber's father (and possibly both his parents) had inducted
young Whitley (probably at around age four) into the secret school of
traumagenesis, how much had he known about what would happen to
his son? Strieber has not talked about it much, but he did address the
question at the Unknown Country Message Board, in February of 2007,
in response to a comment about Ty Brown's research:

> Here is what I believe happened, in essence: During the war, my
> father was involved in a program to prevent US dollars going to
> Mexico from the Texas German community, where this money
> would be used to buy gold to send to Germany. Prior to the war,

during the great German inflation, he had been participating in doing this himself, but certainly never for the Nazis. After the war, he was approached and his patriotism was appealed to, I was enrolled in this program. He did not know what it involved, except that it was important cold war work. I think that he was the victim of Paperclip scientists, who singled us out because of his war work. He did not know that I was going to be harmed, but the stress was so great that my immune system shut down and I was treated in the autumn and winter of 1952 at Brooke General Hospital with gamma globulin injections. I was isolated from other children at that time. (2007a)

In his short story "Pain" (2013), Strieber describes the incident with the photograph but fictionalizes it, saying it is a picture of the main character's uncle. The narrator describes how his uncle lived in Munich in the 1920s, and how the photo is a record of his initiation into the Vril society, a secret occult order behind the Nazis' rise to power. Strieber speculates how the Vril society performed a magical working to "raise a demon" to possess Adolf Hitler, their ultimate goal being to perform an alchemical ritual called "the death of the white king," the final end of which was the detonation of the atomic bomb. The death of the white king relates to the semi-historical practice (famously described in James Frazer's *The Golden Bough*) of *slaying the father in order to replace him*. Also known as the myth of Oedipus.

*

"I call them visitors, but now I am beginning to think that is a misnomer. I have had the impression that they think of themselves as family, and perhaps that is exactly what they are."
—Whitley Strieber, *Transformation*

One of the stranger encounters which Strieber recounts in *Solving the Communion Enigma* is with a weird, feral creature that lived outside his house for several years, chain-smoking cigarettes. As Strieber describes him: *"He looked like somebody who had ceased to age before puberty, and was now not a man but a sort of weathered child"* (2011a, p. 45, emphasis added). Strieber comes to see the weird man-child as his protector, keeping him safe from hostile (probably human) agencies who wish to harm him.

The strange creature seems to live in the forest behind Strieber's house and to be constantly lurking in the vicinity, keeping an eye on Strieber and his family. Strieber first becomes aware of its presence due to the smell of cigarette smoke, which Strieber is allergic to. He goes to investigate the being but is met with a ferocious look and a guttural growl that discourages him from any further attempts. He eventually comes to refer to the being as *"the guardian."*

Like so many of Strieber's encounters, the guardian is an almost spellbinding blend of the mundane with the fantastic. In Strieber's world, creatures that would seem to belong exclusively to the realm of myth have an unsettlingly profane reality to them: bad smells, dirty ships, cigarette butts. While I was looking over the descriptions of this strange withered child, I found myself considering an even more peculiar possibility than that of an objective being "out there." What if—like the daimonic guardian described by Kalsched—the creature was an aspect of Strieber himself? Admittedly, Strieber claims that other people saw the being, and that there was the evidence of the cigarette butts (it seems unlikely Strieber could be smoking them himself without his wife noticing). But in Strieber's world, things are rarely as simple as either/or. Could the creature be an objectively real being (at least some of the time?) while in some strange way being an aspect of Strieber's psyche? Strieber has suggested something similar about other fantastical beings he has encountered, and he speculates on several occasions that the Master of the Key is his "future self." So why not the little shriveled guardian, who at one point he compares to the Master, but who he finds so distasteful?[1] Maybe the answer is in the question?

If Strieber's own psychological development, by whatever means, was deliberately arrested prior to adolescence as part of an inner-outer "archetypal traumatogenic agenda," designed to harvest his psychic energy and redirect it down specific channels (towards the creation of a de-eroticized transhumanist scientific religion, *say*), was this weathered prepubescent what his traumatized psyche might have looked like? A lot more than "the Master of the Key," at any rate?

Towards the end of *Solving the Communion Enigma*, Strieber describes a kind of "mind-meld" with the being. He describes the creature's mind as "a desperate nest of rage and tension." The creature was able to hear thoughts, and at one point Strieber is able to briefly share his experience, "among the most appalling things that has ever happened to me." He hears a cacophony of roaring, snarling, wailing voices, a mix of words

THE SECRET GUARDIAN 57

and feelings, "primitive in the extreme ... savage but ... also in a strange way wonderful" (2011a, pp. 199–200).

He then makes a surprising statement—"*I have wanted to hold him, to bring him some kind of comfort*" (ibid., p. 200, emphasis added). Strange, but if the creature somehow embodied Strieber's own traumatized inner child, the statement also makes perfect sense. Perhaps the weird creature might best be seen as Strieber's "alter"? Psychologically speaking (in Kalsched's model), the "guardian" describes the aspect of the psyche that comes into being in order to protect the conscious mind from reexperiencing the original trauma. It is the way "the secret guards itself." Part of the individuation process, perhaps even the central goal, entails *getting past this defense mechanism and discovering the secret which it exists to protect.* Once the secret is exposed, the "guardian" no longer has any reason to exist. In a sense the secret *is* the guardian, and vice versa. An unconscious mechanism, once it is brought into consciousness, ceases to operate or even to exist. Donald Kalsched describes it this way:

> [T]he original traumatic situation posed such a danger to personality survival that it was not retained in memorable *personal* form but only in *daimonic* archetypal form. This is the collective or "magical" layer of the unconscious and cannot be assimilated by the ego *until it has been "incarnated" in a human interaction* [emphasis added]. As archetypal dynamism it "exists" in a form that cannot be recovered by the ego *except as an experience of retraumatization.* Or, to put it another way, the unconscious repetition of traumatization in the inner world which goes on incessantly must become *real* traumatization with an object in the world if the inner system is to be "unlocked." (1996, p. 26)[2]

This appears to be the underlying dynamic and drive behind the kind of experiences Strieber describes: an unconscious attempt to translate an archetypal ("screen") memory of early trauma into more human form, in order to interact with it and recognize its true nature. This interaction is an opportunity to repeat the original trauma in a new way, to bring it all the way into consciousness, thereby dissolving the defense mechanism (that of the false self or "guardian") created by the early experience of trauma. This can only happen, however, if the individual recognizes the "incarnation" of trauma for what it is, *an image from the past personified in the present* as a means to be understood and assimilated, dissolved, through exposure to consciousness. Ideally, this is what occurs in the psychotherapeutic process through *transference*. Transference is when a safe space is created by the analyst for the analysand to reexperience an original trauma *with a minimal risk of re-traumatization*. Re-traumatization is the result of misattributing the distress that arises during the therapeutic process to a *present* cause, rather than correctly tracing it back to the past and *integrating* it.

Truly distressing as the therapeutic process is, most individuals prefer to experience re-traumatization by projecting their autonomy onto the other—whether alien, spouse, or analyst—and attributing both the "transformation" and the trauma to an outside agency. The alternative is to go willingly back into the original trauma and *reexperience it with full body awareness*, which, by definition, is the most terrifying thing there is. Strieber touches on this in *Transformation* when he reports his wife's suggestion that the contact experience, while stemming from an objective reality, is "changed by the filter of our experience." Expectations distort the ability to see or understand, she says. The visitors appeared to her *"to be using our distorted perception as a vehicle through which they could transmit messages of importance to the inner growth of the individual participant."* (1988, p. 37)

I understand this statement to mean that the visitors were drawing Strieber *into forms of interaction that would allow him to see his own distortions*. Strieber is attributing "messages" to the visitors, but the nature of the therapeutic process is that all such messages must finally be seen as coming from the patient's own psyche and not from any external source. Without this realization, the projected distortion remains in place, and instead of unlocking the defense system and reintegrating past trauma, there is an experience of *re-traumatization* without any resulting breakthrough. New layers of trauma are then added to old, and the guardian becomes a prison guard.

CHAPTER VI

Martian dreams

"[W]here the inner world is filled with violent aggression, primitive defenses are present also. More specifically, we now know that the *energy for dissociation comes from this aggression* .... It seems that as the unbearable (traumatic) childhood experience, or something resembling it in the transference [i.e., during psychotherapy], begins to emerge into consciousness, an intra-psychic figure or 'force,' witnessed in the patient's dreams, violently intervenes and dissociates the psyche."
—Donald Kalsched, *The Inner World of Trauma*

My aim with this exploration has been to uncover the self-protecting traumatic secret hidden behind Strieber's narrative—and by extension my own—in order to unlock it. This inevitably runs the risk of being as invasive—and as uninvited—as an alien rectal probe. If Strieber has constructed a line of defense against seeing the true nature of his experiences—or at least a central aspect of them, one that changes everything about them—then he has done so for good reasons. Tearing down that psychological wall might prove harmful—to him, and therefore to me.

Chapel Perilous is not just any ordinary hall of mirrors; the mirrors are perfectly aligned to create an infinity of reflections, with nothing in between. To really *see* what's (not) there does not mean to shatter the mirror—that would only leave us with a collection of dangerous fragments and a lifetime's bad luck. It means to disappear from view, to become pure perception, without either subject or object because there is no perceivable difference between the two. The author, the subject, and the reader, all vanish into an infinite progression, leaving only the space behind. That is the picture I am trying to hold up to the light, without my shadow getting in the way. It is a picture of infinite space, not only out there but *in here*. The psyche, as within, so without.

When writing psycho-history, the meanings don't make themselves available like ordinary facts and figures. They have to be teased out and then they need to be apprehended, not only with the intellect and the intuition, but with the total body. This exploration is attempting to present the "lost body" of Strieber's work and of my own life simultaneously. With any luck, the *vesica piscis* of our two psyches as they overlap will act as an opening onto the collective psyche. But this will only happen through *an accurate superimposition* of material. If it is more than slightly off, the image will be fuzzy and blurred, and the reader will see only a double distortion.

To spell it out too much means losing the finer meanings that is the subtle body of the analysis. If I don't spell it out enough, those meanings might never be recognized. It is like walking a razor's edge, the razor's edge that Strieber is walking: the edge between "worlds," between the madness of denial and the insanity of going off the deep end. We are walking it together.

What I've done for this chapter is to take a leaf out of Whitley's book. I have turned the focus around and taken it outward, to the stars, specifically to Mars, a planet which Strieber has shown a consistent interest in. Conversely, with fearful symmetry and not without hesitation, I will once again be probing into Whitley's childhood experiences. In *The Secret School*, he describes his ninth year, in 1954, receiving nine lessons from a being, or beings, he later identified as the visitor(s), as part of a group of children being tutored in a sort of cosmic consciousness, beyond space and time. In the first of these lessons, he describes visiting Mars—in non-physical form—and seeing the (now famous) "face on Mars," followed by an encounter with a Martian nun (whom he later identifies as the female visitor he was reintroduced to in 1985). This brings three elements together into a single narrative: Strieber leaving his body (dissociation) as a child; his encounter with the visitors; and his first being seeded with an interest in Mars. Strieber describes how, partially due to the influence of sci-fi movies, he became obsessed with the planet Mars as a child and staged fantasy enactments of being transported there. He recounts in great detail an out-of-body vision of flying above the surface of Mars. In it, he feels a great loneliness and a desire to be back with his parents; he is tormented by "The hollowness that fills children when they are far away ... I could not let myself think about home: I was looking for something and I had to find it because failing would be very terrible. Still, I sure wanted to be home with Momma and Daddy" (p. 5).

The feeling of hollowness causes him to plummet to the surface of the planet. As he does so he sees a huge face staring up at him that resolves itself into a "tumble of low hills." He winds up stranded, afraid he will freeze to death. In his account, he writes: "*I fought with the only weapon I had, my mind*" (1997, pp. 6, 8). This may be a key to Strieber's whole *oeuvre*.

Strieber's Mars vision expresses the separation-anxiety of a child on the verge of growing up. When I was ten or eleven, I was sent away to boarding school. It was excruciatingly painful for me to be away from home. Among the memories I have from that time, there's one that I have never been able to explain of sneaking out in the middle of the night with the boys in my dorm room, into a large field, and running around waving white sheets in the air. Did this actually happen, and if so, what on earth were we doing? It sounds more like something out of Strieber's childhood than my own (I noticed, with a feeling of unease, that the Finders material included photographs of children dressed in white sheets for some sort of "blood ritual"). As if to further insinuate some hidden reality, in a letter I wrote home from that same period, I recount seeing a UFO from my dorm window! I have no memory of the incident—so what else have I forgotten from that time? I wrote quite a few letters during that period, and looking back I realize this was probably how I first learned to express myself through writing. It was a way to be connected to home, to feel less alone and isolated. For me as well as for Whitley, writing (the mind) was a weapon against the cold.

Strieber remembers being a child, traveling to Mars (the planet of war), far from home and the warm comforts of family life, where he discovered "the only weapon" he had. (Besides war, the archetype of Mars represents male sexuality and is associated with adolescence, the period when sexuality awakens.) Evidently, Strieber's profound desire to "get to Mars" as a child was not just the result of too much science fiction; considering the kind of abuse he was being subjected to during this period, was he unconsciously focusing on Mars as the location (internally) of his life force? Was he sensing the need to become a warrior? (Mars signifies the male body, just as Venus represents the female form.) Rather than connecting to his sexuality, however (perhaps because it had already been severely sabotaged by then), he turned to his *mind*. Eventually Strieber became a writer, for whom the pen is mightier than the sword. (Incidentally, this phrase was first coined by Lord Bulwer-Lytton, the author of *The Coming Race or Vril: The Power of the Coming Race*, a book which inspired Hitler and the Nazis, most specifically with its descriptions of the *Vril* force.) Strieber's chosen field was horror, a natural way for someone to use their mind/pen/weapon/Vril to distance themselves (disassociate) from the horrors they suffered as a child, by turning them into *mental imagery*—that is, fiction. (In fact, Strieber describes everything he learned in the secret school in mental terms: "The secret school was founded by the mind, and it lives in the mind …. The mind is the teacher, also the student. Of all the truths that are emerging out of this strange colloquy, perhaps the greatest is that time itself—even time—may become our servant" (1997, p. 191).

In Strieber's childhood vision (which he apparently believes was an astral journey), having used his mind as a weapon to fight his fear in the freezing and hostile Mars environment, he then has an encounter with the "Sister of Mercy" who runs the secret school (the "good" one). The being (whom he later identifies as the female visitor depicted on the cover of *Communion*) is described in the lurid, nightmarish terms of horror fiction. When he first sees her, she is "something like a giant bat with a cloak wrapped around it."

> The voice became a hiss. "You will get to the telescope! You must, do you understand! *Must!*" Her hissing reminded me of the giant lizard at the zoo, the way he hissed when you got him with a mesquite bean. The hand was weird. It was bony and thin, and it was digging hard into my shoulder. This sure didn't seem much like any dream I ever had before. Writhing from the pain, I looked up, trying to see this person. (1997, p. 10)

The guardian figure demands that young Whitley get himself a telescope, which is a way to take the focus *outward and upward*: just how a

lonely, frightened child might deal with unbearable isolation and loneliness, by gazing at the stars, imagining a better life in another world.

> But she pushed my head back down and I found myself looking
> into a huge book made of dark blue leather and crusted with rubies
> so enormous that I could see my own face reflected in them. I could
> see the Sister of Mercy, too, a black shadow in the depths of each
> jewel. Her long, thin hands caressed the cover of the book with the
> care due a fragile, overripe fruit. And yet it did not seem worn.
> On the contrary, the sense of antiquity was combined with a qual-
> ity of the fresh, as if it was both ancient and freshly minted. She
> lifted the cover, revealing supple, curiously floppy endpapers that
> reminded me in a creepy way of skin. Instead of pages in the book,
> there was a strange darkness. (1997, pp. 10–11)

What is the meaning of a book which also acts as a mirror, into which
the young Strieber is forced to gaze? (Rubies reinforce the Mars-theme.)
The child must learn to see himself as a warrior, but a "bookish"
warrior—one whose weapon is his mind, a mentalist, a writer. The
imagery of overripe fruit is both sexual and biblical; it brings to mind
both sex and sin, equating them. Strieber was raised a Catholic, so the
connection would be automatic. The book had skin, like a living thing,
a body. Inside was darkness, that is, unconsciousness, the womb. The
floppy skin-like endpapers brings to mind the female genitalia—inside
of which is "a strange darkness."

> I did not want to look; I didn't even want to be near it. Hands
> grasped my head and pushed it downward. I was aware of suck-
> ing, as if the book were a well and there was a creature down there
> that was going to devour me. I could not prevent it … *because in
> some way the creature was also me.* (1997, p. 11, emphasis added)

The sexual implications here are too clear to need spelling out. And in
The Super Natural, Strieber writes for the first time about being made
to perform cunnilingus on the female visitor, thereby confirming this
interpretation of his encounter with the Martian Sister of Mercy: "Her
hands came onto my head like tendrils of smoke, the hands of a ghost,
but they were paradoxically strong and pressed me towards her lap.
She opened her legs and I saw a darkness within. Not entire darkness,

though. There was a glow there too. She drew my head gently down" (Strieber & Kripal, 2016, pp. 140–141).

In Strieber's childhood account, the child-Whitley does not want to place his attention on the inside of the "book" (the body), or even *be near it*, indicating a child's fear of female sexuality, and by extension of his own body. But he cannot prevent it. As with all of Strieber's encounters, to a greater or lesser extent, the dream-vision has the earmarks of a symbolically reinterpreted memory of sexual interference; and yet, despite the distinctly unpleasant, even horrific nature of the encounter, Strieber sees the being as a benevolent presence. Later he writes:

> There was something about her body—a tickling vibration—that we really liked. We all wanted to be near her, and sitting beside her was a big reward. When she touched us, it would transform us into a state where we felt spectacularly, deliciously alive, as if every cell was conscious. One by one, she would touch us, grabbing our hips, our faces. I remember I saw inside her wimple once, and it looked as if a giant moth was staring out at me. My whole being rocked with terror. (1997, p. 146)

Strieber's early experiences, as described in *The Secret School*, connect various fragments together to indicate a larger picture. His desire to go to Mars shows the desire to become a warrior, discover his weapon (mentalism/writing), and develop a tool for understanding and combatting the forces controlling him at that time.

As a point of comparison, in my adolescence (after I had left boarding school for a local school), my stepfather went off philandering and my mother became suicidal, spending days on end in bed. My brother and sister had left home by then and I was alone with her madness. She was an irrational, unpredictable, and terrifying presence. I had terrible nightmares (as previously described) and took refuge in comic books about superhuman beings and David Bowie songs about aliens (and spiders) from Mars. I became obsessed with Clint Eastwood (a warrior-type who resembled my father) and then with movies in general. This led me to writing (I wrote movie lists, then reviews, and finally scripts). I was also writing short fictional pieces at the time, including one I can remember from the period quite well, about a boy who met a magical teacher, an older man. The man gave the boy a magic watch that could stop the flow of time, and the boy learned to use the watch. He had complete freedom to move through the world, unseen by others. Somehow the watch broke while he was using it, and the boy was trapped. Since his own body was not subject to the ravages of time, he realized he would be trapped there, isolated from all human contact, forever: a prisoner of infinity.

*

"The ego refuses to be distressed by the provocations of reality, to let itself be compelled to suffer. It insists that it cannot be affected by the traumas of the external world; it shows, in fact, that such traumas are no more than occasions for it to gain pleasure."

—Sigmund Freud

In Strieber's follow-up to *Communion*, *Transformation*, he describes a series of experiences from 1986. Having been given a book by the researcher Robert Monroe, *Journeys Out of the Body*, Strieber begins to experiment with the exercises Monroe devised.[1] He has no clear success until one night, while attempting to leave his body, he has a vision of a long, gray hand (a visitor) pointing at a box "about two feet square on a gray floor." The hand is long and thin, with four fingers with black, claw-like nails. The image of the box had caused "an explosive sexual reaction" in Strieber, "a blast of pure sexual feeling." The effect only lasts an instant, but "it had an amazing effect on me ... [It] seemed to loosen connections inside me. I rolled out of my body. It felt as if I had come unstuck from myself. The experience was strange in the extreme—almost beyond description. [T]he vision of the box drew me so powerfully that I literally left my body" (1988, pp. 202, 208)

Strieber then finds himself looking down at his sleeping body and sees the face of a visitor at one of the windows. He interprets the face as a "warning" (like the face on Mars?) and goes out another window instead. He explores the normal world outside and then returns to his bedroom. He looks down at his body. It is so still it looks dead. He finds the thought of reentering it unappealing, and has the feeling he could leave and never come back. "When I dropped down into myself, my body seemed to have an invisible opening in it that I went through. But I was terribly loose inside and I found myself coming out again" (p. 205).

Suddenly he finds himself in a scene from his past, at his childhood home in San Antonio, looking out of his bedroom window at his father, who is mowing the lawn at the crack of dawn. His father looks up and says, "When are you going to come help me?" Strieber shoots back to his body in fright, with the feeling he has touched death. He notices his body is chilled to the bone and that his arms and legs are stiff as if they haven't moved in a long time. When he looks at the clock, he sees that only ten minutes have passed.

The vision begins with a box and ends with his father and a feeling of having "touched death." The image of a box is already connected to Whitley's father by the photograph of the coffin—signifying death and confinement. What is concealed in the box—in Whitley's story—is not only the "dead" father but the living boy—the victim of original trauma. The box, like a picture of a father in a coffin, is the secret that guards itself. Seeing the box activates an intense rush of sexual energy for the adult Strieber. Why? Is it because what was trapped in the box was inseparable from that initial sexual trauma, namely, his Martian life force, his libido?

We've already seen how Strieber's memories of being abused as a child center upon being confined in a box for extended periods of time, and how that led to visions of angels and demons. Was such confinement part of a successful attempt to force children to dissociate and develop an ability to leave their bodies? (Perhaps it was connected to an early remote viewing program?) At the same time, if such experiments were occurring simultaneously with some kind of sexual interference, this might also account for Strieber's strange reaction.

When a child is sexually abused, there is often a sexual response, not merely despite but to some degree *because* of the terror and the violence being inflicted. One way for the child to reduce his distress and to survive psychologically is to *identify* with the abuser. This means the child to some degree *experiences the abuser's sexuality as his own*, which is how the trauma becomes internalized, and why the act of dissociation, as Kalsched describes it, is an aggressive one. It is equivalent to a kind of *involuntary self-violation* on the part of the psyche, a splitting of awareness that allows the developing ego to escape the scene of the trauma, and secure itself from any future incidents. As Kalsched writes, "The full pathological effect of trauma requires an outer event *and a psychological factor*. Outer trauma alone doesn't split the psyche. *An inner psychological agency—occasioned by the trauma—does the splitting*" (1996, p. 14).

The conscious self then becomes *de-eroticized*. This doesn't mean they are devoid of sexual response (the person may even develop a sexual pathology), but only that the libido remains trapped inside the body by, and to some degree *as* (inseparable from), suppressed traumatic memory. The child dissociates. His consciousness leaves the body and enters into (or creates) an alternate, anti-libidinal identity, a "mind-self" that is forever safe from reexperiencing that trauma, but also forever cut off from its own life force and body, like a child, trapped inside a box.[2]

*

> "If we now survey all the far-reaching possibilities of the infantile constellation, we are obliged to say that *in essence our life's fate is identical with the fate of our sexuality.*"
> —Carl Jung, *Aspects of the Masculine*

Unsurprisingly, Strieber's early visions of Mars (which he didn't remember until much later) *connect directly to his first interest in extraterrestrial life.* In *Breakthrough*, published in 1996, Strieber states it plainly:

> The first time that I came across a possible hidden government policy devoted to concealing evidence of extraterrestrials was in 1984. Early that summer, Dr. John Gliedman, whom I had then known for about a year, showed me a photograph that appeared to be of a gigantic sculpture staring up from a desert .... I was soon involved with the group, which was known as the Mars Anomalies Research Society, Inc. (p. 253)[3]

Strieber is confused about the date of this incident, because in *The Secret School* he reports it occurring "on a clear September day in 1985," and states: "*The mystery of Mars and the secret school, it would turn out, were deeply bound together*" (1997, pp. xviii–xix). This date fits better with his contention that the photograph of the face on Mars triggered his 1985 close encounter experience.[4] Apparently being shown the photograph of the face on Mars in 1984 or '85 stirred vague memories of his childhood trip to the planet, which in turn triggered, or paved the way for, his first fully conscious memory of being taken by the visitors in December of 1985.

This strange scenario clearly links Strieber to a group of intellectual elites and intelligence types with *an interest in space travel*. At that time, Strieber was a writer of horror fiction, so how and why exactly did he wind up joining such a group? He doesn't say, only that he was asked to finance their efforts and agreed. He does state that, after *Communion* was published, he "withdrew from direct participation in the committee out of concern that [his] connection with the UFO subculture would embarrass the other members and compromise the already tenuous standing of the project in the scientific community." This raises another question which he doesn't address. In *Communion*, Strieber indicates that he had *no knowledge about UFOs or aliens* prior to his experiences of October and December 1985, stating that, in January of 1986, even *after* doing some research, he "knew almost nothing about UFOs" (p. 39). He was quoted in 1987 saying: "I did not believe in UFOs at all before this happened. And I would have laughed in the face of anybody who claimed contact" (Disch, 1987).[5]

So what is Strieber saying? That he had a formative experience in childhood which he recalled as an out-of-body trip to Mars, during which he was handled by an alien nun and made to stare into an empty book; and that this created a psychological mechanism within him that was "triggered," thirty years later, when he was shown a photograph of Mars by a member of an elite scientific group with a focus on extraterrestrial life and/or space travel—a group which Strieber mysteriously neglected to mention (effectively lying by omission) in *Communion*? And that the Martian-face-trigger then led, in Strieber's own estimation, to his abduction experience, during which he was given a rectal probe by the visitors—an event which to this day he refers to as a rape, and from which he still suffers physical symptoms. It's also worth noting that the incident that immediately precedes the rectal intrusion is that of *having a needle inserted into his brain*.

> If I had been afraid before, I now became quite simply crazed with terror. I argued with them. "This place is filthy," I remember saying. Then, "You'll ruin a beautiful mind." I could imagine my family awakening in the morning and finding me a vegetable. A great sadness overtook me. I do not recall screaming, but evidently I was doing so. (1987, p. 28)

The reason I cite this is because, if the (sexual) violation of his body occurred simultaneously with what he perceived as *an attack upon his mind*, it appears that Strieber's narrative is held together by a common thread, that of a recurrence of trauma. (As Ed Conroy notes in *Report on Communion*, "For Strieber, an intellectual whose livelihood has been gained by use of his mind, brain damage would threaten his entire identity, not merely his professional ability" (1990, p. 302). And these incidents seem to date as far back as Strieber's own memory: When I first dipped into *Solving the Communion Enigma* while working on the first part of this exploration in 2013, I was struck at once by a couple of incidents which Strieber mentioned (in chapter 2, "The Mirror Shattered") from his early childhood. At four, while playing in a kindergarten run by nuns (again), he was made to leave for thrusting a "friction toy under a sister's habit. Her underthings became tangled in the whirring mechanism. To put it mildly, she was agitated" (2011a, p. 18). On the same page, he mentions, in passing, how his "best friend got his penis caught in a bicycle pump" (come again?). These aren't offered up as part of Strieber's fragmented, otherworldly memory set, but as ordinary childhood memories; yet both relate to *technology interfering with the sexual organs*, somewhat eerily echoing the rectal probe of December of 1985.

I am well aware how the rectal probe has become the source of much humor, of the blackest variety, in popular media (including the first episode of *South Park*), and how Strieber has been understandably indignant about it. I am also aware that, despite his belief that it was a medical action, he has frequently described the procedure as "rape," because of how deeply traumatic the experience was for him.[6] While I can sympathize with Strieber, it is also understandable if people have turned his trauma into a joke. The possibility that an otherworldly race of highly intelligent beings took a grown man from his bed in the dead of night and anally penetrated him with a foot-long device for unknown reasons is not something most people want to even think about. But even that scenario (which could be easily placed in the realms of sadomasochistic science fantasy) is preferable to considering the deeper implications of Strieber's *traumata*.

Strieber has stated that a medical examination, taken after his abduction memories surfaced, revealed physical signs of rape. He has said that he suffered side-effects from the experience for years afterward, and that it was his rectal pain (among several other physical symptoms) that caused the memories of his abduction to surface in the first place. Is it fair to say then that this was the most real thing about his experience? Yet such physical symptoms hardly prove conclusively that he was taken by nonhuman beings that night.

While Strieber has described the rectal probe as part of some "medical" action, he also remembered, during the second hypnosis session transcribed in *Communion*, a distinctly sexual element:

> (I could sense them, but I was looking at her. She drew something up from below.) "Jesus, is that your penis?" I thought it was a woman. [Makes a deep, grunting sound.] That goes right in me. [Another grunt.] Punching it in me, punching it in me. I'm gonna throw up on them. [Pause.] (They began trying to open my mouth with their hands.) "What do you keep wanting to do that to my mouth for?" They keep trying to put something in my mouth. They're real. They're real. Put up her cheek right to me, and they're real! That's the incredible thing here. I've still got this thing in me and it'd be nice to take it out. (1987, p. 301)

A little while later, Strieber describes how the beings are asking him if he can be any "harder" (i.e., more erect). In February 2006, on an audio titled "Unpublished Close Encounters: Part 1," Strieber discussed the possibility that he had been manipulated to provide semen to the visitors to impregnate the female being. While exploring his fragmented memories of the summer of 1968 (which I will look at in the next chapter), he remembered being sexually manipulated by strange people for unknown purposes, apparently to impregnate a woman (Róisín). In the audio commentary at the end of his second hypnosis session (2004a), Strieber makes the connection between the rectal probe of 1985 and the semen-extraction process, referring to the procedure known as "rectal electro-ejaculation" (REE), which has been used on humans since 1948.[7] For whatever reason, as far as I know he hasn't referred to this connection since, nor has he addressed the question of why beings able to enter into (and/or emerge out of) the depths of his psyche would need such archaic technology to bring him to orgasm.

While I was working on this material, I suffered from my own rectal pain, which eventually led to inexplicable bleeding. I didn't interpret it to mean that aliens had recently interfered with me, but I did consider that working on this subject matter, since it was undoubtedly stirring up suppressed trauma in my own body, might be causing "old wounds" to reopen. As already mentioned, past trauma will often surface through somatic effects—or *affects*. Freud wrote about this over 100 years ago, and called it "hysterical phenomena." In extreme cases (such as the famous "stigmata"), wounds can open up in the body, bruises may appear, and blood can flow.[8]

Is this a literal, tangible attempt on the part of the psyche to reintegrate the trauma, not just emotionally but viscerally, by reexperiencing it *in and through the body*? If so, where did the limits lie of such a psychosomatic reenactment? Might the "physical proof" of the kind Strieber and other abductees have displayed be proof of something quite different—something that is both *present and past* at the same time?

In relation to this, and to the psychological process described by Kalsched, it is striking to observe how the interactions Strieber has had with the "daimonic layer of reality" (or of his own psyche, assuming there is even a difference), have become progressively *more human* (and correspondingly less traumatic) over the years. His first fully recalled traumatic encounter with alien visitors was in 1985. His experience with the feral man-child was roughly eight years later, around 1993. His encounter with the being he called "the Master of the Key" was five years after that, in 1998. During his alleged conversation with this "radiant being," the Master of the Key told him, "I can imagine no greater honor than to be called human" (2011b, p. 58). Rather bizarrely he also said, "If I were an intelligent machine, I would deceive you." But nothing is ever straightforward in the life of Whitley; we will return to the machine question later.

Just as past trauma can be integrated by the psyche through a reemergence of bodily symptoms, perhaps the dissociated, disembodied, "alien" fragment of Strieber's psyche is assuming a progressively more human form, on its return journey from outer to inner space?

CHAPTER VII

All work and no play: "Pain" & Strieber's missing summer of '68

"The most blessed are those who suffer the most."
—Whitley Strieber, "Pain"

My own father was all work and no play. He had no "time" for children. He did play tennis until his late thirties, but a crippling genetic disease slowly robbed him of the use of his legs, thus ending his play. By the time my memories of him begin (when I was around seven, after he'd left us), he was walking with a cane. Later came crutches, and much later he succumbed to the necessity of a wheelchair. He suffered from an extremely rare genetic disorder, which only one of his siblings, his younger sister, contracted (his two brothers and older sister didn't, nor did either of his parents or his children). When he could no longer play tennis, he played bridge instead. He played for money, and as a child I helped empty ashtrays and refill the players' glasses in return for tips. I was a mercenary child, and regularly stole from my father's suit pockets, where he kept a pound for an emergency cab fare. He had many suits. Like him, I took money seriously.

My father didn't believe in God, aliens, conspiracies, psychic powers, or human potentialities. He didn't believe in the soul or the afterlife. He was a "proud individualist" who saw himself (and was seen by others)

73

as unconventional, a rule-breaker and social iconoclast. I didn't see him that way. I hardly saw him at all: When I spent the weekend with him, he would mostly hide behind a newspaper, and having a conversation with him was practically impossible. I do remember one time, probably when I was a teenager, asking him how he could stand to believe there was nothing after death. "If there's nothing, I won't know it," he replied. "So why should I care?"

He was an advocate of equality and believed that the rights of the individual were more important than the needs of the collective. Yet he was a socialist, with an oft-expressed sympathy for minorities and a loathing of any sort of prejudice. At the same time, he was an intellectual who looked down on the lower classes for their ignorance and lack of education or artistic refinement. He admired social reformers (I can imagine Gandhi or Martin Luther King among the people he respected—though he didn't believe in "heroes"); he also admired artists and pioneers. He respected anyone out of the ordinary, who forged their own path away from the herd and who he saw as "different." That wouldn't have included spiritual or religious pioneers, however, and he would have dismissed Whitley Strieber without a second glance. He was a pacifist who loathed all forms of violence and was unable to watch violent movies. (He once told me that he "hid under the seat" during Stanley Kubrick's *A Clockwork Orange*.) In contrast, I became obsessed with violent movies as a teenager, and eventually wrote two books about them. I tended to see my father's pacifism as squeamishness more than sensitivity. One of his favorite refutations of religion was that it had caused more killing than anything else in history, hardly an original opinion, but one he expressed a dozen times or more to me.

Until he retired he put most of his energy into three things: work, sex, and drinking. He didn't believe in family values any more than religious ones, and he showed no interest in being a father. But he didn't seem to believe in the work ethic or have a high opinion of his own achievements either (though other people did). The company he ran was started by his father, Alec, whom he professed to have always disliked (even in his final years). He took over Northern Dairies, the family business, in 1969, when I was two, and after Alec retired. By replacing his father, he became what he most despised. No doubt this was Alec's wish for his son (and for his family and the business), and my father probably felt like he had no choice. He only joined the company after he met my mother and they had their first child. Before that, he'd been bumming around Canada failing to write "the great English novel." It's tempting to say he sold his soul to gain the world, but I don't think my father was especially interested in worldly power (unlike my grandfather). I think he was running from something and that he jumped down the first rabbit hole he could find. It didn't go to wonderland.

In *A Most Accursed Religion: When a Trauma Becomes God*, Greg Mogenson writes:

> Traumatic events are not all painful. Frequently, the imagination is fixated by events, which stop it from imagining on but do not cause pain. The birth of a child, for instance, may be as overwhelming for the new father as for the mother. The sudden appearance of the new life immediately cancels the conventions of its parents' old life, temporarily bankrupting their previous soul-making. We should not be surprised, therefore, that new parents often admit to being afraid of their children and sometimes even suffer depression or psychosis following a birth they may have joyously anticipated. It is a tremendous responsibility to be the parent of an overwhelming event, the mother or father of God. (2005, p. 51)

I seriously doubt my father ever joyously anticipated the birth of his children—and certainly not me, the last to arrive. I think he let biology take its course and tried his best to keep his end up, so to speak. Mostly this was by bringing home the bacon (literally, once Northern Dairies took over Pork Farms). If the arrival of children bankrupted his "soul-making" with our mother—and more importantly, interfered with their sex—he may even have perceived us as "diabolic" interlopers. Certainly he refused to answer to the word "father." Now I think about it, he probably despised religion as much for its puritanical attitude towards sex as for its justifications of violence. He would have had no time for de-eroticized spirituality, or de-eroticized anything, and if my father had any religious feelings at all, they probably centered on sex. Yet paradoxically, he once described to me falling in love with my mother as "a meeting of minds." She in turn described his arrival in her life as akin to Pluto's abduction of Persephone, and later referred to my father as "a sex addict." Yet despite his sexual addiction, he lived a de-eroticized life, cut off from his own body. In fact, sexual addiction is really a symptom of de-eroticization, which causes a Jagger-esque perennial lack of satisfaction.

In the last years of his life, it would be hard to say what, if anything, my father believed in. Possibly it had to do with the power of human beings to create their own meanings, free from the guidance (or interference) of religious or political authorities. Just as he rejected his father (and his own fatherhood), he rejected God and all other forms of authority. It didn't make him free; it made him groundless, weightless, disembodied. At some level, my father never grew past adolescence, presumably because his father didn't hold the necessary space for him to step into his own authority, his own manhood, his own *body*.

When I asked him once if he thought his father had raised him well, he affirmed it by saying that Alec had insisted on a good education. In the same conversation, however (and in the same context), he described Alec as "a bully." Besides the fact that he loved his mother and disliked his father, I know almost nothing about my father's childhood. It seems likely Alec's "bullying," and his insistence that my father got "a good education," started early on. My father was sent away to boarding school at the age of five, and his younger sister was sent away at three. Is there any relation between this and the fact it was these two who later succumbed to the crippling genetic disorder that took away their legs? *Something* happened in my father's life, something that left him wounded beyond repair, unable to stand up straight or live the life he wanted to live. Perhaps, as in Strieber's case, it related to that early induction?

At one point in his life, my father may have believed in the possibility of creating a system for people to live by without the crutch of religion or the interference of government (he was an anarchist at heart, or so he said). Yet, so far as I know, and besides his unconventional and innovative business methods, he didn't bring about any kind of lasting change in the world or leave it a better place. Unlike Jimmy Savile, no buildings were named after him. He was a humanitarian who would have despised transhumanism with every fiber of his being. He disliked technology, and it took him years to admit he needed a wheelchair. That stubbornness combined with stoicism was part and parcel with his inability to admit that he was, after all, a cripple. I suspect he felt abandoned, not only by God and by his own father, but by his body. He was—in the fullest sense that I have experienced directly—a lost soul. And if you discount the sex and the alcohol, which were really evidence of addiction, of a desperate desire to *escape* the body, then he, like the other men described in this chapter, lived a life that was very much "all work and no play."

When I think of my father as I knew him, it's been hard for me to feel much. It's as if he had already vacated the premises by the time I was old enough to have a conscious relationship with him. I have found it easier to connect to him emotionally when I imagine how he was before I was born, when he first met my mother: full of aspirations and a passionate belief in his own potential. I suspect that having children, the burden of that responsibility (which almost certainly led him to join his father's business), broke his spirit, and that when he found he couldn't carry the burden he'd assumed, his legs gave out and he gave up the ghost. He kept on living but no longer had anything substantial to live for, besides work and pleasure. There was no higher meaning he could believe in, not even the higher meaning of his own spirit. Especially not that.

I see my father's life as a tragedy; but ironically, what makes it a tragedy in my eyes is that he was unable or unwilling to see it that way himself. He not only turned his back on his own spiritual potential (authenticity), he told himself that there was no such thing to turn away from, that it was just empty belief and social control. He turned his lack of faith into an intellectual position. I think that was what really crippled him. A spiritual potential that isn't embodied becomes, by slow degrees, a spiritual disease, a soul sickness. It's a fate that I have devoted my life to avoiding, and it's probably what compelled me to write this account.

*

"You have not lived, my friend, until you have been waked up out of a dead sleep by an alien who seduces you with the precision of a computer and the cunning of a Geisha. Nor would you ever again entertain the idea that such an experience was a fantasy. If it was, and that was ever proved, I have to admit that it would break my heart."

—Whitley Strieber, *Thinking XXX*[1]

Whitley, another wounded soul, appears also to be very much "all work and no play." He is a relentlessly driven worker bee, a man whose world-saving, soul-rescuing mission consumes him and (arguably) threatens to drive him mad. Perhaps there is something about wounded souls that drives them into activity, into "work," as the surest way of escaping their pain?

My father rarely ever mentioned his physical condition, and many people around him saw this as stoicism, a brave refusal to complain. But he drank heavily every day of his life and died in a state of insensibility from drugs, and avoidance is not stoicism. In contrast, Strieber appears to be obsessed with pain, primarily his own, and to like nothing better than to talk about it, often in a shrill and lamenting tone, sometimes (as more recently) in a creepily orgiastic way. Where my father was an atheist and saw nothing ennobling about suffering, Strieber is a "secular" (lapsed) Catholic who has created a veritable philosophy out of the transcendental power of pain, of ecstasy through agony. He even named a story after it. "Pain" is the story Strieber was working on in December 1985, when the memories of his alien encounters first began to surface. It was published in 1987 (and was nominated for a World Fantasy best short story award) as part of a horror anthology called *Cutting Edge*, roughly around the time *Communion* came out. I had heard about it (he mentions it in *Communion*), but I knew almost nothing about it until recently. This is how he describes it at his website:

> Pain was written between mid-December 1985 and mid-January 1986. It is the last thing I wrote before becoming conscious of the close encounter experience I had on December 26, 1985. While I was writing it, uneasy and confused memories of that experience were flowing through my mind, and I was beginning the process of research that would eventually lead to recollection of the close encounter and the writing of *Communion*. The story contains a great deal of unconscious material about the experience. In fact, my entire unconscious understanding of close encounter [sic] and its connection to the dangerous sacred is contained in the story .... It is among the most important things I have ever written about the visitors, because it contains so much truth coming straight out of my unconscious recollections of what happened to me. (Strieber, 2013.)

In the spoken introduction to his reading of "Pain," Strieber states emphatically: "This is not a personal narrative." He adds that, when he first released it, "sleazy people" tried to claim that he "was somehow involved in sadomasochistic sex," and that this disturbed him so much that he put the story "on ice" for twenty-five years. He insists, somewhat indignantly, "It is not a sex story. It is about the dangerous sacred" (Jeffrey Kripal's pet subject, please note). After twenty-five years of silence, Strieber made "Pain" available as an audio reading at his website; as it happened, I was working on this present chapter, and it was two days after I re-subscribed to Unknown Country after more than a year's absence. The timing was so exact, it felt as if Strieber was co-operating with my exploration.

The story reads exactly like Strieber's nonfiction narratives (which he invariably dramatizes), complete with commentary on the nature of the aliens and occult-religious-philosophical asides. As Strieber acknowledges, it is a sort of symbolic retelling (or foretelling) of his "close encounter" experiences, while also invoking childhood memories of "initiation-by-trauma" government abuse and/or psychic training under the "Sisters of Mercy" at the Secret School. In "Pain," Strieber's surrogate character is researching a piece about prostitution (Sisters of Mercy) by interviewing working girls when he falls under the spell of "Janet O'Reilly." By the end of the story, the dominatrix has been revealed as a supernatural being—or alien.

Since I know better than to take Strieber at his word when he insists the piece is not a personal narrative, I did some online research and turned up a host of curious facts (or factoids, much of this is anecdotal and difficult to verify). First off, in the bio notes on the inside back cover flap of the first edition (1981) of *The Hunger*, I found this:

> [Strieber] has traveled through many parts of the world, working in fields as diverse as intelligence and filmmaking. His underground films were shown frequently in England in the late sixties. His other work includes a documentary on the Process Church of Final Judgment, an unusual religious group that has been connected with satanism.

Strieber is on record as stating that he didn't write this bio and that his publisher had "sensationalized some parts of his life ... particularly the part about having worked in fields 'as diverse as intelligence.'" If so it's likely they also exaggerated his reputation as an underground filmmaker—particularly since Strieber claims to have only spent a year in London studying film (he graduated from the University of Texas in 1967), a year in which he was apparently also studying at the (Fabian) London School of Economics![2]

Going back a year or two, to 1966, there is a great deal of confusion around the question of whether or not Strieber witnessed the infamous

Charles Whitman shooting at Texas University in Austin. In *Communion*, he wrote how for years he had told of being present at the shooting. "But I wasn't there. Then where was I?" In *Transformation*, he changes his mind again, but he remains unsure of what he is saying:

> For years I'd remembered being there but hadn't been able to find witnesses who could place me. At the time I was writing *Communion* I concluded that this must be another screen memory [so] I carefully reported that I hadn't been there even though the memory was so realistic that I had actually given interviews describing the event in detail. (1988, p. 92)

Having concluded he was there after all, Strieber describes the incident in detail, including spotting someone he knew (who later confirmed their presence). He describes leaving the scene at once and driving back to San Antonio, hanging his head out of the car window and screaming. Why, with memories as vivid as this, did Strieber ever doubt his memory? If he could be unclear in his mind about something of such profound personal significance, how are we supposed to know *what* to believe about his accounts?

At the same time, Strieber as a 1960s underground London film-maker hanging out with The Process Church seems supremely unlikely, in light of his known history and personality (Strieber is about as far from a Sixties swinger as it is possible to imagine). As for The Process Church, any researcher into conspiracy and occult lore will tell you that this shadowy group is like a "strange attractor" for weirdness, and its brief history overlaps with everything from Scientology to the Son of Sam. This isn't the only unexpected overlap with other areas of my research either: William Sims Bainbridge, the transhumanist who had such a strong influence on Ray Kurzweil, did a five-year ethnographic study of The Process. He even took some pages out of their book when he adopted the term "religious engineering."[3] In "Social Construction from Within: Satan's Process," Bainbridge writes:

> Popular consensus held that [Process members] were dangerous Satanists, and their black cloaks and the red man-goat heads they wore on their chests gave no lie to this image. An antisatanic book claimed to know the truth about the group: "Savage and indiscriminate sex is forced on the entrants into the cult not as a means

of religious communion but as a means of purging any residue of Grey Forces that might be latent in them." (1991, pp. 297–300)

The Process Church was founded by two Scientology "apostates," Mary Ann McLean and Robert de Grimston Moor. Moor and most of the other founding members—just like Charles Whitman—were architecture students. Mary Ann McLean was born in Scotland and worked as a dominatrix and prostitute (Esther, 2010.) The Church established their headquarters in London in 1966 (when Strieber was in Texas witnessing the Whitman shooting—if he was). In late 1968, the senior members of the Church, including McLean, left London and traveled around Europe, eventually settling in a basement in Rome (Feral House, 2013). In the summer of 1968, Strieber had a series of strange experiences of missing time, starting in London, and leading to a collection of bizarre and fragmented memories traveling around Europe with a young woman, *ending up in the catacombs of the Vatican, in Rome.* In *Communion,* Strieber first mentions this period of his life in typically mysterious terms: "In 1968 I ended up with four to six weeks of "missing time" after a desperate and inexplicable chase across Europe. This is associated with a perfectly terrible memory of eating what I have always thought was a rotten pomegranate, which was so bitter that it almost split my head apart" (p. 119).

Pomegranates are associated with Persephone's "rape" and her journey to the underworld. Various winding roads converge in Strieber's narrative at an already strange and perplexing juncture in his life, the summer of 1968. It may be time to pause to reorientate.

*

A few days after listening to "Pain" and discovering these peculiar facts, while reworking this current chapter, I listened to a 1986 recording of a hypnosis session between Strieber and UFO-researcher Budd Hopkins. The focus was on Strieber's missing time experience in the summer of 1968. During the session, Strieber remembers traveling to Rome with a mysterious woman and being joined by some other people. He is able to remember these people only peripherally, as shadowy figures at the edge of the scenes. He remembers telling his "life story" in great detail to the woman, "twice or three times." He recalls that the woman told him she grew up in Ireland (McLean was Scottish, the fictional Janet is given an Irish name), and describes having sex with her more than once. On at least one occasion, he remembers other people in the room, directing the sex act and manipulating his body! One of the rooms he finds himself in was reportedly an "operating theater that was supposedly a bedroom." (In the introduction to the audio recording, Strieber suggests that he was supposed to impregnate the woman. Conversely, during his recall of the events, he describes withdrawing from her in order to ejaculate, and seems puzzled why he would do such a thing. In *The Super Natural* (written with Kripal, 2016, p. 212) Strieber's only reference to this meeting is described as "a couple of weeks in Florence, we had a lovely time, living together in chaste intimacy"!)

In a line that would be quite at home in "Pain," Róisín asks him, "What would you do if I told you I wanted to cut you in half?" Strieber describes a feeling of being under the "absolute control" of these people. He recalls visiting an apartment with skulls lined up on shelves (as well as art books), and being shown off by one of the group, "like a prize." He recounts being interrogated by a man with a New York accent about New York, and being terrified. He and the woman (whom he calls "Róisín"—an Irish name meaning Rose) go to the Vatican, where Róisín gives him a history lesson. They go down into the catacombs and Róisín disappears into the shadows. He encounters another woman who tells him he will find Róisín "on a street corner." While he is in the Vatican basement, Strieber recalls looking up at some glowing lights and seeing "the face of the devil ... a red face." A red "Baphomet" head with goat's horns was part of the Process iconography. The imagery also, quite tellingly, echoes the "trigger" of 1984 or 1985, the supposed "face on Mars."

Strieber stares into the face's deep, dark eyes. As he recalls this part of the experience, his voice becomes progressively quieter and more trance-like. *"This is so secret ... you would hurt yourself so much, if you knew this ... sssshhh shhhhh ... [inaudible] close the door ... "* Although his voice has been quite normal until this point, it here becomes almost inaudible, very much like someone going into a deep hypnotic state. After about half a minute, his voice grows strong again and he describes hearing someone telling him to go back up to the main floor. (Imagining climbing steps is a standard way to bring someone out of a trance state.)

Strieber returns to his *pensione* and there, in his room, he finds a black, box-like piece of luggage belonging to Róisín. He opens it and sees a "liquid eye" looking up at him. He describes it to Hopkins, in stunned tones, as a living being folded up, as if made of paper. Hopkins suggests (leadingly) that it may be a costume and Strieber agrees (as if the idea hadn't occurred to him until then). Whatever it was, it was apparently so lifelike that Strieber mistook it, even in folded up form, for a living being. The impossibility of what he was seeing (and the thought that his female companion was carrying such a thing around with her) frightened him so badly that he fled Rome the following day. (In *Transformation*, Strieber writes that he no longer credits his recollection of what he saw in the room. In *The Super Natural*, Strieber retells the story, replacing the staring eye "costume" with a nun's habit!) Weird discrepancies notwithstanding, the similarities of this fractured account with the story in "Pain" are striking, to say the least.[4]

The first thing that struck me when I heard Strieber's 2013 reading, however, was that it contained a very clear description of government secrecy around UFOs, along with an elaborate hypothesis about the nature of the inhabitants. Once again, this gives the lie to Strieber's statement that he had dismissed the whole subject of UFOs before his close encounter experience of 1985. And while Strieber insisted in his preamble that "Pain" was "not a personal narrative," the rest of the audio clearly suggests otherwise. For one thing, he recounts an experience of finding a photograph of his "uncle" lying in a coffin in North Africa and his uncle's reaction when he showed him the photograph. Besides the switching of father with uncle, it's an exact replica of the experience recounted, twenty-five years later, in *Solving the Communion Enigma*. Strieber goes on to make explicit what is only implied in the later work: that the photo is a documentation of his "uncle's" initiation into the Vril society, adding a lurid detail about "raising a demon" to take possession of Hitler, alchemical rituals, and the atomic bomb.

"Pain" goes on to describe the nature of the otherworldly beings in more baldly horrific (and also more religious) terms than probably anything Strieber has written since (not counting his novel *2012*). He refers to "something higher than man [that] fed on human souls." He describes "the prime aesthetic of death," an alien culture "designed for the purpose of causing us suffering," for which human beings are the "prime energy source."

> Perhaps there is a burst of very fine energy as the soul explodes from the body, an energy which can be used for the most subtle and powerful purposes? Or perhaps the soul is simply food for finer

bellies? Our suffering does not benefit them directly but rather the growth our suffering brings us. To reap mayhem in the world is not the responsibility of demons but of angels. It is their greatest and most painful duty ... This is a slaughterhouse. But we the victims are not gainsayed [sic] the blessing of a quick club to the head or the slitting of the throat. The greater our learning, the happier the angels.[5]

So let's take a step back. In a story he allegedly began before he even suspected their existence, Strieber describes the visitors in unequivocally maleficent terms, while simultaneously identifying them as "angels." In the same context, he describes himself— the character who is emphatically *not* Strieber, that is—as "ear-marked for special suffering," and recounts how, in the end, he comes "to love [his] tormentors and share with them their own sorrow." The rest of "Pain" recounts how the central character (not Whitley!) meets a beautiful and enigmatic woman and is initiated, through pain, into a higher understanding of reality. "Pain breaks down the barriers of the ego, of personality, of false self," Strieber's alter ego realizes. "It separates ourselves from ourselves and allows us to see deep. Witness the Book of Job, which in the secret texts which Janet used is called '*the Book of Man*.'"

Listening to Strieber's reading of "Pain" is reminiscent of Whitley's experience of the ruby-crusted book on Mars: it is a bit like being sucked into a dark well. One thing I found myself wondering, while considering the strange mixture of religious imagery with sadomasochism and thinly veiled occult teachings: Was this part of what Whitley learned in the Vatican basement, while he was hanging out with The Process Church in the summer of 1968? And what does any of this have to do with nonhuman beings?

CHAPTER VIII

A wound in the soul: the Master of the Key & the Oedipal Project

"When we can't follow in the father's footsteps, when a trauma has erected a 'Do Not Enter' sign above reality's door, we must regress to the mother's bed, dip our pens into the psychic gene pool of the collective unconscious, and return to the surface to write our personal mythology. As the fatality of the traumatized soul, the Oedipus complex is less a complex to be resolved than a psychology to be affirmed."

—Greg Mogenson, *A Most Accursed Religion*

In *The Inner World of Trauma*, Kalsched cites the psychoanalyst Sandor Ferenczi, an associate of Freud. Ferenczi observed in one of his patients how, when subjected to unbearable trauma and on the point of "giving up the ghost," a new element entered into the fray. He called it "the organizing life instinct," or "Orpha" for short. In place of death, Orpha "chopped up the personality, dispersing it into fragments"—thereby splitting the psyche into three: the ordinary ego self, the traumatized child self, and a "higher" self which comes to the rescue of the child self. The "destroyed" child part is "a being suffering purely psychically in his unconscious, the actual child of whom the awakened ego knows absolutely nothing." Orpha, on the other hand, is

... the part that "sees" the destruction. "She" is a supra-individual being, apparently without time and space, who, at the moment of unbearable pain, "passes through a hole in the head into the universe and shines far off in the distance like a star," seeing everything from outside, all knowing. This "Astral fragment," Ferenczi says, leaves the selfish spheres of earthly existence and becomes clairvoyant—"beyond understanding the aggressor, to an 'objective understanding' of the entire universe, so to speak, in order to be able to grasp the genesis of such a monstrous thing." Orpha, says Ferenczi, has only one concern and that is the preservation of life. She plays the role of the guardian angel. She produces wish-fulfilling fantasies for the suffering of a murdered child, she scours the whole universe seeking help. (1996, p. 121)

Orpha can't be dismissed merely as a delusional state, but is better seen as "part of a regenerative universal 'intelligence' [that] makes use of a deeper wisdom in the psyche at moments of traumatic distress ... It represents a factor truly 'superior' to the ego" (1996, p. 122).

The darkness at the end of Whitley's tunnel would seem to have come knocking on his hotel room door, in the wee hours of June 6, in Toronto, Canada, while he was on a book tour for *Confirmation: The Hard Evidence of Aliens Amongst Us*, the fifth in his "visitor series" (not counting *Majestic*, a novel about the Roswell crash). As Strieber presents his 1998 meeting with the Master of the Key ("a true encounter" is the subtitle of the book), it is very much the capstone of his otherworldly, transcendental or daimonic experiences up until that point. When I first read the book in early 2001, I was so impressed that I made photocopies of it and handed it out to people. I have read it at least a dozen times over the years and it has had a profound impact on my thinking. Initially, I took the book for what it purported to be, the faithfully transcribed words of a perfectly realized being: God in human form (the Master even speaks in the first person of/as God).

Strieber certainly appears to believe his encounter was a literal, factual event in his life, which is how he has chosen to present it to the world, and becomes defensive at any suggestion he made it up. At the same time, his inability to be coherent about the event, and incidents surrounding it, begs the question of why an actual, flesh and blood encounter would be so shrouded in mystery, confusion, and obvious contradiction. (An obvious example: his memory of the Master of the Key's height varies from 4 foot to 5 foot 8 inches.) Strieber is the proverbial unreliable narrator, whose constantly shifting story and voice throws the narrative into question. Whether this is deliberate or not, and whether the Master of the Key is a real being "out there," a concatenation of Strieber's mind, a literary device, or a strange psychoplasmic blend of all three, is something I suspect even Strieber may not know for sure.

The psychoanalytic school of thought observes how the male child, trapped inside the once-nurturing, now-stifling symbiotic union with his mother, creates an "imago" of the father in his own image—a stern but powerful presence to rescue him from drowning. As Jung writes in *Aspects of the Masculine*, the role of the father-imago is an ambiguous one.

> The threat it represents has a dual aspect: fear of the father may drive the boy out of his identification with the mother, but on the other hand it is possible that his fear will make him cling still more closely to her .... This double aspect of the father-imago is characteristic of the archetype in general: it is capable of diametrically opposite effects and acts on consciousness rather as Yahweh acted towards Job—ambivalently. And, as in the Book of Job, man is left to take the consequences. (2015, pp. 74–75)

Norman O. Brown wrote, after Freud, that "Psychoanalysis must always take the position that the Child is Father to the Man" (1985, p. 120).[1] The Master of the Key is Strieber's idealized image of himself *as* the father—he even speculates it may be his future self. In light of Strieber's fragmented personality—his strange blend of guru-like wisdom and childlike histrionics—the Master of the Key, and the artifact Strieber created to represent him (*The Key*), might be seen as an embodiment (in book form) of the split in Strieber's psyche, *transformed into a literary device*. *The Key* purports to be a transcript of a real-life conversation, and maybe it is. But it reads like a dialogue between Strieber's regressed, child self and his progressed, father self, or Orpha: the guardian in its benevolent and angelic form. The Master even refers to Whitley as "child."

After the encounter of June 6, Strieber claims he woke to find his hotel room floor covered with notes. He found them illegible, but not useless. When he looked at the notes, he says, whole chunks of the conversation came into his mind as if the notes were "a mnemonic device." He called his wife, described the meeting, and told her that a day would come when he would try to dismiss the encounter as a dream, and that she must never let him do so. She followed his instructions, and *The Key* is dedicated to Anne Strieber, without whose "insistence, it would have been neither written nor published." Here Strieber is in classic infant-to-mother relationship to his wife: that of *having her affirm his reality for him in times of doubt*.

Strieber's recollection of the incident, outside of the transcript itself, certainly resembles a dream. He has stated that the whole conversation took roughly half an hour, yet reading the book out loud would take at least three times that. He claims that the words of the Master communicated far more information than mere words could communicate, that each phrase was like a soft bullet that exploded in his mind and filled it with imagery and associations. When the 2011 edition came out, he claimed that the first version had been interfered with without his knowledge, "censored" by "sinister hands." And yet he had been reading from the supposedly censored edition for years, and even claimed to remember phrases the Master used, phrases *he later claimed had been falsely added or altered by those sinister hands*. So all the evidence suggests that Strieber himself is unsure what happened that night, and that the only solid evidence he has is whatever he managed to write down. In other words, and whatever real-life basis there may be to the encounter, he *wrote* it into being, and has since adopted that literary version *as* reality. This is not meant as a criticism: It's what we all do, all of the time. As Greg Mogenson writes in *A Most Accursed Religion*, memory is a form of imagination:

> The psychological motto "we act out what we can't remember" becomes for us "we are determined by the literalness of events (physical, emotional, intellectual, social, etc.), which we cannot imagine." Memory, or *memoria* as it was once called, is a form of imagination .... Though we tend to reify history, thinking of it as what "really happened" in the past, history is not static. Inasmuch as it touches us experientially, it must enter into the imaginative modes of recollection, thereby becoming psycho-history, a history of soul. (2005, p. 19)

Strieber admitted this in a 1988 interview when he said about the visitor experience: "Not only does it trigger memories, it also triggers the imagination and you can't tell which is which" (Blackmore & Curtis, 1988).

*

"Whatever we do not face but gain salvation from remains unredeemed and becomes satanic. Evil is the excrement or waste product emitted by the salvation process itself. Ironically, the more we are saved, the more there is to be saved from."
—Greg Mogenson, *A Most Accursed Religion*

Whatever happened that night of June 6, 1998, whatever strange child was born from Whitley's psyche—Archangel or Legion—it may be that Strieber *had* to grant it concrete reality by writing *The Key* (and later labeling it "A True Encounter," the final nail in the coffin of the subjective). He had to because the forces were already set in motion: at the secret school in 1954; in the catacombs of the Vatican in 1968; after he wrote *Wolfen* and *The Hunger* in 1981–83 and Hollywood turned his dark dreams to reality; as he stared at the face on Mars in 1984/5, and then gazed into the black eyes of the visitor that Christmas night in 1985—all the forces of the unconscious that carried him to the top of his profession and down into the depths of his soul *demanded* that God-the-father show up and *make sense of it all*. The child cannot face the chaos of the world and the mother's psyche combined. His life *depends* on receiving the key to unlock the mysteries, from a good father who shows the way through, into the light.

In *Communion*, during the second hypnosis session, Strieber describes an exchange with the female visitor:

I want to go *home.*
"What if we don't let you go home?"
But I don't know if she said that or not. I think I think that she said it. (I was shown that door again, which for some reason terrified me. I was asked if I wanted them to *open the door.*) "*I do not want you to open that door! I belong with my momma* and my wife … and my boy. That is where I belong. [Sobs.] I don't belong here. I don't know how I ended up here. What the hell did I do to attract all this?" (1987, p. 84, emphasis added)

Whitley wants to go home to his momma/wife. Whitley cannot face the door opening. Whitley is still waiting for the key. But what *is* the key that will open the door? In *The Key*, Strieber expresses a feeling of helplessness in the face of the enormous stakes which the Master is describing to him (the extinction of "a living world," and worse).

"My God," Whitley says. "Can anybody do anything?"

"You can write," the Master tells him. "*Use your tool.*"

He adds further incentive: "But also, you will see the demon revealed in those who refuse to acknowledge the signs" (2011b, p. 133). The Master is confirming Strieber's divine (Martian) calling to bring order to the chaos and slay the dragons of denial, using the fiery sword of writing. The fate of the world hangs on Whitley using his tool right; and should he fail to penetrate, he can always blame demons! (Which brings to mind Strieber's manipulation by–what sounds a lot like–a shadowy cult to perform sexually during his 1968 Rome odyssey.)

 If writing is the way Strieber makes sense of the chaos and brings light to his darkness, if it's the key to his own psychological survival (though also his psychic-imprisonment), it was inevitable he would eventually write himself a salvific in the form of a key-carrying God-man—*his own perfected image of himself.*

Aggressive dissociation is how the traumatized boy-child first learns to use the mind as a weapon—against his own *eros* or life force. Strieber's tragicomic self-emasculation/aggrandizement process echoes what Freud (and Norman O. Brown after him) describes as "the Oedipal Project," the infant's attempt to "transform passivity into activity ... by becoming father of oneself." The infant feels God-like when still immersed in the mother's psyche—his every wish granted. The threat of impotence which accompanies his first steps towards autonomy all but demand a compensatory "will to power" and the creating of a God-the-father imago to conquer and claim the mother imago which is about to be forever lost. From *Life Against Death*:

> The essence of the Oedipal complex is the project of becoming God ... By the same token, it plainly exhibits infantile narcissism perverted by the flight from death. At this stage (and in adult genital organization) masculinity is equated with activity [e.g., Mars]; the fantasy of becoming father of oneself is attached to the penis [or the pen?], thus establishing a concentration of narcissistic libido in the genital (p. 118). [The Oedipal project is] the *causa sui* (father-of-oneself) project, and therefore in essence a revolt

against death generally, and specifically against the biological principal separating mother and child …. "All the instincts, the loving, the grateful, the sensual, the defiant, the self-assertive and
independent—all are gratified in the wish to be the father of himself." (1985, pp. 127, 118)

*

> "I will never really understand the relationship between mother
> and son. I will never part easily from her."
> —Whitley Strieber, *Transformation*

In *Communion*, when Strieber describes his first remembered encounter
with the visitor, he makes a series of striking statements (1987, p. 106).
He first of all remarks that the being "was undeniably appealing" to
him and that he felt love for her, "almost as much as I might my own
anima." Yet he also experiences "the same feelings of terror and fascination that I might toward someone I saw staring back at me from the
depths of my unconscious." He states: "*In her presence I had no personal
freedom at all.* I could not speak, could not move as I wished" He admits
that to surrender his "autonomy to another" would provide him with
"not only fear but also a deep sense of rest." To be with this being, he
writes, was "… like dying. *When they held me in their arms, I had been
as helpless as a baby, crying like a baby, as frightened as a baby.*" He goes
on to describe how the visitor's gaze "seemed capable of entering me
deeply … *as if every vulnerable detail of myself were known to this being.
Nobody in the world could know another human soul so well … I could actually feel the presence of that other person within me—which was as disturbing
as it was curiously sensual*" (1987, p. 106, emphasis added).

Strieber's "Pain" contains the following passage:

> She came to me and supported me while one of the others loaded a
> high powered rifle. I was slack with terror. The bullets clattered into
> the magazine, and one of them clicked into the breach. She held me
> under my arms, keeping me erect so that the bullet would pierce
> my chest in the right place. (2013)

Janet—the angelic initiator-dominatrix of "Pain"—holds him erect
(obvious sexual connotations, linking mother with lover in later life);
she holds him like a mother holds a baby that can't stand on his own

power, teaching him to walk. Those first few steps are the beginning of the end of symbiotic union with the mother. While still enmeshed in the mother's psyche, the baby experiences himself as all-powerful: The mother's body is an extension of his will and she seems to move according to the infant's every desire. To begin the process of leaving the mother's body is to experience the exact inverse of that feeling: total powerlessness—like a bullet to the heart. If the child is overwhelmed by this feeling, he will desire one thing only: to be enveloped again in the mother's embrace.

In Strieber's latest work, *The Super Natural: A New Vision of the Unexplained* (with Jeffrey Kripal, see appendix), Strieber describes a vision he had which he interprets as a memory of entering into his mother prior to his birth. It begins with his disembodied form hovering over her, leading to "a violent embrace, as if her soul was coming around me, drawing me to her. Then, in an act beyond anything I have known since, I penetrated into her." Strieber is aware of the Freudian connotations of this when he adds:

[P]erhaps coitus, in its desperate urgency, and in the sense of annihilation that accompanies it, is a striving to return to this extremely secret moment that is hidden within us all .... Ah Oedipus, sweet child of longing, and dear Dr. Freud, peering with his crystal light into these dark, uneasy halls. Even if it unfolded only in my imagination, that penetration of the womb exposes, I think, a deeply human and probably universal longing. (2016, p. 242)

It is a longing that appears to have remained unsatisfied in Strieber. A few pages later, he goes on to state: "My mother did not leave me when she died." He then describes how he became aware of her presence after her passing, watching over him. "My mother was my advocate," he writes. "She understood that my mind needed food." His father, he adds "felt that I should stay with children's books, but she defied him. I was so grateful to her, and I still am ... So we were very close, and *I just cannot tear myself away from the belief that it was her on that night, doing her part to help me awaken to a very real world* that continues to seem to me to be entirely impossible" (p. 246, emphasis added).

Strieber is stating here a strongly held belief: Just as his mother brought him into physical existence, she is now performing a similar role on the *other* side, drawing him into a *new* existence, that of "the super natural." Strieber views the visitors in a similarly maternal light: In his introduction to the 2008 edition of *Communion*, he recounts the painful moment in 1988 when (in his own estimation) he failed to "cross the threshold" and enter into a conscious, fully consensual relationship with the visitors:

> The moment I turned away from them that morning, I entered into a school, which I have been in ever since. My matriculation was symbolized a few moments after I retreated, when I found myself vividly recalling something that had been lost for many years in the natural amnesia that surrounds our childhoods. I remembered—or they gave me to remember—the first steps I ever took in my life. For a couple of wonderful and profound moments, the glorious experience of walking from the edge of my mother's bed to the towering leg of her desk was returned to me as vividly as if I were re-experiencing it, but with my adult's mind. So I knew, at least on that bitter morning, where I actually stood. (2008, p. xviii)

The word "matriculation" is striking in this context. It means to be enrolled or registered in a university or college, but it comes from the Latin *matrix*, meaning womb, which shares a root with *mater*, mother.[2] Strieber's professed inability to take those final, decisive steps towards the visitors leads to his being *matriculated* and returned to the matrix of the mother's psyche. The same thing appears to be indicated by "Pain," following the piercing ritual.

> As the ritual moved slowly along, she spoke kind words to me.
> "Is there anything we can do to help you?"
> "Somebody could hug me."
> "Oh, ok, I can do that." (2003)

As Strieber points out, this passage directly echoes a scene with the visitors which he later reported in *Communion*, when the female "master" asks him (in a subtly electronic tone of voice) what they can do to help him stop screaming, and he replies that she can let him smell her.[3] "What can [I] do to help you stop screaming" is a question every mother (internally) asks her infant child, 100 times or more. Strieber's desire to smell her may not be "a normal request" for a grown man, but it is perfectly normal *for a baby* seeking reassurance of the presence of the mother. In Strieber's account, he first describes a *male* visitor putting its hand against his face; in the transcript of his second hypnosis session, however, it is the female being who puts her cheek up by his face (1987, pp. 28, 83). This discrepancy is never addressed. Nor is the still more disconcerting moment in which Strieber realizes that the being he thought was female has a *penis*, which he then experiences being punched into him repeatedly.

After his own penetration by the bullet, Alex, Strieber's *fictionalized counterpart* in "Pain," experiences an infantile immersion into the mother's body:

> As we remained there together something quite unexpected happened to me. My will, the core of my identification as a separate self, ebbed slowly away. The ebbing of will was like black water revealing a drowned cathedral .... My whole will was in her hands: I was so free of myself that I even lost the wish to beg her for my life. (2003)

The experience is comparable to how Strieber describes his first reaction to the visitors in *Communion*, albeit in far less blissful terms, when "'Whitley' ceased to exist. What was left was a body in a state of raw fear ... I do not think that my ordinary humanity survived the transition to this little room. I died, and a wild animal appeared in my place."(pp. 26, 29). A wild animal or a wild infant? And in a conversation with Ed Conroy reproduced in *Report on* Communion (p. 340), probably from 1989, Strieber recalls his "impression that one of the beings was my mother and another was my sister. I had that impression, even though I don't mean my human mother and sister. I didn't say anything about it at the time because it seemed so bizarre, but now it's beginning to make a little sense."

In *A Most Accursed Religion*, Greg Mogenson describes trauma as "the body of the world and the body of man." He pictures a self that "splits off from the body and hovers above it—a false self. World becomes mere worldliness, and a transcendental, heavenly world is split off and affirmed" (2005, p. 56). The projected "heavenly world" of the false child self is an image of the mother's body, and of itself *becoming its own father and conceiving itself*. It is an imaginary future projected from a traumatic past, recreating itself in its own image, mirrors within mirrors, gazing, abysmally. The image of the mother-bonded child projected outside the reach of the mother, incorporeally, is eternally rejecting his own body in order to escape the body of the mother; yet paradoxically, the attempt only ensures he remains forever bonded to her.

*

> "[W]hatever traumatizes us becomes our parent. Or, putting that another way, let us say that whatever we cannot master with our creating will, we will turn into a super-parent or god and be infantilized by it."
> —Greg Mogenson, *A Most Accursed Religion*

Before the Master of the Key, there was another being that Strieber wrote into existence, one he described as "the greatest master I have ever known": the female alien pictured on the cover of *Communion*. In fact, I was surprised to discover that he used this phrase to describe her at his website in December of 2001, three years *after* meeting the Master of the Key. Characteristic of the separation-individuation process, Strieber appears to have experienced divided loyalties.

> The woman whose portrait is on the cover of *Communion*, which I am looking up at now as I write, was without a doubt the greatest master I have ever known. Her being projected devastatingly powerful knowledge. A great part of the terror that I knew when I was with her came not from the situation, but from how it felt to be seen by her. In fact, she and those around her were trying to calm me down in some ways, even as they engaged in very quick but also very intrusive medical actions. (2001)

In the same post, Strieber immediately goes on to describe the rectal probe. He then makes a striking statement: "Looking back over these years, two things have entered the culture from my experience: her face and the rectal probe." It's a grisly juxtaposition of imagery; typically, Strieber attributes the dark association to the world at large: "I have been both amused and disgusted by the eagerness with which elements of our human community seek debasement, by concentrating on whatever they can find that offers them the potential to lower themselves further." (Seeking debasement—a demonic predilection if ever there was one—provides a stark contrast to the "ascension" prescribed by the Master throughout *The Key*.)

Strieber also refers to the female master as "somebody very great ... somebody whose life is vastly larger than a human life," which is a pretty good match for how an infant child must experience his mother. After several more sentences, Strieber points out how the visitor experience was complex and varied: "Some of them are not like the woman I met and her staff. Some of them qualify as what we would call monsters, in every sense of that word" (2001). Considering the ignominies which Strieber endured at the hands of the "the greatest master [he had] ever known," the imagination pales to think what these *other* monsters might have in store for us!

Strieber's supreme veneration of the female being who helped abduct him and presided over his "rape" in 1985 is surprising, to say the least. It's especially so since, in *The Key*, Strieber asks the good father if he was "in the company of demons or aliens that night" (in 1985) and the Master of the Key infers he was by telling him to love his enemy as "your best friend." In fact, the first words which the Master of the Key says to Whitley are: "You're chained to the ground"—that is, bonded to the mother (earth) (2011b, p. 41). The next thing the Master states is his benevolence: "I am here on behalf of the good." The good father has come to "fish" the child out of the mother's psyche, as echoed by the imagery of Aquarius (the zodiacal sign most closely equated with aliens) pouring the little fish of Pisces out onto dry land. The Master calls the planet "a death trap," the only possible escape from which is *to develop the technology to leave the planet and venture into space* (2001b, p. 42). Later, Strieber is told that "the extinction of mankind," if it happens, will be due to "your inability to expand off the planet" (p. 132). The reason the Master gives (p. 43) is that the child who would have "unlocked the secrets of gravity" was never born because his parents were killed in the Holocaust!

The lunar-vaginal mother debases, violates, drags down into the earth. The solar-phallic father ascends, sets free, lifts up to the heavens. Earth and sky are seen as split, at odds, and the child-psyche is torn between the two. The child has reached the end of a healthy symbiotic union with the mother. He was meant to have acquired the ability to separate-individuate from her body and psyche, but he has not. She can no longer support the child, yet without the intervention of the father, the child will be unable to leave the mother. He will enter into symbiotic psychosis, "mother bondage." This is akin to the death, or stillbirth, of the child's psyche.

*

> "Mahler, Pine, and Bergman viewed the father as 'a knight in shining armor' coming to the child *'from outer space'—rescuing the child from the symbiotic tie to the mother*. As the child moves from infant to toddlerhood, the father is differentiated from the mother as an exciting, mysterious other ... the task of separation-individuation might be *'impossible for either [mother or child] to master without having the father to turn to.'"*
> —Christine C. Kieffer, *Psychoanalysis and Women*

In *The Key*, just before referring to the Earth as a death trap, the Master gives Whitley what might be *the key* to *The Key*, and even to this whole convoluted psycho-history. He tells Strieber that humanity "bears a wound in its soul that makes you deny the reality of the past that is plainly visible all around you." Mars was murdered by us, he says, at which point, "intervention occurred, as it will happen again when you destroy this planet, as will probably happen. This is *the trigger* for intervention, the destruction of a living world" (2011b, p. 111). As is becoming increasingly clear about everything in Strieber's work—most especially *The Key*—this passage appears to be concealing a deeper, more intimate meaning behind an *apparently* cosmic narrative. The narrative, like all good sci-fi, is metaphorical. The galactic-spiritual language of the Master of the Key, and of Strieber's other writings (including his early horror fiction), is what I have called Whitley's "cosmic lens," as symbolized by the telescope the Martian nun told him he *must* acquire at any cost, immediately after he realized his mind was the only weapon he had. Whitley's telescope allows him to see what is far away; but it also prevents him from seeing what's in front of his eyes.

Strieber's writings might be seen (inadvertently) as an example of how the intellect, when trained to act as a sophisticated mental-literary dissociation device, makes it possible for us to hear, and report, what would otherwise be too painful to allow into consciousness. The problem is that this distancing device also greatly reduces the chances of our understanding our experiences—most of all because the cosmic narrative is so arresting and urgent *on its own terms* that it never occurs to us to look beyond it. The mystery, dear Whitley, is not in the stars but in ourselves (and not our interstellar selves either). Whitley is convinced that "the key" he was given is meant to save the world. In fact, if I am right, it was meant exclusively to help him save *the inner world* of his psyche. For everyone else, it's manna laced with strychnine: truth seen through the distorted patterns of personal trauma.

Repressed material can only resurface into consciousness in an atmosphere of denial and negation (that cosmic lens, in Strieber's case, and my own). The only way the daimonic guardian allows suppressed trauma to come back into consciousness is by first denying it and/or by representing it as *something else*. That resistance strengthens what's being resisted and ensures it eventually *break through*—because denying something affirms it by admitting something is there to be denied. Awakening, integration, individuation invariably threatens to bring about ever greater levels of denial, resistance, and distortion, and an increase in neurosis.

The Master of the Key describes an ancient cosmic event in which Mars was about to be murdered and "intervention occurred." This, he says, is "the trigger for intervention, the destruction of a living world." Strieber described in *The Secret School* seeing the photograph of the face on Mars as a *trigger* (like the photograph of his prostrate father?) which led to the *intervention* of the visitors (including an Ishtar-like female Master[4]). This intervention was not so much divine as bodily, taking the form of a traumatic anal violation apparently intended for *healing* purposes. If so, it gives a fair indication of both the type and scale of trauma which Strieber needs to be healed from. The living world that is in danger of being destroyed, evidently, this dark and stormy Christmas night, is the world of Strieber's psyche—specifically that aspect corresponding with *Mars*, namely, his sexuality and "manhood."

This more intimate and disturbing narrative, hidden behind the cosmic one which Strieber's books present as fact, has several diverse, overlapping, and recurring elements:

- Early trauma involving some kind of sexual interference, possibly using technology
- The absence, passivity, or complicity of the father, resulting in a lack of protection and an unhealthy bondage to (identification with) the mother's psyche
- Veneration of a controlling and terrifying female presence

- Aggressive dissociation (psychic fragmentation) necessary to the child's psychological survival
- The resulting disconnection from the body, life force, and libido
- The imprisoning and rechanneling of the libido into mental activity (writing, out-of-body experiences) as a form of offense-defense
- A preoccupation with the demonic, the horrific, and with soul damnation
- The equation of the body and the Earth with a "prison"
- The sustained attempt to escape the body/become the father/ become God through a variety of visionary scenarios and other-worldly encounters
- A recurring series of sexually tinged traumatic reenactments
- A consistent and growing preoccupation with overcoming death and leaving the planet.

Strieber's oeuvre is thematically bookended by the mother-father dyad of *Communion* and *The Key*. In its entirety it offers a coded narrative of indefinitely prolonged mother-enmeshment, or "matriculation." This includes an internally generated "Godhead" of a rescuing father, an image which perpetuates the infantile oedipal project of mother-possession via the creation of a womb-like matrix identity, based on that projected image.

Embedded in these cosmic narratives is the supposed "proof" of their own pseudo-empowering message. Strieber is a culturally significant figure whose tales of power have widespread influence, so they reinforce the notion that such a belief system (Strieber's interpretation of trauma-events as a cosmic alien drama) is eminently desirable, since it allows for apparent "autonomy" (social advancement, super-powers, etc.). Yet this is only true insofar as these tales of specialness are legitimized by the same systemic cultural pathologies which created them (and to a degree, Strieber himself), systemic cultural pathologies which they were created precisely in order to serve.

CHAPTER IX

Padre nostro castrato: the name of Whitley's game

> "They are forcing me to grow. Stressing me so much that my mind is evolving. Rats—there were tests of rats in the seventies. Stress tests. Rats were stressed with electrocution. Day after day they were made to suffer for long periods of time. They grew stronger, their brains got larger, they became better rats .... And suddenly a voice–a tired, young voice says as clear as day: 'Thank you.' Them. *Their function is in some way to make us evolve.* And now at last I know a little something."
>
> —Whitley Strieber, *Transformation*

While I was working on what became the first part of this exploration, I came across a used copy of Strieber's *Transformation* in the local bookstore. I bought it and started rereading. Like *Communion*, I read the book many times in the past; it has had a formative influence on me, and I was curious to see how it would affect me after more than ten years, in light of recent discoveries and my changed spiritual perspective. Many of the passages still impressed me with a genuinely "magical" flavor, and once again I was struck by how much Strieber had gone through and the degree of apparent "soul-growth." At the same time, it drove home just how little, from my point of view, it seemed to have actually benefitted him in terms of personal development.

In chapter 17 of the book, "Fury," Strieber describes a disturbing series of incidents. He has already recounted how the visitors told him to give up sweets and that, if he eats chocolate, he will die. Strieber makes a couple of attempts to obey these unexpected demands, but he soon realizes he is addicted to sugar. He receives further admonishments and tries again. He wonders if the visitors are only attempting to show him how addicted he is to externals, or whether there is an actual, physical state they want him to enter into that can't be accessed without giving up sugar. He continues to eat candy, however, and eventually the visitors react.

Strieber wakes to find one of the beings in the corner of his room. He feels "an indescribable sense of menace." The next moment, inexplicably, he feels "… mothered. Caressed." He experiences a "light, electric pressure" between his eyes and instantly finds himself on a stone floor with a stone table in front of him. There are iron shackles attached to it. A man is led up some steps by another man dressed in black. The first man is shacked to the table and the man in black begins to beat him violently with a whip, until he is "almost torn to pieces."

Strieber is told that the man is being beaten because he failed to get Strieber to obey him. Strieber understands it is because he failed to give up sweets. The man continues to be beaten, coming in and out of consciousness. Strieber hears a voice in his head, the female visitor, telling him: "It isn't real, Whitley" over and over. Strieber writes that the voice doesn't help, that he had "never felt such raw humiliation and guilt"; he would have done anything, he writes, to have taken the beating in the man's place. The next thing, he is back in his bed and the female visitor is smiling at him sardonically. He hears his son screaming in another room. The being tells Strieber, "He is being punished for your transgression." Strieber closes his eyes. "The sense of being infested was powerful and awful. It was as if the whole house was full of filthy, stinking insects the size of tigers." The screaming stops. He tries to get out of bed but is hit in the face and falls back (1988, pp. 190–192).

The next day, his son appears to be unharmed, and Strieber expresses love and gratitude for the visitors and what they have done for him.

> I had the sense that they had on my behalf turned away from perfect love, and that they had done this to help me. If they are an element of the divine, to come into our world would be like penetrating perfect darkness. I realized that I was isolated in myself, turned away

from the light that surrounds us. I suspected that the ugliness I had seen last night was not them, but *me*. I was so ashamed of myself that I almost retched. (1988, p. 193)

Previously, when I'd read this book and *Communion*, I had fully accepted Strieber's view of the visitors' harsh treatment of him as a kind of cosmic tough love. I had even tried giving up sweets: *I* wanted access to that "place." Now it seems more as if Strieber unconsciously found a way to interpret the events in a favorable light, because (as he admitted) he desperately *needed* to see the visitors as benevolent. The alternative would be intolerable. This isn't necessarily as simple as rationalization, because it might be a *pre*-rational process. There is an exact match for it when a small child is abused or neglected by a parent or other adult caregiver: Since the child's survival depends on the adult, he can't allow the possibility that the caregiver is anything other than perfect and benign ("an element of the divine"). The child then sees *himself* as bad, as *deserving* the punishment he receives. As Kalsched writes, "It is an almost universal finding in the literature of trauma that children who have been abused cannot mobilize aggression to expel noxious, 'bad,' or 'not-me' elements of experience, such as … hatred of an abusive father." Because the child is unable to hate the parent and sees them as good, "the child takes the father's aggression into the inner world and *comes to hate itself and its own need*" (1996, p. 17).

For alien beings to enforce a strange, seemingly random discipline—getting Whitley to give up sweets and punish him when he failed—is like a grotesque caricature of bad parenting. If Strieber is unconsciously protecting these "visitors" by blaming himself for their abusive treatment of him, then all the "spiritual evolution" he is supposedly undergoing becomes part of that same unconscious cover-up: evidence of his own complicity with the abuse. It is the irrational, or *pre*-rational, circular logic of the child: since they *are* good, what they are doing to him is for *his* good; since their harsh treatment of him is for his own good, they must be good.

The appliance of control and discipline *can* be parental and it can be a form of love. But it can also be done for very different ends, as is the case when such discipline crosses over into abuse. In a 1988 interview, Strieber discussed the incident:

I mean, like the business of eating sweets, which is so stupid. How dare they do that? And yet it became finally so terrifying that I was sort of forced into doing something about it because of my child and now as time has passed what happens when I eat sweets is that I ... I go into a decline. I mean I just can't do it and it's because— I'm convinced it's psychosomatic but still it's—I've just lost that ability. I can't do it because of what happened, and I don't understand why it happened; there isn't any explanation for that anywhere in my understanding of what I've experienced. It's almost as if by forcing me to do something that was apparently difficult for me in the physical world, this force gained strength. (Blackmore & Curtis, 1988)

The statement is chillingly concise.

*

"When we examine closely the specifics of the events which have overwhelmed us, we find them to be the causes—efficient, material, formal, and final—of our so-called first cause, God. Yes, the image-less God is an image *for us*, albeit an intolerable image. The jungle fire-fight, the early morning rape, the speeding automobile of the drunk driver—all these images may be God images if, like God, they create us in their image, after their likeness."

—Greg Mogenson, *A Most Accursed Religion*

In Strieber's 2011 book, *Solving the Communion Enigma*, he revisits the question of "who are the visitors," promising (in title at least) to provide a final solution. Sure enough, in the last section of the book, he writes this:

If you actually wanted people to increase the use of the right brain, then stressing them would be a way to do it. [I]f you apply trauma *in the right way*, what you are actually doing is *reengineering the brain*. [O]ne thing the visitors are doing is creating situations that are designed to increase our left-brain functioning. They are trying to improve our ability to think logically. But for those of us who have *the correct response to trauma*, it doesn't end there. We are also being given shocks that induce [posttraumatic stress disorder], thus causing an increase in right-brain functioning as well. (2011a, p. 196, emphasis added)[1]

This idea can be traced back to the Gurdjieff Foundation and "the Fourth Way," which Strieber participated in during the Seventies, and is known as "intentional suffering" and "the second conscious shock." Apparently the name of Whitley's game is "Pain," and without it, no evolutionary gain is possible. What exactly does Strieber believe "an increase in right-brain functioning" allows for? He doesn't specify, but presumably one thing it facilitates is encounters with demons and God-men in the middle of the night. In the passage immediately before that quoted above, however, he makes a characteristically candid statement:

> After my 1985 close encounter, I had a galloping case of post-traumatic stress disorder (PTSD). Unfortunately, the various treatments I have tried have failed, probably because the stressor—the encounter experience—could always happen again at any moment. Thus, to this day I have terrific nightmares and wake up at the approximate time the encounter happened, usually with my heart hammering, waves of fear coursing through me. (2011a, p. 196)

Strieber is not offering this description as an example of being "evolved" through trauma. He merely includes it as a preamble to the remarkable statement that follows it. Before that, however, he writes that "Among other things, some sufferers of PTSD can experience flashbacks and hallucinations that seem real." "Hallucinations that seem real" is a curious turn of phrase, and it begs the question of how real such hallucinations might seem. Real enough to write a string of "nonfiction" books to persuade others that they *are* real? If Strieber's statement is accurate, how would he *know* what was hallucination and what was real? No wonder Strieber is desperate for some sort of physical evidence (outside of the implant in his ear, which had "military" written all over it). Strieber adds, "They [PTSD sufferers] are thrown off the road of the real, and exist instead in an awful twilight of memories and illusions, and have no way to tell the difference between them" (2011a, p. 195).

How much might a person with no way to tell the difference between memory and illusion be willing to *do* to feel like there was *some* solid ground to stand on? Strieber is painting an inadvertently self-damning picture, even as he moves towards his primary point about evolutionary engineering through trauma. Strieber writes that there is *a correct response to trauma* that doesn't involve being thrown off the road of the real. Our concern should be less what Strieber believes, however, than what can be reasonably deduced from his accounts, fictional or otherwise. The evidence he presents for the realness of his perceptions, so far, is a series of wildly improbable, fantastic, and otherworldly accounts of nonhuman interaction, and a body of scientific-mystical literature that, while impressive, is deeply confused, highly disturbing, and riddled with contradictions. Wouldn't it be more logical to deduce that Strieber is exactly the sort of PTSD sufferer he describes, and that perhaps he is implicitly leading us to this conclusion without realizing it (or at least without admitting it)? There is a desire in all of us to come clean and be clearly seen, free from all masks, and maybe the enigma Whitley wishes to solve—and that prevents communion with his soul—is the enigma of Strieber himself?

"I have lived this for a long time," he writes. "In fact, though, it is further support of the reality of my experiences. *If nothing had happened to me, I wouldn't suffer from PTSD. You don't get it from bad dreams*" (p. 195, emphasis added). I doubt if anyone who has been paying attention is likely to suggest that nothing ever happened to Whitley Strieber. The question is—*what*? Strieber sees it as a form of sadomasochistic angelic intervention by a complex intelligence that has our spiritual evolution at heart. He is a "true believer" that the end justifies the means, and his end is now to sell those same means to us.

> Perhaps it isn't improbable that the same complex intelligence that we are facing would act in many different ways, some of them tremendously challenging for us. If contact meant that what is apparently happening in Sulawesi and in Brazil [i.e., death and mutilation] would extend to the entire world, or abductions and implantations would become a general human experience, then the danger is incredible. But if it means that *millions of people will end up in a school such as the one I have attended*, then a case can be made for embracing it. (2011a, p. 211, emphasis added)

Strieber is making the case for the embrace. But what sort of school is he recommending for the unenlightened masses? One in which he "was raped, my sexual materials taken from me, subsequently shown a baby and left to live in a permanent state of stress but also shown new ways of thinking, and a hidden level of being that is sublime" (ibid.). Strieber is certainly communicating a permanent state of stress. His delivery style is histrionic, and the message of hope and transcendence he offers filled with horrifying narratives and doom-laden scenarios; it is as if his trauma has been *sublimated* into, and *as*, a series of crucial, pseudo-spiritual fictions. In *The Key*, Strieber asks why the (human) agencies enforcing "mankind's blindness" are harming us so terribly. The Master tells him, "The objective of resistance is to make you strong. The weight lifter puts more and more weight to himself, so that he'll be able to lift more and more" (2011b, p. 82).

As with so many of the passages in *The Key*, for years and over the course of countless readings, I accepted this line at face value. In fact, comparing spiritual development to weight lifting is a disastrous analogy, and if it is really the reasoning of an advanced intelligence, then it's not a very compassionate one. A few weeks before working on this chapter, I met a young Native American in the local sauna whose physique was obviously the result of lifting weights. I'm a painfully skinny guy (my build is like one of the visitors), and we had a brief conversation about working out. He told me that heavy lifting repeatedly tears the muscles in the body and the scar tissue causes the increase in size. Hearing that pretty much confirmed my opinion that bodybuilding is a neurotic pursuit that, besides boosting self-confidence, intimidating bullies, and scoring with chicks, offers no real physical advantages. But while it's a strange metaphor for an ascended master to choose for spiritual growth, there is one thing it has in common with Strieber's "no pain, no gain" school of evolutionary progress: *trauma*.

While it's plausible that intense stress can and does change the chemistry and/or wiring of the brain, thereby allowing access to larger, deeper, or alternate fields of perception, the question left unasked in Strieber's recipe for evolution is: What about the body? Isn't Strieber making the most fundamental mistake that a scientific mystic (or mystical scientist) can make (and the one they always seem to) by assuming, implicitly, that consciousness resides primarily in the brain and not in the total body? Trauma has to do with energy *trapped in the body* that causes distortion, contraction, and dis-ease. The purpose of traumatic reenactments is not to increase brain power but to *release that emotional energy trapped in the body by the original trauma.*

Maybe this is why Strieber's little gray aliens look the way they do: because they engineered their brain-evolution and forget all about their bodies, until their heads swelled up like over-inflated balloons and their eyes popped out of their heads. Maybe an endless series of "evolutionary" shocks reduced their bodies to feeble, ghostlike shadows of organic life. In *Solving the Communion Enigma*, Strieber offers up this grisly picture of de-eroticized, disembodied existence as our future. He presents tormenting, malformed, sexually abusive angels as the butterflies to our caterpillars, yet he doesn't take this peculiar idea all the way to its logical conclusion; he never asks how, or why, our trauma-engineering, disembodied future selves are directing our evolution. Is it, like the abuser with the child abused, to ensure we become *just like they are*?

For the sons to castrate their fathers is a reversal of the Saturnian myth, but the end is the same: to terminate the lineage. Strieber's "future man" appears to be trying to murder his own past in a kind of cosmic retroactive suicide. The child whose libido is abducted by sexual abuse grows up prematurely, which is the same as saying, does not grow up at all.

CHAPTER X

Whitley's baby: the unholy junction of 1968

"A traumatic event is not pushed out of awareness; it is too big to register in awareness. Traumata only return from repression when a sufficient inventory of comparable events provides a reality schema that can more or less absorb them. The so-called repetition compulsion is a way to trying to create the field of comparable events in whose terms the traumatic event can be relativized and experienced."

—Greg Mogenson, *A Most Accursed Religion*

A psychic healer I met once in Navarra, Spain, in response to a question about my chronic health issues, told me, without explanation, that they were the result of my having "seen the devil" ("*viste el diablo*") when I was one year of age. I was one in 1968—the year Strieber saw a devil's head in the basement of the Vatican. There be great mysteries here?

In *Transformation*, Strieber mentions a couple of names from his 1968 London period, one of them in relation to his sugar addiction. Briefly, he describes how the visitors get a "message" to him by appearing in the bedroom of an old lady diagnosed with diabetes. The story gets back to Strieber because of the similarity between the old lady's experience and his own; when he looks further into it, he discovers she was the grandmother of an old friend, Martin Sharp. Strieber mentions that Sharp lived in The Pheasantry on King's Road, a place he frequented in 1968. I hung out a lot on King's Road in my late teens (it was where the gorgeous "Chelsea girls" were), and I visited The Pheasantry night club more than once. Not only that, but during the same period the house I lived in in Yorkshire during my adolescence was also called The Pheasantry.

Martin Sharp was an early innovator of the hippie-style poster/ album art, and a highly influential artist. He was one of the cofounders of *Oz*, "a scandalous magazine and a major part of the '60s underground scene" (the same scene Strieber's films were supposedly part of). *Oz* was first published in 1963 in Sydney, Australia (Sharp was Australian), and in London from 1967 to 1973. Richard Neville, a "futurist," was the editor, and Strieber's other friend, Philippe Mora (who directed the film version of *Communion*), was a major contributor along with Germaine Greer. As well as contributing cartoons (as "Von Mora") to the magazine, Mora made a short film called *Passion Play*, shot in The Pheasantry around 1967 or 1968, with Jenny Kee as Mary Magdalene, Michael Ramsden as Jesus, and Mora himself as the Devil.

This seemingly trivial detail brings up another curious connection: Roman Polanski (who was living in London during this period, and married Sharon Tate there) shot *Rosemary's Baby* (in New York) in 1967–68. In the film, Anton LaVey, the head of the Church of Satan, was a "technical advisor" and allegedly played the Devil who impregnates Rosemary (this may be apocryphal, Internet Movie Data Base credits the role to an unknown actor, "Clay Tanner"). LaVey was tenuously connected to the Manson family via Susan Atkins (who was present at the murder of the pregnant Sharon Tate in August 1969), and Charles Manson lived two blocks from a branch of The Process Church on Haight-Ashbury in 1967.[1] Manson, who studied Scientology in jail prior to creating his Family, allegedly stated that he and Robert Grimston (the cofounder of The Process) were "one and the same."[2] (He also wrote an article for The Process magazine.) This brings us back again to Strieber, who in 1968 was getting intimate with the inner works of The Process. It's also curious to note how closely Strieber's path came to crossing that of William Sims Bainbridge: Bainbridge spent four years with The Process Church, from 1969–1973. Inspired by the experience, Bainbridge developed the notion of religious engineering and proposed the creation of a Galactic Religion via UFO cults. But that will have to wait until Part Two ...

The Pheasantry was a melting pot for many influential artists of the period: as well as Martin Sharp, Eric Clapton (who later did the music for *Communion*) lived there briefly, on the top floor with the *Oz*-ies, as did the famous rock 'n' roll photographer Robert Whitaker. Sharp and Whitaker created an album cover for Cream and a three-minute film with Germaine Greer called *Darling Do You Love Me*, directed by Sharp. A synopsis of the film (at IMDB) bears some similarity to Strieber's "Pain": A vampire-like woman, with deathly pale skin and jet-black eyeshadow, harasses a deadpan young man wearing a straw hat and horn-rimmed eyeglasses, continually asking him, "Do you love me?" She follows the man and sings the question out of tune over and over. He remains impassive, only holding up a little stick with the picture of a smiling, toothy mouth, which he puts over his own mouth while hysterical laughter plays in the background. Her question grows more frantic, desperate, and pleading as she dances about him, tackles him, and presses her face to his through the bars of a gate. She manipulates his face, which remains expressionless. Finally, she grabs him by the throat and shakes him repeatedly until he succumbs.

Richard Neville wrote a memoir of his time with *Oz* called *Hippie, Hippie, Shake*, which was made into a movie of the same name in 2007. Although it has never been released, I knew about the movie because they'd shot part of it on the street in London where I lived, during the same period I wrote my first piece about Strieber! I had hung out for an hour or so, making eyes at the star, Sienna Miller, before being moved along by one of the security staff. Before I left the set, I found out that the director was someone I used to play with as a child in Yorkshire named Beeban Kidron! What are the odds? It was Chapel Perilous: Whitley's and my paths were slowly but surely converging. But what did it all mean—besides that "the coincidence goblin" was getting involved?

The coincidence goblin is something cited by H. P. Albarelli Jr. in his review of Peter Levenda's *Sinister Forces*: "a peculiar and recurring phenomena by which one experiences odd and disconcerting coincidences, which quickly lead into still odder coincidences until one gets the overwhelming and unshakeable sense that one has been ordained by some invisible higher power to write his or her book ...." As it happened, Levenda was one of two writers (the other being Kripal) I contacted before beginning this present work. My correspondences with Peter Levenda about Strieber were frustrating and only slightly fruitful. Levenda (like Kripal) seemed either unable or unwilling to acknowledge the nuances of my arguments, and responded as if I were reducing abduction accounts to mere hallucinations. Later on, while working on the book which I hope will follow this present work (goblins permitting), Levenda and I crossed pens over the question of Aleister Crowley's complicity with child abuse. I eventually came to see Levenda as seriously compromised as a researcher, a fact I mention here only because the rather esoteric (and fanciful) notion of a "conspiracy goblin," while having *some* merit, may also be a means for redirecting attention away from any possible real-world implications of the data (such as those outlined in this current chapter), by passing them off as evidence of goblins (the implicate order of things) rather than of any human-based conspiracy. In most cases, I find it is not a case of either/ or, but both/and.

Returning to the matter at hand, I looked into *Oz* magazine and discovered that, surprise, surprise, they ran a piece on The Process Church in the May 1967 issue—one month after I was born. The cover of the issue was done by Sharp; at the end of the article there was some artwork that included a flying saucer. On the page before, there was a short fragmentary piece which began with these lines: "In common with Steve McQueen, Lee Marvin, Dean Martin 'and a lot of other cats,' Norman goes on UFO hunts. Recently in a field near London, Norman says he was sure *they* were there, but for some reason would not show themselves. 'Maybe they didn't want to frighten us.'" Norman gives an anecdote about the aliens' sense of humor and says, "'They're *so* human.'" The piece ends with the words, "'What we need is religion rather than religions—the gods are only shorthand for the gods inside your head—and more contact with ourselves.'"[3]

When I read the piece on The Process, I found an even more striking passage:

> The faction is divided—more than once it seems—first of all there's the desire to tell humanity about this divine revelation, then there's this anti-grey masses scene which means no one is actually very keen on mingling with *the 'greys'* in order to put across the message. Thus a Process magazine is born. A lovely, remote way of making the word Process known—just pay your thousands and have it printed on glossy paper, without actually having to touch the outsiders your-self. Then you sit and wait for the right ones to come pouring in: all those *Gurdjieff initiated meditating hippies* ... (etc.; emphasis added)

As it happens, Strieber allegedly spent thirteen years studying with the Gurdjieff Foundation immediately *after* this period, from roughly 1970–83. Meanwhile, another significant figure who lived at The Pheasantry during this period was David Litvinoff, an adviser on the production of the cult movie *Performance*, shot in London in autumn of 1968 around the time Strieber was scattering his marbles across Europe. The film was made by Nicholas Roeg and Donald Cammell; Cammell was in Kenneth Anger's *Lucifer Rising* as Osiris, along with Manson family member Bobby Beausoleil, who played Lucifer. Cammell was the son of Charles Richard Cammell, a close friend and biographer of Aleister Crowley, and in fact Cammell was Crowley's godson. For his role in *Performance* as "Chas," a violent organized-crime figure, actor James Fox was trained by Litvinoff, an associate of the notorious Kray brothers, and Fox spent time with the Krays.[4]

Mapping these same shadowy and labyrinthine connections, comic book writer Alan Moore included Litvinoff as one of the characters in his *League of Extraordinary Gentleman* series:

> Litvinoff is one of the few concrete real life examples of the process Moore is trying to describe in 1969. The archetypal London face, he was a living link between the various contemporary, queasily cohabiting underworlds of criminality (boyfriend, or at least some-time arm candy of Ronnie Kray), showbiz (the *Performance* film-making/art scene connections) and psychedelic occultism (probable sideline in good acid). He somehow survived getting heavily in debt to the Krays, but speculation remains that the eventual reason for his demise was the embarrassing secrets supposedly revealed in an exposé he was writing based on his experiences and insider knowledge of these various nefarious milieus. (*Mindless Ones*, 2011)

To top it all, the Krays, like the Finders, were reputed to have been involved with supplying children to pedophiles and pederasts via the notorious Jersey care home.[5] A letter sent by a prominent conservative politician, Lord Robert John Graham Boothby, to Ronnie Kray on *June 6*, 1963 (the date, though not year, of Whitley's visit from the Master of the Key) was discovered in 2009 in which Boothby—whose sexual perversion was already common knowledge—thanked Kray for an invitation to "Jersey."[6] The Krays were reputed to have "paid informers on every level in the force," and to meet with police detectives at the

Jersey home to do business.[7] I mention this mainly because of another high-profile entertainment industry player who has since been implicated in the Jersey home scandal and who has been discussed in the present work: Jimmy Savile. (Jimmy Savile was interviewed for a 1969 issue of The Process magazine, in the "Sex" issue. The piece was called "The Natural Life of Jimmy Savile.") This places Savile in the same circle as the Krays, the Cammells, and the Claptons—the foxes in with the pheasants—during roughly the same period. And Whitley Strieber?

Strieber's forgotten London odyssey now showcases not only strange occultists, UFO-heads, and leading entertainment industry players, but organized London criminals and pedophiles. It places him, as a twenty-something "underground filmmaker" making a documentary on The Process Church, at the very heart of the scene in the years 1967–69. How did he get there? What did his involvement consist of? Was he out in the field with Norman and the other Gurdjieff-initiated hippies, dropping LSD and looking for UFOs; was he getting glimpses into the world of hardcore criminality via Cammell and Litvinoff? If not, why not? If he was too square for all that, how did he wind up hanging out with Sharp and Mora and Eric Clapton at the center of the London Sixties scene? Most puzzling of all, why has this period of his life been all but stricken from the record?

For all his outré encounters and unconventional perspectives, Strieber comes across as a very proper, Texas-born-and-raised, red-blooded Catholic American—a square. What happened to that secret life? Did he forget it along with so much of the other high strangeness of his past? Or did he deliberately sweep it under the rug, for reasons as yet undivulged? Or, as seems more and more evident with Strieber, was it a little of both, and a little of neither? The only mention he makes of this period of his life in Communion is suitably bizarre:

> Then, in July (of 1968), there was another incident. I cannot recall what happened with any clarity. It was simply too confusing, too jumbled. I was at a friend's flat in the King's Road, Chelsea. For years I have described it as a "raid" from which I escaped by "crossing the roofs." What I actually remember is a period of complete perceptual chaos, followed by the confusing sensation of looking down into the chimney pots of the buildings. Then there was blackness. (p. 137)

A little digging uncovers the fact that there *was* a massive series of police raids in early May of 1968 (directed by one John du *Rose*) targeting the

Krays' London operations (*BBC Home*, 2003). The Krays were the first to be arrested but many other homes were targeted. Litvinoff, who lived at The Pheasantry, was allegedly running a gambling joint for the Krays *at that time on the King's Road* (*BelleNews*, 2013).

Strieber recounts waking up the next morning in his apartment with no idea how he got there. Whatever happened in the flat (whether it was The Pheasantry, The Process's Mayfair apartment, or somewhere else) was never referred to by anybody there ("with one exception," Strieber adds, cryptically). The next day, he says, he decided to leave London for the Continent. He was unable to stand England "for another week, not another hour." A friend warns him against going, saying he will never come back, and threatens to get a witch to cast a spell to bring him back. Strieber thinks *"What superstitious nonsense"* (1987, p. 137).

It was about then that another piece of the puzzle fell into my lap. In a 2006 interview with Peter Levenda, the author of *Sinister Forces*, Strieber mentioned having had "a certain involvement" with The Process Church. He described being a film student in London in 1968 when he and his partner, "Mike Smith," "happened upon the existence of this mysterious organization." Strieber doesn't seem sure how he heard about it but suggests it was via "a strange ad ... while reading the back pages of some local equivalent of *Time Out*." Considering that he was hanging out with Martin Sharp at The Pheasantry, it seems likely he heard about The Process via that connection or read the article in *Oz* magazine. Strieber recalls going to a meeting "in a fancy house in Mayfair ... run by a beautiful woman."

> A few young men were around all looking longingly at her, as we were. She tried to induce us to join and then, we decided ... because we were in film school and we had a documentary to make, that this would be our subject. And we began making our documentary. Soon we were called, or more accurately I was called, by a gentleman in the British Foreign Office, to come and meet with him. It was rather surprising because how they found me and, etc., etc., I never found out. In any case, we met with him and he told us this: he said that in their opinion The Process Church of the Final Judgment was seducing young people and taking them to Mexico, wealthy young people on a yacht that they had access to, and in Mexico, they were sacrificing these young people in pyramids in the Mayan country. And a number of young people had disappeared as

a result of this. We finished our documentary and I ended up—Mike got away Scott free but I ended up being chased. They unleashed dogs on me in their building in Mayfair and I ended up having to escape across roofs. It was really pretty dramatic. (Strieber, 2006b, six-minute mark)

As far as I know, this is the only time Strieber has gone on record about his "involvement" with The Process Church, and typically, he throws it out as one more bizarre incident in a life overflowing with anomalies. Was this the event he described, as a fragmented memory, in *Communion*? If so, why did he describe it as "a raid" in 1986 if he remembered the incident with the Process dogs which he described to Levenda in 2006? If he only later had a full recall of the event, why didn't he mention having misreported it and set the record straight at his website? Were the events connected—for example, did The Process come looking for him with their dogs at his friend's flat in King's Road? If not, and the incidents are unrelated, exactly how many rooftops did he end up running across during his year in London? Was there any connection between rumors of Strieber's "intelligence work" and his being "contacted" by someone in the British Foreign Office? Or between his eulogizing of sacrifice in "Pain" and what he supposedly discovered about The Process Church, back in 1968?

Only in a life as fantastic and incoherent as Strieber's could these be considered minor questions.

*

"Has the Space Age at least fostered—especially among young people—a sense of awe, wonder, curiosity, and impatience to know, an urge to explore and a rekindled faith in progress, the future, and human nature, or perhaps even a postmodern, gnostic religious vision conflating transhuman evolution, biological or post-biological immortality, space colonization, and contact with extraterrestrials? ... Perhaps the Space Age will alter the consciousness of a critical mass of people. Perhaps, as William Sims Bainbridge eloquently contends, such a quasi-religious consciousness may give rise to a new social movement transforming the scale and priorities of the human presence in space."
—"A Melancholic Space Age Anniversary," Walter A. McDougall, *Remembering Space Age*

While I was writing about *The Key* for this present chapter, I noticed the date Strieber gave for the Master's appearance, June 6, and initially believed that same date (in 1966) was the birthdate of Rosemary's baby, i.e., the antichrist, in the *1968* Roman Polanski film. I somewhat jokingly speculated that, since the Master of the Key was presented as an omniscient god-being, he should have been aware of the fact and that, someday, some occult-versed movie buff would find an unholy significance in it. However, while there is some online attribution of the antichrist's birthday to that date, the correct date is actually June 25. By that time it was too late, however; this whimsical association (though it was more than whimsical, as I will explain) had led me into a spaghetti junction of interlacing threads, complete with witches, warlocks, and sacrificial victims.

For one thing, I re-watched *Rosemary's Baby* in the interests of research and noticed some clear parallels between Rosemary's and Strieber's experiences. Rosemary is drugged with a bitter tasting liquid (a chocolate "mouse") and then abducted from her bed. She is carried naked from her room and then led into an underground chamber where she is surrounded by shadowy figures, all the while dreaming (screen memory) of being on a yacht (ship) floating in the ocean. She is raped by a nonhuman, predatory entity (the devil) and inseminated with a child, a half human, half "alien" *hybrid* being. She remembers the experience only as a particularly vivid nightmare, yet she has marks on her body when she wakes. There is even a curious correspondence with the name: Strieber's female companion (abductor?) in Italy of 1968, whom he believed he was supposed to inseminate, was called "Róisín," or Rose.

Returning to that date: Robert Kennedy was assassinated sometime after midnight on June 6, 1968 (thirty years before the Master of the Key came knocking on Whitley's door); the previous evening, Kennedy (as reported in Peter Levenda's *Sinister Forces*) had dinner with Roman Polanski and Sharon Tate at the home of John Frankenheimer, the director of *The Manchurian Candidate*. Kennedy's alleged killer (evidence suggests another shooter was involved) was Sirhan Sirhan. Sirhan has been connected, somewhat tenuously, to The Process Church: A chapter of the 1971 edition of Ed Sander's *The Family*, omitted after The Process Church took legal action, stated that Sirhan was known, "in the spring of '68, to have frequented clubs in Hollywood in the same turf as The Process was proselytizing. Sirhan was very involved in occult pursuits," Sanders wrote, and had "talked several times subsequent to Robert Kennedy's death about an occult group from London which he knew about and which he really wanted to go to London to see."

In the 2002 edition of Sanders's *The Family* (following a cue from author Adam Gorightly), I found still more clues linking the Manson murders to Sirhan and (maybe) The Process Church, as well as to the group Strieber discussed in *Solving the Communion Enigma*, the Finders. In 1974, Sanders learned about an investigation being conducted by one Richard Smith, of the Immigration and Naturalization Service (INS) into a "satanic group of English origin that had oozed to America in 1967, 1968, and 1969." According to Sanders, Smith wanted to launch a "full-scale investigation" from Germany to London, with an office in Mexico City to investigate the Mexican operations of the group. When one of Smith's superiors saw the name of a US congressman included in the investigation, however, Smith was told to cease and desist. Fortunately, Sanders's inside source had gotten a look at Smith's report before the investigation was shut down.

> The report stated that English satanist cult members invited Sirhan Sirhan to a number of parties that were sponsored by television people in LA area, and that one of these parties took place at Sharon Tate's residence. At these parties, it was averred, sexual and ritualistic activities were reported to have occurred. These assertions were apparently based on an FBI report done during the initial investigation of the RFK assassination ... Smith's report stated that a Los Angeles law-enforcement agency had an informant who averred that the English satanist group had commissioned Manson to kill Sharon Tate ... The reason for the contract ... was "something that she unfortunately overheard that she was not supposed to overhear in regards to Sirhan Sirhan." (Sanders, 2002, pp. 483–484)

Smith could not provide any more details, Sanders's source said, citing it as "a matter of national security."

In 2012, Sirhan Sirhan was diagnosed by Dr. Daniel Brown[8] as acting under hypnotic suggestion the night he shot (at) Kennedy. Dr. Brown described Sirhan as "uniquely suited to mind control, one of the very small minority of the public deeply susceptible to programming" (Morales, 2012).

[H]is firing of the gun was neither under his voluntary control, nor done with conscious knowledge, but is likely a product of automatic hypnotic behavior and coercive control. I am convinced that Mr. Sirhan legitimately recalled a flashback to shoot at target circles at a firing range in response to the post-hypnotic touch cue and did not have the knowledge, or intention, to shoot a human being, let alone Senator Kennedy. Even after 40 years Mr. Sirhan still is confused when told by others that he shot Senator Kennedy.[9]

In the process of taking a more nuanced and depth-psychological look at Strieber's alien contact experiences, I have somehow wound up mapping the underground nexus of mind-controlled assassins, child-sex rings, satanic cults, and celebrity murder. How has this happened? It's a neighborhood I have frequented in the past, but not one I'd originally planned to return to again. The funny thing is that, in a sense, I have been frequenting this neighborhood my whole life. My troubled adolescence, fraught with fever nightmares, was leavened by a penchant for Hammer horror films and James Herbert novels, an infatuation with David Bowie (especially his "occult" period from 1968–75, roughly), and a full-blown obsession with Clint Eastwood. At first, I was only interested in movie stars, but I soon developed a more serious interest in the filmmaking process; the first movie director I was seriously drawn to was Roman Polanski. Now here I am, in my late forties, going over exactly the same ground, having arrived at it from a completely different departure point. Like attracts like, and birds of a feather hunt (or huddle) together.

I am beginning to think there is a simple, if unorthodox, reason why the usual suspects—Aleister Crowley, Polanski, Manson, the Kennedys, The Process, Charles Whitman, David Bowie, Nic Roeg, Jimmy Savile, Stanley Kubrick, William Sims Bainbridge, L. Ron Hubbard, Aldous Huxley, Gurdjieff, and now Whitley Strieber!—keep cropping up wherever I seem to look. For all the billions of people on the planet (allegedly at least), are there only a few hundred, at best, who play any sort of visible role in the grand theater unfolding before the public eye? And of course they would all hang out together, formally or otherwise, literally or not, because they are in the same business—that of socio-spiritual engineering, or "culture-making." It might *seem* like world history is far too vast and complex a meta-organism to be reduced to a handful of players, but is that just part of the illusion? Actors on stage exist in a world of their own, complete unto itself, while the audience exists in a kind of limbo realm, having no say about how the story unfolds. Even so, the audience's attention is essential to the maintenance of the illusion. The audience is complicit in its own irrelevance—it has to "disappear" from the scene in order for the surrogate reality to take hold.

Insofar as my own psychic development has been informed (let's not say hijacked) by all of these cultural influences or "players," it is perhaps inevitable that, someday (in the process of trying to become a "player" myself, that is, have some cultural influence, a goal I have pursued ever since I first discovered Polanski, roughly), I would wind up struggling to identify those agents, and the shadowy agendas behind them, in an attempt not to secure my future, but to make sense of my own past.

*

> "Because the psychogenic theory makes the individual psyche both the source of variation and the unit of selection, it posits that childhood is the central focal point of social evolution."
> —Lloyd de Mause, *The Emotional Life of Nations*

So where in the performance have we left Strieber? Fleeing London, after which he fled Rome and wound up in a hotel in Barcelona, "holed up in a back room." He remembers "nights of terror, being afraid to put out the light, wanting to keep the window and the door locked, living like a fugitive, never wanting to be alone." The rest of his memory is "a jumbled mess" in which he "lost weeks of time." He recalls "something about being on a noisy, smelly airplane with someone who called himself a coach, and something about taking a course at an ancient university." He recalls "little adobe huts, and expressing surprise to somebody that their houses were so simple"[10] (1987, p. 138).

Strieber remembers returning to London "in an odd way," weeks later than planned, with no way to explain the missing time and no memory of how he got back. He found himself outside a hotel at about six in the morning, got himself a room, and slept until noon. (Very precise recall for someone whose memory was a jumbled mess!) The next day he went to his former lodgings and found that his room had been let and his belongings "stored in a trunk in the basement" (1987, p. 138).

On June 5 (note the date) 2004, Whitley Strieber's website aired an interview with author Donald Bain about "CIA mind control" and the case of Candy Jones (Strieber, 2004b). Strieber told Bain that, like Sirhan (whom they discussed on the show), he was among the "5 percent" of human beings who are highly susceptible to hypnotic suggestion. He described having been subjected to the same sort of procedures as a child at the Randolph Air Force base, under the direction of "Dr. Antonio Krause," and then told about having a total memory blackout while driving with his wife and winding up at Randolph, with no idea of how he got there. Strieber then went on to describe a friend he had at the University of Texas "who recruited for the CIA—we both did this together." (Apparently this was a slip of the tongue and Strieber meant to say "applied for" the CIA!). He described receiving a dire warning from a "rather famous man" who told him flat out, "You will be killed, you will not live, if you join the CIA." (His friend joins and is killed ten years later. Strieber doesn't specify but it's likely this is the same "CIA friend" whom Strieber saw in the presence of the visitors, on one of his first adult encounters, and who he later found out had died, i.e., had been dead when he saw him.)

Regarding the question of his having been mind-controlled, Strieber told Bain: "I don't know what I did in connection with this, in terms of intelligence. Apparently nothing. I can't remember anything at all, not even a snatch of anything." Like the lost summer of '68, or his on-again, off-again memory of witnessing the Whitman shootings in 1966, the question of what, exactly, Strieber was being trained and/or programmed for at Randolph Air Force base during his childhood remains obscure and elusive, in equal measures tantalizing and forbidding. At his public forum in 2007, he touched upon the subject only briefly:

> What happened was, essentially, a Bluebird-style effort to fracture me and the other kids into multiple personalities. This "Krause," I believe, had done this for the Gestapo, in order to create children who could be made to be unwitting spies on their parents. The children were tormented in this way, then let go. They absorbed information that could later be "downloaded" from the hidden personality, with the child's normal personality never knowing what had been done. [I]t is no "experiment." It is something much larger. And it DOES lead to contact, and whoever is behind this assault on children knows this, and is, I believe, intentionally putting people in harm's way by methodically shattering their grip on reality

when they are children, then monitoring them and learning from the contact experiences they then have. (Strieber, 2007a)

On an audio recording he made for his website called "Intelligence Community Child Abuse" (2010), Strieber stated that "bad things" had happened to people from his past when he tried to get in touch with them. He recounted an odd story about a close friend from his time in London who he had regained contact with. He received an email from the friend with some photographs of their activities, including a photograph of Strieber with his (the friend's) son and grandson. There was also a copy of a letter, supposedly written by Strieber sometime in the past; it referred to his "CIA activities ... back in London in 1968." Strieber dismissed the idea—just as he dismissed the same inference on his author's bio in 1981[11]—saying that he was just a boy at the time (he was twenty-three). He suggested that the letter was meant as a warning to both him and his friend (who claimed to know nothing about it) to stay away from each other: "There might be something you'll [sic] remember that somebody doesn't *want* me to remember."

Note here how Strieber shifts the focus mid-sentence, from second to first person, suggesting a lack of certainty about the subject of his recall—was it him or someone else? As to what the something he was not supposed to remember might have been, Strieber offered no opinion. The idea that it might relate to his having worked for the CIA didn't seem to even enter his mind. By this point, it probably makes him the only person whose mind it *hasn't* entered.

*

"Unable, as Freud said, to 'distinguish between truth and fiction that has been cathected with affect,' we feel as buggered by the father we never knew as by the pedophile we did know. For, inasmuch as the angel that we also are demands a union that we can never fully realize, the pain of its yearning will register itself in our dreams, fantasies, and the constructions of analysis as a sexual trauma. No wonder the religious instinct so readily expresses itself as pedophilia. No wonder that on the way to rebirth we are always complaining that it is Rosemary's baby."
—Greg Mogenson, *A Most Accursed Religion*

In Amy Wallace's account of being married to Carlos Castaneda, *Sorcerer's Apprentice*, she recounts how Castaneda confessed to having worked as an assassin for an unnamed government agency (on other occasions he mentioned the CIA and US military intelligence). A friend who roomed with Castaneda in 1957 said he had heard similar stories from Carlos. Castaneda's first wife, Margaret Runyan, recounted a story he told of being seriously wounded while serving in "an intelligence division" in Spain or Korea. According to Wallace, Castaneda even confessed his secret to his "nagual" (sorcerer master) don Juan. Wallace quotes Carlos as saying:

> Later, when I had met don Juan, I told him I had a terrible secret. Terrible, the worst, and I had never confessed it. I had been don Juan's apprentice for years before I found the courage to speak of this horror. "Tell me, *estupido*," said don Juan, "what can be so bad, eh? Is this why you're always so heavy, so *pesado*? Why do I have to stand on my head to move you an inch? What is it, this terrible thing you did?" "I killed people, don Juan. Lots of people." "That's *it*?? You killed people? *Carajo*, Carlos, you killed *apes*. That's what you're so ashamed of? Killing a few apes? Believe me, there are always plenty more to take their place. And you're making yourself sick with this Great Big Secret?" (2003, p. 96)[12]

According to Wallace, Castaneda was trying to turn his experiences with the CIA (or whoever) into a novel in his final months of life. He called it *Assassin*. I mention this in passing as a parallel example to Strieber that once again involves a foremost literary influence. How, or why, have I chosen these role models? On the other hand, if we are drawing our models out of the mold of popular culture, are there any other kind? Is this perhaps the unavoidable dark side of both the mystical path and the individuation journey? My early heroes, whether Elvis or Bowie, Eastwood, Polanski, or Peckinpah, were all associated with one form of self-destructive excess or another. I have always been drawn to the dark side to see what is in my unconscious, what is controlling me and leading me into aberrational or self-destructive behaviors. So perhaps not to follow such dubious "leads" might be as fatal as to follow them blindly?

Our minds always tend to want to focus on simple moral questions, such as whether the aliens, or government agents, or sorcerers, or teachers (or parents), are acting for good or evil. But if the psyche is beyond good and evil, the real question is a question of fragmentation or wholeness. A fragmented psyche can do no right, a whole psyche can do no wrong, and the greatest "evil" of all stems from a fragment that takes itself for the whole. When a shattered psyche looks for symbols of wholeness outside of itself, it finds, inevitably perhaps, only the fragments of a shattered mirror.

The guardian protects the wounded child-self. To do so it adopts a dual guise as angelic, wise, and caring, and also as demonic, deranged, and destructive (though still protective). An "alter" (as in the case of programmed shooters such as Sirhan, but also many of us who grow up with unbearable trauma) is created to do the "dirty work" which the conscious personality won't, and can't, do. Like Norman Bates, the alter "cleans up" all the bloodstains, the loose ends, inconsistencies, and awkward or compromising elements (the "leaks") that threaten the illusion of the benevolence of the guardian. Anything, in short, that interferes with its rule over the divided and conquered kingdom of the psyche. The "progressive" or "benevolent" guardian (the spiritualized ego) is like a politician or a movie star whose spotless public persona is dependent on a covert agenda of bribes, blackmails, illegal wiretaps, harassment, and assassination. The "light" side *depends* on the dark.

This leads me to what seems like an unavoidable question: Is programmed murder the necessary flip side of self-engineered spirituality (killing the ape of the ego), if both are fuelled by the guardian in its unbending "will to power"? When I first decided to include my 1993 dream of the intelligent limbs in this series of essays, I left out the part about programmed killer robots. It seemed unnecessarily dark and I thought it would distract the reader from the main narrative—that of childhood trauma informing quasi-memories of nonhuman beings. I'd posted the whole thing at my blog a few days before, however, and a reader who had been helping with the investigation messaged me: "One thing from your blog that keeps repeating in my mind is the phrase 'I'm not a girl. I'm a boy!'" He described the detail as "haunting." I asked if he thought I should reinstate the fragment into the current work. "It's a dream," he replied. "Err on the side of accuracy."

His point was that the unconscious knows things which the mind has difficulty letting into awareness, and that the smart move is to let the dream speak for itself. It *is* unthinkable, but so is everything else we have suppressed from our awareness. If "alien-programmed killers" are becoming an integral part of the dream-narrative, Magonia is starting to look more and more like Manchuria.

PART II

CRUCIAL FICTIONS

"It is obvious, therefore, that in order to be effective a doctrine must not be understood, but has rather to be believed in. We can be absolutely certain only about things we do not understand."
—Eric Hoffer, *The True Believer*

CHAPTER XI

The ones who must lie: alien abduction & MKULTRA

In Julian Jaynes's influential work, *The Origin of Consciousness in the Breakdown of the Bicameral Mind,* he presents evidence that

> Consciousness is a much smaller part of our mental life than we are conscious of, because we cannot be conscious of what we are not conscious of. How simple that is to say; how difficult to appreciate! It is like asking a flashlight in a dark room to search around for something that does not have any light shining upon it. The flashlight, since there is light in whatever direction it turns, would have to conclude that there is light everywhere. And so consciousness can seem to pervade all mentality when actually it does not. (2000, p. 23)

In terms of conditioned learning, Jaynes argues, not only is consciousness unnecessary, it actually *prevents* learning from occurring. The more conscious we are of being conditioned, the less susceptible we are to it. This brings us back to the question of belief, and how the idea that we have consciously chosen to believe something is, nine times out of ten, an error. We believe or disbelieve because, at one time or another, it was *necessary* to do so.

129

Everyone knows that, to some degree at least, we respond to far more than we are consciously aware of. We all know what it's like to experience irrational anger, to fall into despair for no apparent reason, or to find ourselves doing things with no idea of why we are doing them (and sometimes no memory of having done them). We are all, to one degree or another, aware that there is far more to us than we are ever able to observe, much less categorize or explain, with our conscious minds. Yet we are also able to conveniently—and somewhat miraculously—ignore this fact throughout most of our lives.

All that we know of the UFO and the alien—outside of any direct experiences we might have—comes from stories, that is, from accounts of eye witnesses and experiencers, some of whom have, I think beyond all doubt, experienced something. These partial descriptions of unclear perceptions have then been collected, organized, and interpreted by researchers and, over time, been turned into hypotheses and, in most cases, articles of belief.

My own investigations—partially reported in Part One—lead me to the following hypothesis: It is not possible to separate the faculty of perception from the element of belief, because we not only develop beliefs based on our perceptions, but our perceptions are, to an unknown degree, limited, directed, and shaped by our beliefs. Both perception and belief develop in human beings at an early age, at a pre-rational stage of development. During this early stage of development, there is a primary experience of powerlessness and of the corresponding potential for trauma. There is also the near-inevitability of at least *some* degree of trauma informing our psychological development, limiting our abilities to perceive and giving rise to a certain set of beliefs. To an unknown degree, both our perceptions and our beliefs are shaped early on, then, to protect us from the full traumatic brunt of reality, and from being overwhelmed by a feeling of powerlessness.

The depth psychological view sees early trauma, and the resulting psychic fragmentation and dissociation, as at base of all our subsequent experiences, perceptions, and beliefs. This is most evident in the way we encounter divine or transcendental realities, for the simple(?) reason that the way we deal with early trauma is via *dissociation*, by calling upon and/or withdrawing into the realm of phantasy. Through phantasy, the greater, more transcendental part of the psyche intervenes and rescues us from intolerable reality by "abducting" us into its realm. This is not an unreal realm (the psyche is real), but it *is* a dissociated one.

An experience of the psyche that isn't grounded in the body cannot become fully real, because it will always be diluted, or polluted, by the defensive fictions that have arisen to keep the trauma out of our awareness. These "crucial fictions" extend to every aspect of our existence (starting and ending with the ego itself), and the UFO is a perfect opportunity to map the ways in which such fictions are created and made "crucial," that is, become articles of faith, fanaticism, irrational conviction, and out-and-out obsession.

What I discovered in the writing of and dialogues around the first part of *Prisoner of Infinity*, and which I hope is being communicated to at least some of my readers, is how the experiences of Strieber (and by extension other abductees), whether phantasy, reality, or some little understood combination of the two (the model I lean towards), are filled with very clear "symbolic" elements. These symbolic elements point towards early childhood trauma (possibly universal) that the psyche is attempting to address and integrate through *psychic reenactments*. This requires reexperiencing trauma in an unconscious attempt to *make conscious* the original experience. If psychology is accurate about this, then early trauma is the basis, the driving factor, not merely behind UFO encounters but *all* human history and experience, at least until that early trauma is made conscious and can be integrated.

The purpose of the UFO experience, then, like all other traumatic/transcendental encounters, is a reexperiencing of trauma to bring about healing in a conscious, contained fashion. This can be compared to the many types of initiation through trauma found in shamanic traditions, and even in Masonic and other Western forms. However, it's essential to point out that it is not the trauma *per se* that allows for integration, but the erasing or dissolving of previous "traumata" trapped in the body, by way of the "traumatic reenactment." If this subtle distinction is missed, new trauma is caused, and what occurs is merely a new layer of conditioning to override the old, likely only to bury it still deeper in the unconscious. This can *appear* to be effective, however, because experiencing a new trauma will sometimes reactivate the dissociative mechanism developed in childhood to escape the original trauma. The person may then have a "transcendental experience"; but if so, the danger is that it will take them *further* from embodiment, and not closer to it.

I have come to see Strieber as a clear example of this in the way that his later trauma at the hands of human agencies and/or "the visitors" can be mapped onto (and feeds into) his earlier Catholic conditioning. (And many of Strieber's experiences, both early and later, entail out-of-body journeys, which seems to mirror the early experience of dissociation.) In the case of many other abductees also, I would suggest there's more evidence for the experience being unbalancing and deranging than "initiatory." It may activate "psychic potential," as many experiencers report, but activating psychic potential, also from what I've seen, is as often as not deranging rather than conducive to a person's psychic wholeness or embodiment.

It's here that the alien abduction lore overlaps with that of the infamous intelligence programs such as MKULTRA, which often entail, or at least hint at, the conditioning-via-abuse of children (which Strieber also believes he was subjected to). Such programs are aimed at tapping into the psychological survival mechanism of dissociation, by which the psyche summons "daimonic complexes" from "the Beyond" (the deeper unconscious) to bring about some kind of healing intervention for the child. If so, it may be that Strieber, along with thousands of others similarly interfered with (and not necessarily by government), has unwittingly summoned his own "visitor" phenomenon, one which is both highly personal and, paradoxically, universal—since the human psyche reacts to trauma in more or less the same way every time.

The danger in this is obvious. People who have suffered such early fragmentation, by whatever outside agencies (I include myself in this camp), and who are then exposed to the alien abduction literature, are likely to reframe their trauma within the new context, as a way to reexperience it "safely." As a result, the phenomenon will then, over the generations, become "viral" and, as already suggested, generate its own proofs. If abductees on the whole seem closer to what we've seen or heard about victims of mind control than to shamanic initiates, the "aliens" must be deduced to be closer to CIA agents than to shamans or "spiritually evolved" beings.

This may all be part of the larger plan, and it's certainly worth looking into for anyone who wants to get to the bottom of the UFO bottle. But what's more interesting to me, at this stage, is how all of this can be seen to demonstrate the way the psyche works. Because if the UFO is evidence not of outer but inner space, then the psyche becomes, almost literally, the creator and destroyer of worlds.

*

"Most of you are not like that. Most of you have gone farther and a lot of you have gone *really* far. So this is a really unique group of people here. These are the people the visitors are really interested in because you're the ones that made it. The whole school of fish is swimming along, and the sixteen people at the front, the little fish at the front, they're you. So, you're very interesting and they'll be interested in even having you listen to this to see how you react."

—Whitley Strieber, 2016

I should make it very clear at this point, once again, that I am in no way suggesting that abduction experiences are merely mental fantasies created as a screen through which to revisit past experiences. There is abundant evidence that something "objectively real" (so far as we can even talk about such a thing) is happening, something that, by the nature of the evidence, clearly involves some sort of agenda both hidden and "advanced"—something that entails either technological or natural means beyond our common understanding of what is possible. What I *am* saying is that these anomalous or otherworldly experiences are echoing—feeding into and potentially exploiting and exasperating—original traumas that may be independent of these hidden forces, and therefore much closer to home and easier to identify.

So while I don't intend to suggest that the abductee experience is less real than, say, an ordinary human kidnapping, it is clearly less "provable," because the UFO and the "alien" do not adhere to the rules of reality as we have come to accept them. The usual explanation for this maddening lack of proof is that "ETs" belong to some higher level of reality. I would argue that it has less to do with any magical qualities we assign to hypothetical outside agencies, and more to do with the fact that we have, to a great extent, denied the reality of the psyche. As a result, we are unable to grasp, or even fully recognize, its manifestations.

I believe that the desire to prove that these experiences are *real*, while perfectly natural and to some degree unavoidable on the part of the experiencer, is a dead end that leads only to undirected obsession. As the man says, "What is real?" If the psyche is real, then whatever it experiences is real too. Seeking validation from outside is not part of the solution but part of the problem. And not a small part, either.

Suppose we juxtapose reports of alien abductions, and the wide-spread belief in them, with the question of institutionalized child abuse (ritual or otherwise). There is growing evidence all around us for the latter; it is a largely overlooked part of human history (see Lloyd deMause's *The Emotional Life of Nations* for a starting point). In contrast, there is relatively little evidence for alien abduction as an actual, physical occurrence (as compared to an insufficiently understood psychic one). Yet belief in alien abduction—while not yet embraced by the so-called "intelligentsia"—is far more widespread than belief in (or rather awareness of) systematized child abuse (though this is changing fast, in the UK at least). There may be different reasons for this, but the one that interests me relates directly to the psyche, and that is that stories about alien abduction, though no less preposterous than stories about institutionalized abuse of children, are considerably more *palatable* to most people.

As Martin Cannon wrote in his classic, unpublished work *The Controllers*:

> Many books have been written about abductees, yet few exist about the victims of mind control. I cannot understand this situation; the reality of UFOs is still controversial, yet the existence of mind control was verified in two (heavily compromised) congressional investigations and in thousands of FOIA documents. Nevertheless, the abductees find many a sympathetic ear, while those few who dare to proclaim themselves the victims of known government programs rarely find anyone to hear them out. Our prejudices on this score are regrettable, for if we listened to the "controlees" we would hear many details strikingly similar to those mentioned by UFO abductees. (1990)

One argument given by believers for the paucity of evidence for alien abductions is that the aliens in question are good at hiding their traces. Very well, and so we will counter that those involved in child trafficking, mind control, and other forms of exploitation—being merely human—must surely be considerably *less* efficient than such alleged "aliens." So why do we hear so much about aliens and so little about exploiters of children? I think there's an equally "magical" explanation, but one which we can all identify to one degree or another in our own lives. The conscious mind has *extremely* strong defenses, and equally ingenious subterfuges, to prevent it from seeing what it does not want to see, in this case, the reality of trauma and its impact, both directly and indirectly, on our lives.

Alien abduction may be a way for some of us to allow such traumatic material into our awareness in a more "magical" (transcendental) guise. This would account for the inescapable overlap between abduction narratives and systematized child abuse, for which Whitley Strieber, once again, is exhibit A. An NBC *Section Three* report aired on October 11, 1977, called "The Children and the CIA." It describes MKULTRA's "sub-project 102" a "study of how youngsters behave without adult supervision" conducted in San Antonio, Texas and two other Texas cities. Strieber was born and raised in San Antonio; in 1958 he would have been thirteen. In the CIA documents, "No child is identified by name" (NBC, 1977).

Strieber's accounts of "the visitors" are undeniably horrific, or at least they would be if he didn't constantly frame them in the language of shamanic initiation, evolutionary engineering, spiritual midwifery, and cosmic intervention. Such ambiguity is essential for the psychological survival of the child who suffers abuse (he *has* to believe in the goodness of those who have power over him); and logically, it's easier to feel ambiguous about beings who are outside our ordinary frame of understanding than ones who are not. Hence Strieber and others frame the visitors, in Nietzschean terms, as "beyond good and evil."

This is a form of circular logic when it comes to presuming that actions or events we cannot comprehend or assimilate (which include traumatic experiences) must be sourced in something that is equally beyond our comprehension, and therefore also beyond judgment. But even if there *is* a nonhuman element in all of this, it doesn't mean an all-too-human element isn't cynically manipulating—and even simulating—some of these experiences for its own, more comprehensible ends. Or cynically exploiting those who have suffered these experiences.

In the years since I first began digging in the unknown country of Strieber's extended opus, I have encountered at least one person, LilyPat, who has run the spectrum from being a devout believer in the alien abduction interpretation propagated by Strieber, and a devoted follower of Strieber, to a considerably more qualified perspective.

> I believe that a lot of survivors of systematized traumatic abuse
> were deliberately manipulated into believing it was aliens who'd

abducted and abused them. To me, Strieber's site looks an awful lot like a honeypot to attract and keep tabs on us, especially any who are waking up enough to remember human beings during those abductions. When I did, I was already a longtime member of the site, but I was first attacked and shunned, then unilaterally banned by Whitley even though I'd done nothing to violate his published site rules. It could have been that I'd triggered him really badly, but it also could have been a callous silencing of any alternate viewpoints that might have poisoned the honeypot by him or by a handler. (personal correspondence)

LilyPat was not alone: "Several other people who'd wakened up from Whitley's alien dream and remembered people from alphabet agencies messing with them from childhood on" were also removed.

*

> "To the ones who have slipped into the mirror
> And the ones who reflect it in their eyes.
> to the ones who must hide everything,
> And to the ones who lose what they hide
> To the ones who cannot be silent
> And the ones who must lie."
> —Whitley Strieber, dedication to *Communion*

The Canadian therapist Allison Miller has worked for many years with victims of mind control and organized ritual abuse at the hands of cults (including the government kind). In at least one case, she had a client who eventually confessed to having kept quiet about memories of alien abduction because she didn't want to throw her other claims into doubt. Together, they worked through the abduction memories until they "discovered that the 'spaceship' was parked in the courtyard of the cult training center." In case she began to remember her experiences of abuse, the client had been instructed to remember an alien abduction event, "so that nobody would believe her account of ritual abuse" (2012, p. 55). This doesn't prove that all (or even most) experiences of alien abduction are screen memories concealing memories of ritual abuse. But it does indicate that at least *some* of them are, and that any sincere exploration of these phenomena has to explore this possibility thoroughly. Strieber (and Kripal after him) do not allow themselves to do so. In fact, throughout Strieber's countless books, the possibility is never addressed in any depth, not even once. Presumably the reason is that, potentially, this interpretation throws all testimonies of alien abduction, including Strieber's, into serious question. Yet *not* addressing this possible interpretation only makes the evidence for it all the more compelling for being excluded. It begins to seem as if it has been deliberately omitted. Who are the ones who must lie, and why?

There is a thin line between validating someone's experience and feeding their delusion. Many researchers (and a researcher-experiencer such as Strieber) may jump to too many conclusions too fast. One of the reasons they are able, or even forced, to make such leaps is from underestimating the power of the psyche to generate experience. The other reason, perhaps connected, is that the mind experiences profound discomfort when forced to leave an unknown *as* unknown. It relentlessly seeks answers and, when it doesn't find any, has no qualms about inventing them and then forgetting it has done so.

While many abduction researchers may very well be sincere in their attempts to get to the bottom of what's happening to experiencers and to help them to make sense of it, this doesn't mean they aren't susceptible to delusion, or to external manipulation, or capable of unconsciously manipulating or deluding their witnesses. The recent disclosures around Budd Hopkins's and David M. Jacobs's work with abductees have provided extremely damning evidence of this. What makes me suspicious of the work of many researchers is that they frequently choose to frame the abduction experiences in terms in line with (what I see as) an overarching agenda: that of sowing the seeds of a new scientistic religion. John Mack, for example (giving the benefit of the doubt), recognized that the abductees he interviewed were reporting something real, and that it was a real unknown. He then got busy interpreting it to make it into a "known," and of course, he couldn't help but refer to previous interpretations, both fictional and not, to do so.

I have dealt with people who believe they are abductees (I even have my own abduction-like experiences), and from what I've seen, interpreting the experience as an external, "objective" reality tends to exacerbate the tendency of the mind towards rigidity, projection, delusion, and obsession. The person will often become comfortably immersed in a fantastic narrative about space brothers, hybrid aliens, government conspiracies, and the like, which removes them further and further, not merely from consensus reality (which is not always a bad thing), but from their own *inner* reality (as any obsessive external focus does). The reason for this tendency to take refuge in convincing fictions or partial truths may be straightforward: to connect fully to one's inner reality—to become fully embodied as a psyche—means returning to and fully rein-tegrating whatever early traumas prevented that embodiment from happening, at an early age. All of our fictions are designed to protect us from that mind-shattering—and soul-rescuing—event.

So while I can admit to the possibility of actual, nuts-and-bolts aliens, I'm not really interested in exploring this possibility, at this time, espe-cially because, as every ufologist knows (though only if he or she admits it), there's almost nothing to go on. As Sherlock Holmes says, we need to first rule out all of the improbables before accepting the impossible. And yes, I'm aware that, for many people, the idea of extraterrestrials visiting Earth and using super-advanced technology to hide their pres-ence is less improbable than that of autonomous psychic fragments. But I still argue there's more evidence for the latter, and that the primary criteria for accepting a given hypothesis is that *it fits the data better than the others.*

As a one-time believer in Strieber's *Communion* narrative and the "magical," nonhuman nature of his experiences, I have been surprised how, through the course of this written investigation, allowing for extremely sophisticated human manipulations as a possible explana-tion has been sufficient to account for most if not all of the evidence. Admittedly, the human explanation itself requires allowing for meth-ods and technologies that might be indistinguishable to many people from magic, and specifically from occultism, ancient and modern. It isn't really either/or, however, even if generally these subjects are kept apart because serious UFO researchers (if that's not a complete oxymoron; George Hansen and John Michael Greer come to mind as exceptions) tend to stay away from deep, parapolitical analysis and social engineering (unless it is by nonhuman agencies). But then as far as I know almost no one has looked into the possibility of social engineering that goes back as far *as* history, and so might *in some sense* encompass the entire UFO phenomena, and faery lore too. This is not to suggest that it was all fabricated as a folklore and myth for the masses (though I think it was partly that), but that "psychic-hacking"—which relates to inducing trauma within ritual context—could have *created* it. This might have occurred first unwittingly and then, on being observed over time, intentionally, reaching its apotheosis, the state of the art, with MKULTRA, which coincided with the first modern UFO wave and contact phenomena.

At the very least, if it can be shown beyond reasonable doubt that childhood trauma informs at least *some* of these experiences, we now have a new element to bring to the table when considering all other cases. It may be that "the ET hypothesis" is *entirely unnecessary* based on the evidence (that's my position; I believe it was Jacques Vallee's too). Of course that doesn't rule out some other, nonhuman unknown; but again, the sensible way to proceed would be first of all to see if we can account for all the evidence *without* resorting to "magical" hypotheses. The fact that, to some people, the psyche is a magical hypothesis itself makes it doubly ironic that it's not being allowed into the debate, because it may be that all the magic and mystery which we are projecting onto the UFO is already here, at the center of our lives, in the form of the psyche.

Accepting the reality of the psyche and learning more about how it works is, I think, indispensable for making meaningful headway in this field, and for helping experiencers deal with their experiences. In contrast, I have seen very little evidence that anyone was helped by fully embracing a belief in nonhuman entities having control over their bodies and minds in a totally random way, or at best as part of some nonhuman design. In most cases (Strieber being an example), all this really does is allow the person to get swept away by a grandiose personal narrative partially formed by lurid sci-fi magazines and movies, and largely informed by religious/spiritual indoctrination and a (trauma-based) need to feel powerful or special.

To give an example: One way in which experiencers get swept up by a sense of being on a world-saving mission is by trying to get the government (and other people) to see what the aliens are doing. Scratch the surface of this phantastic narrative and underneath we may find something more mundane and tragic: the frustration and torment of a child, unable to get his parents (or other adults, if the abuse or neglect is by the parents) to *see* what's happening to him. The experiencer's experience then becomes part of a larger, unconscious reenactment, meant to bring about whatever resolution failed to occur when it was most needed.

This doesn't make the experience unreal; on the contrary, it makes it *more* real, but only if it's seen in the proper psychological context. We can even allow that the hypothetical aliens are real without invalidating this reading, since it re-contextualizes them as outside agencies assisting the experiencer towards healing by re-staging a psychodrama *for* them. Without this extra layer of meaning to flesh it out and give it body, however, the alien abduction narrative is a two-dimensional and bloodless affair—little better than a B-movie rendering of profound psychic truth.

CHAPTER XII

Finding the ground/leaving the ground: "Mind at Large" & the Overview Effect

"The work on trauma is a repetition compulsion of ceaseless mental fight. Interminable analysis, interminable writing, interminable soul-making is the only medicine—there is no antidote. The transmuting of trauma into creative affirmations, the mutual transformation of trauma and soul, is a process that like poetry 'survives the valley of its own saying.' To put it another way … and another way … and another way is what soul-making is all about."

—Greg Mogenson, *A Most Accursed Religion*

The first draft of the piece that became *Prisoner of Infinity* was a little over 4,000 words. It is now over 100,000 and still growing. I didn't intend for this to take over my life. In an email to Ty Brown, I wrote that "This current work is like being abducted—it has a life of its own and it won't let me go—like an octopus, once you grab onto one of the tentacles." That's what happened: I grabbed onto what I thought was a snake but it turned out to be a limb of a much larger beast. I had two choices then, either let it go, or get a hold of the rest of the limbs so I could see the whole thing in all its slithering glory: a fully-rounded picture of the infiltrated psyche. I chose the latter path, and here we are.

Writing this book is like being a slave to a pharaoh who won't let me quit until I have built his pyramid. Except this isn't a creative process but a destructive one, so a much better metaphor would be that of gold-prospecting, something I was doing in my spare time before this work took over my life. When I first started digging I didn't really know what I was looking for. The more I dug, the better an idea I got. Gold is deposited from higher up as waters drag the dirt and sand down the mountain, and since gold has a greater atomic weight than just about anything else, it always sinks as far down in the dirt as it can go, towards the bedrock. To get to the bedrock you have to remove regular dirt, rocks and boulders, then there's clay, then there's black sand, which has heavy metals in it, and amid the black sand, there's the gold (if you are digging in the right spots). In order to find out if you are digging in the right spot you have to get to the black sand and pan it. Your pans are like the trail of clues a detective follows to get to the body. There are other things too, like the shape and position of rocks and the color of the dirt, the smell of sulfur; but the panning is the main part.

What happened as I continued to dig, and learn from digging, was that we started to uncover the bedrock and even caught sight of the pay streak (yellow dirt, where the gold has passed through on its way to the bedrock). At that point, I became more motivated and the digging took over. I wasn't looking for gold as yet (I knew I probably wouldn't be able to recognize it if I saw it), but now I was looking for something concrete: bedrock. When you are uncovering bedrock you don't want to risk a landslide so one of the things you have to do is work at it in "tiers" or stages. You uncover a little here then move higher up and dig a ledge. This way you won't undermine the dirt above you and risk getting buried; but also, you have ledges to stand on while removing the dirt above you. It gets tricky because, as you're shoveling dirt away, you don't want to end up covering the bedrock below you which you've just uncovered. You want to get a clear idea of the shape of the bedrock so that, when you find the pay streak, you can follow it (you can also use the shape of the bedrock to help you to find the pay streak). When you're removing dirt, you get to rocks of different shapes and sizes which are both clues to follow (river-smoothed rocks indicate the pay streak is near) and obstacles to move. Sometimes you might start to remove one rock and realize that it's pinned by another; you have to disassemble the terrain in the right way, not only to reduce the work but also to make sure you don't wind up dodging falling boulders and other heavy objects.

All of this provides a reasonably close analogy to how writing this book unfolded. At a certain point, I spotted what looked like a pay streak, and I also hit bedrock. Now I am doing the necessary work to clear away the dirt: digging, moving rocks, collecting samples, panning them, and reading the fine gold, getting closer and closer to exposing the bedrock and hitting pay dirt. Just as all that glitters is not gold, not everything that looks like dirt *is* dirt. It's all a learning process, and what I'm learning is how to train my eyes to *see* in a new way.

*

Marilyn Ferguson's *The Aquarian Conspiracy* describes how

> A leaderless but powerful network is working to bring about radical change in the United States. Its members have broken with certain key elements of western thought and they may even have broken continuity with history ... Broader than reform, deeper than revolution, this benign conspiracy for a new human agenda has triggered the most rapid cultural realignment in history. The great shuddering, irrevocable shift overtaking us is not a new political, religious, or philosophical system. It is a new mind—the ascendance of a startling worldview that gathers into this framework breakthrough science and insights from earliest recorded thought. (1980, p. 23)

The original essay which this book grew uncontrollably out of, you may dimly recall, was a response to Jeffrey J. Kripal's article "The Traumatic Secret." It was sparked among other things by Kripal's citing of Aldous Huxley and his "human potentialities," "psychedelic solutions," and "perennial philosophies." Because of the momentum of this excavation process, I didn't find time to investigate Huxley's history in detail (you can't always take the time to pan every pile of dirt); but even on the surface I found plenty to wonder about.

Huxley is most famous for two works: his technological dystopia novel, *Brave New World*, and *The Doors of Perception*, which advocates the use of hallucinogens as a means to shut down the "reducing valve" of the brain and enter into an experience of what he calls "Mind at Large." (In passing, psychedelics might be seen as a form of chemically induced trauma to the body.) Huxley, as Kripal points out, was one of if not *the* major influence on "the human potential movement" which eventually became the New Age movement. Along with organizations such as Esalen, he was responsible for introducing Eastern spirituality to the Western world. Huxley belonged to a famous aristocratic family, and his brother, Sir Julian, was a member of the British Eugenics Society, a fact that has been largely stricken from the record. Sir Julian also coined the term "transhumanism"! (In the two volumes of Huxley's autobiography there is no mention of eugenics in the index, and the subject has been omitted from many of the obituaries and biographies.)

For all the Eastern spiritual jargon favored by these individuals and institutes, the aims they put forth (in common with those of transhumanism and the Singularity) are really indistinguishable from the aims of Western occultism (and groups like Scientology): namely, the development of superpowers. In the West, we tend to confuse psychism with spiritual attainment. Yet from an Eastern point of view, they are seen as *at odds* with one another—hence the many warnings about "*siddhis.*" (Even in the East, *siddhis* are often seen as proof of spiritual progress, even if not quite as equivalent to it.) Enlightenment is liberation from the false self—the defensive ego-self *created by trauma*. Psychism—which can easily be confused with "human potential"—is all about enhancing and improving the self to create a kind of "super-self." Enlightenment is said to entail a total openness and the corresponding vulnerability: The sensitivity it brings isn't just psychic but emotional, psychological, and physical/energetic. Psychic superpowers—including the power to leave the body (dissociate) *à la* remote viewing—seem like a movement in the opposite direction, towards becoming *in*vulnerable. Which is a traumatized individual more likely to gravitate towards? What are Strieber's tales of power but accounts of a kind of *siddhi*-wielding, alien-engineered *übermensch* whose only weapon is his mind?

Huxley took the title *The Doors of Perception* from Blake's *The Marriage of Heaven and Hell*, which is presumably why Kripal refers to Huxley's work as "Blakean." But compare Huxley's term, "Mind at Large," to Blake's *Marriage of Heaven and Hell*: "Energy is the only life and is from the Body and Reason is the bound or outward circumference of Energy. Energy is Eternal Delight." Where is mind here, little or large? Huxley and the perennial philosophers posited "Mind at Large" as an understandable reaction against the reductionist equation of consciousness with the brain, combined with a (equally understandable) rejection of religious dogma about the soul. (I don't necessarily include Strieber here, since as a Catholic, he is "all about" the reality of the soul.) Instead, they posited a mind that is everywhere. By choosing to use the word mind, however, they appeared to equate consciousness with *the structure and content of their own minds.*

Where, or what, is mind? Is it necessarily a materialistic view to say that it is only a side effect of the body? Animals possess consciousness, and obviously they have brains; but what sort of minds do they have? The mind has very much become interchangeable with the self (and even the *psyche*, though the latter means "soul"). When we think of who we are, we don't generally think of our internal organs or the shape of our limbs but of our thoughts and memories. The mind, like the self, is a construction built of associations, beliefs, images, and memories. It seems to be *largely dependent upon language to maintain its coherence.* (Freud believed it to be the breeding ground of delusions, and most psychological models would agree.) Take away our power to think in words and what does that leave? Madness, or at best, *dreams.*

But if consciousness doesn't stem from the brain *or* the mind, where does it stem from?

Huxley's Mind at Large is another way of saying the Godhead, the quasi-religious concept that God has a head (or penis), which presumably is where His mind (and brain) is located. This phallocentric view brings us to the core of the matter (pun intended): *the de-eroticization of spirit.* Like Carlos Castaneda's old seers, the philosophers, both ancient and modern, are as persistent as they are perennial. As the basis for all of their projected perfections of both nature and spirit, there lurks a Norman Bates-like mortification of/entrapment by the feminine. This form of mother-bondage requires a corresponding creation of an idealized father figure—a "Godhead"—in their own infantile image. To possess the mother, they must become their own fathers. To do both, they must create internally generated images—mortifications and idealizations—to relate to.

Where flesh is seen as inherently "sinful" or corrupt, only fantasy will do. Rocket ships pushing through space to reach the Moon; Hadron colliders smashing matter in an unconscious striking back at the mother (*mater*) who spawned and spurned them; the creation of technology to dominate Nature, liberate "the spirit," and resurrect "the body" (in digital form); all partake of the same agonizing attempt of the disembodied intellect to feel *potent* in the absence of a life force.

Isn't the mind's refusal to live in the body a refusal to be absorbed into the continuity of being of the body? If so, then the mind's refusal to be absorbed into the body may be *one and the same with the rejection of the erotic dimensions of spirit and spirituality.*

Since sexuality remains in the form of libido (the body can't exist without energy), the libido is now possessed not by the body, Eros, but by the mind. As long as the mind experiences itself as separate and isolate from the body—through the fragmentation of trauma, or rather its insistence on keeping trauma secret from itself—it remains under the dominion of Thanatos. And death is the one thing that energy (eternal delight) can never know.

*

The Aquarian Conspiracy promotes the notion that "Real revolutionary activity ... consists of transforming reality, that is, in making reality conform more closely to one's ideal."

In the section on Strieber in Peter Levenda's *Sinister Forces*, there is the following passage:

> On the one hand you had the Pentagon and the CIA monitoring UFO reports and massaging data, and on the other hand you had the same agencies racing to dominate inner space, as well. If the UFO phenomena partakes of both the scientific (space flight, faster-than-light travel, alien visitation) and the psychological (hallucinations, visions, spiritual encounters and illumination), then the US government had all the bases covered ... The civilian would have had one of the most profound experiences of his or her life, and be unable to put it into any kind of context. [They] would have no knowledge of how to interpret the event, and would thus be left in the dark having received no input from either the government or the scientists ... or the church. (2006, p. 270)

It's worth noting that Levenda begins this chapter on Strieber, UFOs, and intelligence psi-ops, with a discussion of Christianity and *the formation of a new religion.* As for the idea that the UFO experiencer had no official context in which to place his or her experience, surely that depends on exactly what we consider official? Doesn't the idea the US government "had all the bases covered" imply, not that it was preventing any sort of context, but that it was busy creating one?

In 2007, while Ty Brown was doing his piece on the Stanford Research Institute, "10,000 Heroes—SRI and the Manufacturing of the New Age," and his "Nazis from Outer Space" Strieber piece, blogger Justin Boland (a.k.a. Brainsturbator) wrote "Scientists on Acid: The Story Behind *Changing Images of Man*." The article mapped some suggestive ties between SRI-employee and coauthor of *Changing Images of Man*, Willis Harman, and OSS/CIA agent Al Hubbard:

> One associate of Hubbard's was New World Order theorist Willis Harman at the Stanford Research Institute. SRI had earlier received grants from the US Army to research chemical incapacitants. When visited by a representative of the underground press at SRI, Harman told the man, "There's a war going on between your side and mine. And my side is not going to lose." (Keith, 1997, p. 98)[1]

Boland also quotes Todd Brendan Fahey on Hubbard, who "was specifically assigned to the Alternative Futures Project, which performed future-oriented strategic planning for corporations and government agencies." Harman's and Hubbard's shared goal was to provide the LSD experience to political and intellectual leaders around the world. In Harman's words, "Al's job was to run the special sessions for us" (Fahey, 1991).

According to Boland, *Changing Images of Man* coauthor O. W. Markley

> ... left behind a very curious paper entitled "Visionary Futures" that outlines some other SRI "alternative methodologies"—including "channeled material in the book *Seth Speaks*, by Jane Roberts (1972)." This is the same SRI who employed top Scientologists, Hal Puthoff and Ingo Swann, to develop their Remote Viewing program. Channeled material, after all, is mainstream today. (Witness the bestseller success of the *Conversations with God* series.) (Brainsturbator, 2007)

A couple of years prior to this, in 2005, Canadian author Jeff Wells wrote a post called "Before the apex stone is fitted" about Harman's belief that "humanity is embarking on a period of 'global mind change,'" and that people could reorder the world "by deliberately changing their internal image of reality." (Hence the title of the infamous tract.) Wells quotes Harman:

> Whether it's psychic phenomena, mystical experiences, communications with the dead ... whatever it is, you're implying that reality is different from the way they taught you in school. Sooner or later we're going to say 'Well if all of that's so, then our emphases in business and economics have to be different, as well as our emphases in politics, education and healthcare.'

In other words, to quote Wells, "How to anticipate and capitalize upon the revolution in worldviews in the dawning post-industrial era is the question Harman's SRI team set to answer"—to change the image of man from one of industrial progress to one of "spiritual" progress. From *The Aquarian Conspiracy*:

> [*Changing Images of Man*] laid the groundwork for a paradigm shift in understanding how individual and social transformation might be accomplished. "The emergence of a new image and/or a new paradigm can be hastened or slowed by deliberate choice," the study noted, adding that *crisis can be stimulated* [emphasis added] ... The difference between transformation by accident and transformation by a system is like the difference between lightning and a lamp ... The intentional triggers of transformative experiences are numberless, yet they have a common quality. They focus awareness on awareness—a crucial shift. [T]he now classic report issued by SRI ... described a new transcendental social and business ethic characterized by self-determination, concern for the quality of life, appropriate technology, entrepreneurship, decentralization, an ecological ethic, and spirituality. The report urged a rapid corporate understanding of this emergent order, "probably the most important observation of our time." (Ferguson, 1980, pp. 61, 85, 342)

Among the intentional triggers Ferguson lists in her best-selling book are: sensory isolation and sensory overload; biofeedback (the use of machines to monitor bodily processes so they can be controlled by the mind); autogenic training; music; hypnosis and self-hypnosis; meditation; seminars "like est, Silva Mind Control, Actualizations and

Lifespring"; Theosophy and Gurdjieffian systems; A Course in Miracles; and Esalen. "All of these approaches might be called *psychotechnologies*—systems for a deliberate change in consciousness" (1980, p. 87). A little further into her treatise, Ferguson introduces a much more general tool for accelerating evolution: stress.

> *Punctuationalism* or *punctuated equilibrium* suggests that the equilibrium of life is "punctuated" from time to time by severe stress. *If a small section of the ancestral population is isolated at the periphery of its accustomed range*, it may give way to a new species [emphasis added]. The new paradigm attributes evolution to periodic leaps by small groups. This changing view is significant for at least two reasons: (1) It requires a mechanism for biological change more powerful than chance mutation, and (2) it opens us up to the possibility of rapid evolution in our own time, when the equilibrium of the species is punctuated by stress. Stress in modern society is experienced at the frontiers of our psychological rather than our geographical limits. Pioneering becomes an increasingly psychospiritual venture since our physical frontiers are all but exhausted, *short of space exploration*. (1980, pp. 158–159, emphasis added)

Applied stress, isolating sections of the population, a new emergent species of humanity, accelerated evolution, and space travel. Sounds like science fiction. Speaking of which ... Joseph Campbell, one of the listed authors of *Changing Images of Man*, was also an alleged inspiration (along with Carlos Castaneda) for George Lucas when he created what is probably the most far-reaching and influential myth of the twentieth century (one that effectively fused science and mysticism), *Star Wars*. As researcher Tim Boucher put it, *Star Wars* was an "international myth to contain all the societal changes and upheavals that [occurred after] the explosion of the consciousness movements and the New Age." The New Age became the New *Space* Age. In *The Power of Myth*, Campbell told Bill Moyers: "When you see the earth from the moon, you don't see any divisions there of nations or states. This might be the symbol, really, for the new mythology to come. That is the country that we are going to be celebrating. And those are the people that we are one with" (Campbell & Moyers, 1988, p. 41).

*

"This noetic discovery [the existence of God] is at the heart of science and religion. It is the only thing that will counteract contemporary crises and bring meaning, direction, and fulfillment to people. Psychic research can play an important role in helping people make that discovery."

—Edgar Mitchell, *Psychic Research: Challenge to Science*

The correlation between space travel and spiritual evolution/mystical states of consciousness is an obvious enough one in terms of metaphors; but there is also a quite literal correlation being made by those who claim to have crossed "the final frontier." *The Overview Effect* is a 1998 book by Frank White based on interviews with, and writings by, thirty different astronauts, describing how the experience of leaving the Earth and seeing it from space (or from the Moon) profoundly affected their perceptions of themselves and the world. The book argues that the rest of humanity "who have participated imaginatively in these great adventures [through popular sci-fi!?], have also been affected psychologically by them." From the back blurb of the book:

[White] provides a powerful rationale for space exploration and settlement, describing them as the inevitable next steps in the evolution of human society and human consciousness, as the activities most likely to bring a new perspective to the problems of life on Earth. White goes on to consider the possible consequences of a human presence in space, both for the pioneers who settle there and for those who remain on Earth. He imagines how having a permanent perspective from outer space will affect our politics, our religion, our social relations, our psychology, our economics, and our hard sciences. He confronts the possibility of rebellion by a space colony and of contact with extraterrestrial beings. And, finally, he makes it clear that our fate is in our own hands, that we will shape our future in space effectively only by fashioning a new human space program, free of excessive nationalism and dedicated to the peaceful exploration of the space frontier.

The primary astronaut testifying to the wonders of the overview effect, and who has jumped aboard White's evolutionary spaceship, is Edgar Mitchell, the alleged sixth man to walk on the Moon (Mitchell is also rumored to have planted a Masonic flag up there). In Mitchell's own words:

> For me, seeing our planet from space was an event with some of the qualities traditionally ascribed to religious experience. It triggered a deep insight into the nature of existence—the sort of insight that radically changes the inner person. My thinking—indeed, my consciousness—was altered profoundly. I came to feel a moral responsibility to pass on the transformative experience of seeing the earth from the larger perspective. But further, the rational man in me had to recognize the validity of the nonrational cognitive process. (1974, p. 34.)

So what do we know about Mitchell? That he was in the Navy, for one (like L. Ron Hubbard); and that after he left, in 1972, he founded the Institute of Noetic Sciences "to sponsor research into the nature of consciousness as it relates to cosmology and causality" (Mitchell, 2009). Based on what I can glean, he even coined the word psychonaut, though he spelled it *psychenaut* (Mitchell, 1974, p. 35. It's currently attributed by Wikipedia to the Chaos magician Peter Carroll). As for the Institute of Noetic Sciences—Willis Harman was president from 1975–1996, and (according to Harman himself) they were "heavily involved in the psi testing of the 1970s, partly funding the [Uri] Geller experiment at SRI and, until the CIA came clean about their involvement in the remote-viewing experiments in the mid-1990s, it was the Institute of Noetic Sciences that claimed to have funded the initial program" (Picknett & Prince, 1999, p. 235, citing Harman's introduction to *The Mind Race*). Jeffrey ("I don't 'do conspiracy'") Kripal has also spoken there.

In 1974 (the same year *Changing Images of Man* was written), Mitchell published *Psychic Research: Challenge to Science*, a 700-word compendium of the results of IONS' psi research, by various authors including Hal Puthoff, Puharich, and Willis Harman. (*Challenge to Science* was also the title of Jacques Vallee's second book on UFOs, released in 1967.) In the introduction, Mitchell argues that psychic research is "an important element in the long-sought formula for enriching human awareness, reconstructing society, and generally aiding nature in the great work of evolution" (pp. 43–44).

Now is the time for us to begin building a single whole of humanity. Now is the time to develop our nonrational abilities into a "subjective technology," which will be the wedding of science and religion, reason and intuition, the physical and the spiritual ... [A]s science approaches omniscience ... the universal man of cosmic consciousness can then emerge. (1974, p. 49)

Besides his work with IONS, Mitchell was also involved (until his death in 2016) with the Overview Institute, whose goal is to induce or produce the Overview Effect in as many of Earth's citizens as possible in order to bring about a "paradigm shift"—in Mitchell's words, "the transformation of human consciousness that is necessary for solving our critical dilemma" (1974, p. 48).

Only when man sees his fundamental unity with the process of nature and the functioning of the universe—as I so avidly saw it from the Apollo spacecraft—will the old ways of thinking and behaving disappear. Only when man moves from his ego-centered self-image to a new image of universal man will the perennial problems that plague us be susceptible of resolution. (1974, p. 31)

At the Overview Institute's website, it describes how the advent of a commercial space industry will soon begin taking "tens of thousands of people into the near-space environment, far enough to grasp some aspects of the Overview Effect," and how zero-gravity flights will make it "available to many more."

This is only the beginning of the historic human evolution into space, and the resulting transformations of human culture and consciousness as we become a space-faring culture. The second major advance is the rapid maturation of high-definition digital media, from the internet-connected desktop to three-dimensional simulation media and virtual reality. These new technologies, together with other forms of art, media, entertainment and education will soon provide new and more powerful tools to immerse Earthbound audiences in a close approximation of the space environment and potentially bring the Overview Effect to many millions around the globe. (*The Overview Institute*, 2012)

Besides the obvious indifference to any distinction between a physically embodied experience and a mentally simulated one, there's no mention of the (I would think unavoidable) stress of leaving the planet and entering into zero gravity through rocket propulsion—a symbolic/literal tearing away from the mother's body. Or of the profound isolation of it. It's all about togetherness. Yet the idea of an overview effect is a remarkably concise way to equate internal liberation/enlightenment with the capitalist expansionist drive to conquer space. It even manages to make the one dependent on the other. At the very least, it makes enlightenment appear to be attainable by wholly material, technological means—means dependent on a massive, billion dollar industry!

One way or another, the space agenda appears to be underway. At publication of John Ollie's *Time* article in May of 2013, there were already said to be 78,000 volunteers. There are currently plans for a volunteer immigration program to Mars called Mars One, to embark by 2032 (the current date, which has been moved forward several times from the original one, 2022). Mars One selected 1058 astronaut candidates in 2013 (586 men and 472 women from 107 countries) from an alleged 202,586 volunteers. Former Mars One candidate Dr. Joseph Roche claims the number of initial applicants was only 2,761 (Keep, 2015), which Mars One later conceded via YouTube video (Martian Colonist, 2015). In the beginning of May 2014 this number was down to 705 candidates (418 men and 287 women), 353 allegedly removed due to personal considerations. After the medical physical requirement, due either to financial, health, or access reasons, only 660 candidates remained. Notably, some applicants were notified of life-threatening conditions such as early-stage cancer and were able to immediately begin treatment (*Mars-One*, 2015). On June 30, 2014, it was made public that Mars One seeks financial investment through a bidding process to send company experiments to Mars. The experiment slots will go to the highest bidder and will include company-related ads, and the opportunity to have the company name on the robotic lander that is proposed to carry the experiments to Mars in 2018 (Boyle, 2014). Mars One selected a third-round pool of astronaut candidates in 2015 of 100 people— "50 men and 50 women who successfully passed the second round. The candidates come from all around the world, namely 39 from the Americas, 31 from Europe, 16 from Asia, 7 from Africa, and 7 from Oceania." In a video posted on March 19, 2015, Lansdorp said that because of delays in the robotic precursor mission, the first crew will not set down on Mars until 2027 (Wall, 2015). In August 2015, Lansdorp reiterated that their twelve-year plan for landing humans on Mars by 2027 is subject to constant improvement and updates. Following the criticism reported in *The Space Review* in October 2016 about funding mechanisms (Carberry & Zucker, 2016), Mars One created Mars One Ventures. As of late 2016 Mars One had changed its first date to send humans to Mars to 2032 (Boyle, 2016).

The reason given for the trip to Mars being a one-way is that the physiological changes caused by space travel are irrevocable. No trauma here then.

Edgar Mitchell seems to have been a key player in the shadowy narrative of enlightenment via ET intervention and space travel. As improbable as it may sound, Mitchell was born in Roswell, New Mexico. In 1998, he told *The Ottawa Citizen* he was "90 per cent sure that many of the thousands of unidentified flying objects, or UFOs, recorded since the 1940s, belong to visitors from other planets." He claimed to have witnesses, "many of them from intelligence agencies and the military— who convinced him that the American government has covered up the truth about UFOs for 50 years" (*The Ottawa Citizen*, 1998). I have been unable to ascertain whether Mitchell belonged to the mysterious Mars Anomalies Research Society along with Strieber, John Gliedman, and Richard Hoagland, and where Strieber claims he was first triggered (by an image of the face on Mars) to re-access his "buried memories." But Mitchell is "old friends" with Whitley Strieber and appeared on "Dreamland" in 2008 to discuss the quantum mind (i.e., the overview effect) and the Roswell crash. In 2012, he publically endorsed Strieber's *Solving the Communion Enigma*—along with Graham Hancock, the author of *The Mars Mystery*. Hancock is also quoted in the afore-cited *Ottawa Citizen* article. Many faces, one agenda?

Edgar Mitchell was also a consultant on *The X-Files*. Besides his continued affiliation with IONS and the Overview Institute, he participated in an organization called FREE, the Foundation for Research into E.T. Encounters (www.experiencer.co). Like Mitchell (who died in 2016), this site is no longer operational. While it was, it was similar to Strieber's Unknown Country in offering refuge and support to "experiencers," formerly known as abductees. Its (purported) primary aim was "to assist the Experiencer/Contactee/Abductee to understand his or her experiences, to provide assistance in the form of information or personal support, and to conduct comprehensive academic research on the 'ET Contact Phenomena.'"

Among the essays at the site, there was one by Ken Wilbur, whose literary agent used to be John White, editor of *Psychic Research*. There were also several by Mitchell, including one called "The Intersection of Science and Religion," in which Mitchell writes:

> Human beings must evolve or perish—we must swiftly evolve to the next level by eradicating pervasive ignorance concerning who we really are and why we are here, or face the extreme likelihood of mass death and destruction, if not extinction all together [sic]. Humankind's next phase of evolution will be more an evolution in thought, knowledge, spirituality and consciousness than one involving our biology or physiology. (2014)

CHAPTER XIII

Old seers, death defiers, open doors, & machine intervention

"The stakes are very high indeed. They are as high as stakes can get. Unless we can find ourselves before earth ceases to be able to support human bodies in numbers, we are going to find our journey very rudely interrupted ... It is my impression that much of the sexual manipulation our visitors have engaged in has been about creating bodies not that would enable them to live here but rather that would enable us to continue our quest elsewhere, if we lose earth."

—Whitley Strieber, *Solving the Communion Enigma*

In the last chapter, I mentioned in passing Carlos Castaneda's old seers. Now I feel compelled to say a little bit more about the subject, because of how much it overlaps with the primary themes of the second part of this book. Before I do, however, I should point out a couple of facts. Castaneda is the author who, along with Strieber but even more so, had the most formative influence on my mystical beliefs. Like Strieber, I eventually came to understand that his writings, besides inspiring me, had filled my head with half-baked truths and helped generate a deceptively coherent fantasy of supernatural self-empowerment. Castaneda wound up as the shadowy head of a cult-like organization whose principal members (Castaneda's "witches") reputedly all committed suicide after his death. In his final years, based on one of the group's testimony at least (Amy Wallace's *Sorcerer's Apprentice*, which Strieber reviewed[1]), Castaneda went barking mad.

It would be unwise therefore to view the descriptions in his books—most of which are supposed to come from Castaneda's superhuman *nagual*, "don Juan Matus"—as any more reliable, in terms of factual information, than Strieber's "Master of the Key" material. On the other hand, some of these descriptions (specifically the ones about the old seers and the inorganic beings) have some very striking parallels both with Strieber's experiences and, even more acutely, the immortality dreams of Kurzweil and the transhumanists. What follows is a summary of those teachings, paraphrasing Castaneda while keeping all of his original terminology and most of the phrasing intact. The material comes from two of his later books, *The Fire from Within* (1984) and *The Art of Dreaming* (1993).

As "don Juan" (Castaneda) describes them, the old seers were terrifying men, and in fact are terrifying "even today" (1984, p. 103). Their bid is to dominate, to master everybody and everything. The problem with the old seers is that, while they accessed transcendental knowledge of the universe and of themselves, they put it in service to their lower selves (1993, p. 67). Much of this knowledge came to them via communication and interaction with what they called "inorganic beings," beings that possessed consciousness but no organic form, that were a kind of conscious energy with structure and cohesion but no "opaqueness," making them both invisible and intangible to human beings (1984, p. 163). The old seers encountered these beings through what they called the art of *dreaming*, that is, by exploring other realms via *the projection of their consciousness into those realms*. They eventually learned to enter these other realms with their total being, that is, *physically*. The inorganic beings which they interacted with became their "allies," and, "by means of deliberate examples" (1993, p. 67), the inorganics taught the old seers to perform marvels. The allies performed the actions, and the old sorcerers were guided step by step to copy those actions, without changing anything about their basic nature, in a form of interspecies mimesis.

The ultimate goal of the old seers was immortality. This they attempted to achieve by manipulating their own energy bodies. By using *will* to alter the form of their energy bodies from a "luminous egg" to a straight line, the scope of what the old seers were able to perceive and do, as lines of energy, was "astronomically greater" than before (1993, pp. 12–15). Since they were motivated by greed and the desire for power and personal gain, when they came to a crucial crossroads, they took the wrong fork (1993, p. 69). Castaneda writes that everyone who is on the path of self-discovery has to go through the same steps as the old seers, however, because they were the ones who invented *dreaming* (1993, pp. 79–80).

The old sorcerers portrayed the inorganic beings' world as a blob of caverns and pores floating in dark space, and the inorganic beings as hollow canes bound together, "like the cells of our bodies" (1993, p. 100). The realm of inorganic beings was the old seers' field, and to arrive there, they tenaciously fixed their "dreaming attention" on the items of their dreams. By this method they were able to isolate "the scouts," which is to say, the allies that journeyed into the realm between humans and inorganic beings (the dream realm) so as to make contact with humans. Once the old seers had the scouts in focus—once they isolated a real energy from the empty projections of the dreamscape—they voiced their intent to follow them. The instant the old seers did so, they were pulled by that foreign energy into another world (1993, pp. 97–101).

Awareness grows when we perform conscious dreaming of this sort; the moment it grows, something out there acknowledges its growth, recognizes it, and *makes a bid for it*. The inorganic beings are the bidders for that new, enhanced awareness. The inorganic beings are like fishermen: They attract and catch awareness (1993, p. 124). Of all the transcendental observations of the men of ancient times, Castaneda writes, the only one with which we are familiar, because it has filtered down to our day, is the idea of selling our souls to the devil in exchange for immortality (1993, p. 173). This comes straight out of the relationship of the old sorcerers with the inorganic beings. Part of the strategy of the inorganic beings to trap dreamers is to give them a sense of being unique, exclusive, and, more pernicious yet, of *having power*. "Power and uniqueness are unbeatable as corrupting forces" (1993, p. 101).

According to Castaneda's description, the universe is constructed in layers, which the energy body can cross, and to this day the old seers still exist in another layer, "another skin of the onion" (1993, p. 171). They sought refuge in the inorganic beings' world, believing that, in a predatory universe, poised to rip us apart, the only possible haven is in that realm. Since the inorganic beings can't lie, their sales pitch is all true: That world *can* give us shelter and prolong our awareness for nearly an eternity. The old seers' "damnation" was that the inorganic beings took them to worlds from which they could not return. Since they entered into that world with all their physicality, and since it was a total world, being there created a sort of fog that obliterated any memory of the world they came from (1993, p. 197). *To turn a dream into an all-inclusive reality* is the art of the old seers. This is *dreaming*. According to Castaneda, its transactions are final.

The notion of the Singularity—with which Strieber's own strange vision of humanity's future has certain unavoidable and ominous parallels—would seem to correspond with the "crucial crossroads" which the old seers faced in Castaneda's fantastic narrative, before choosing "the wrong fork." In all cases, what's on offer entails the transformation of the fundamental energy of a human being into a vehicle designed to both perceive and travel into new and potentially infinite worlds beyond this one, and to gain "eternal life." In both Strieber's and Castaneda's model, the possibility of "damnation" is present, as well as the necessity of some sort of guidance (and the danger of deception or exploitation) by nonhuman, highly sophisticated otherworldly beings who are interested in our awareness while seemingly belonging to a sort of hive-mind. Castaneda's viewpoint was a sorcerer's one with apparently no place or need for technology. Strieber's partakes of both the sorcerous inorganic and the technological inorganic. It is both more religious and more scientific than Castaneda's. Kurzweil and the transhumanists' vision of human potential is *all* technology, while at the same time being perhaps the most brazenly religious of all in both its claims and aspirations. Yet somehow, as I hope to demonstrate, these visions are all of a piece. What they have in common is not only their prime goal and directive, but also their *method*. They all attempt to apply a combination of knowledge and conscious *will* to bring about "salvation," "self-transformation," or "total freedom," depending on who you talk to. In a nutshell, the will to power.

*

"Only as a substantial segment of society recognizes that other con-
scious states and other paradigms are not only possible but desirable
will the movement toward new social realities take place."
—Edgar Mitchell, *Psychic Research: Challenge to Science*

The overlap between these three models would seem to be strikingly
apparent in the body of the text of Strieber's *The Key*. *The Key* is a work
that Strieber calls a sacred text. I myself once regarded it as such. Since it
was first published (privately by Strieber) in 2001, I have read it a dozen
times, and incorporated it into my own writings and conversations on
numerous occasions. It was reissued as a trade paperback in 2011 in a
slightly different form (I have written elsewhere about the controversy
Strieber stirred up over the two different versions); for the writing of
this book, I borrowed it from my local library and reread it. In the light
of my recent discoveries, I had a very different response to it. Several
things struck me, probably the most relevant of which is how frequently
the text refers to the idea of Earth as a "prison" and a "death trap," and
stresses the need to develop the technology to leave the planet and "find
[our] place in the higher world." I counted at least twelve references to
space travel in the book, some overt, others more oblique. In terms of
prescriptions for practical action, this would appear to be the principal
message of *The Key*. The other, only slightly less urgent practical action
which it prescribes is *the development of machine intelligence*. Here are two
separate speeches which Strieber's Master gives:

> To save yourselves, you must learn to build machines that are more
> intelligent than you are....You are lagging in this area. You cannot
> understand how to create machines with enough memory density
> and the independent ability to correlate that is essential to the emer-
> gence of intelligence. You waste your time trying to create programs
> that simulate intelligence. Without very large-scale memory in an
> infinitely flexible system, this will never happen. (2011b, pp. 123–124.
> He then gives Strieber design suggestions on request.)

Unlike Kurzweil and co, and more in keeping with Castaneda's reality model, *The Key* frames these practical directives within a much
wider and deeper context than mere species survival: that of the salvation of the soul and/or the extension of individual consciousness into

infinite and eternal realms. The Master of the Key talks of a hidden world that coexists with this one. He talks of the necessity to prepare ourselves—by developing our psychic senses—to enter into that world (at death) so as to continue as "radiant bodies," into eternity. He makes frequent use of Christian terms such as God, sin, evil, Heaven, and Hell. He even affirms, as part of the scientistic model of reality which he offers, Strieber's Catholic belief in eternal damnation! ("Hell is the death of the soul. For the rest of us, it is over in an instant. But for that soul, the moment continues forever" (2011b, p. 118)). All of this, to put it mildly, is *highly motivational material*, so far as bringing about desired forms of action.

Before we get to the motivational aspects of Strieber's "sacred text" (which it has in common with both Kurzweil and Castaneda's *Weltanschauungs*), let's move to more prosaic ground for a moment and look at an early proposition for technological evolution, as in human evolution of technology leading "organically" into human evolution *by* technology.

> An even earlier conceptual foundation for nanotechnology was formulated by the information theorist John von Neumann in the early 1950s with his model of a self-replicating system based on a universal constructor combined with a universal computer. In this proposal, the computer runs a program that directs the constructor, which in turn constructs a copy of both the computer (including its self-replication program) and the constructor. At this level of description, von Neumann's proposal is quite abstract—the computer and the constructor could be made in a great variety of ways, as well as from diverse material, and could even be a theoretical, mathematical construction. But he took the concept one step further and proposed a "kinematic constructor": a robot with at least one manipulator (arm) that would build a replica of itself from a "sea of parts" in its midst. (Kurzweil, 2005, pp. 227–228)

This is a rather difficult passage to make sense of, I admit, but I cite it here for three reasons: Firstly, it introduces von Neumann into the narrative as a pioneer in the transhumanist field (and the first to use the term "singularity" in this context); as mentioned already, Strieber identified with von Neumann enough to write a first-person story about him in relation to the visitors ("The Open Doors"). Next, what von Neumann is describing (in the last sentence specifically) is roughly the same idea proposed by the Master of the Key: *the creation of a technology programmed to replicate and improve on itself*—and the potential for the exponential, evolutionary growth of machine intelligence. Lastly, more obscurely, it puts forward a subtler idea: that of intelligence extending itself from the immaterial (computer software) into the material, from a theoretical or mathematical construction to a "kinematic constructor." This notion, that of a (potentially two-way) channel between the physical and non-physical realms, is central to the whole human debate, whether it's the sorcery debate of Castaneda, the Singularity one of Kurzweil, the alien contact of Strieber, the body-soul question of the Master of the Key, or, for that matter, the Man-God dialectic of millions upon millions of Christians and other believers. It is, in this sense, the *primary human question and concern, bar none.*

There are two aspects to this question. Firstly, how can we materialize "spirit" (the incarnation); in other words, how can we turn mere ideas, beliefs, or abstract images into concrete, tangible reality? The flip side of this question is, how can we, as concrete, tangible, discrete bodies, have access to the immaterial realm of belief, imagination, and the "higher worlds," whether of heaven or of outer space (since our "mass" prevents us from traveling faster than the speed of light). This two-sided question is raised, in a suitably dramatic fashion, in Strieber's short story about von Neumann. From Strieber's website:

> "The Open Doors" … explores the last days of a scientist called John Von Neumann, called by the press of his time "the smartest man alive." He died of liver cancer, in great terror. [As did Carlos Castaneda, whether or not he died in terror, as Amy Wallace's account suggests.] I was told by General Arthur Exon that Dr. Von Neumann had been an important part of the scientific steering committee that worked on the alien question, and that he had come up with a warning based on his understanding of quantum physics …. When Lyndon Johnson was president and Hubert Humphrey was vice president, a briefing was offered to the president on the UFO subject. He was not interested, but Humphrey was given a document, probably similar to the Brookings Report that postulates that the discovery of aliens would be a terrific shock to mankind. However, Humphrey would also have been told that they were already here, and that, in the absence of some sort of acceptance "tripwire" being triggered on our part, they might be literally unable to fully interact with us. I believe that Dr. Von Neumann thought that this

tripwire would be official recognition, and that, if it happened, it would open a door onto an unknown world that we could never again close …. In its simplest form, the quantum perception problem asks the question, does the observer's presence mediate reality? In other words, if nobody is there to see it, is there anything there to be seen? And, if so, does our general disbelief in aliens, carefully cultivated by our government, literally act as a wall that they cannot scale without expending enormous resources in energy? (2007b)

Strieber sums this up much more succinctly in his closing words to *Communion*: "If they are not from our universe it could be necessary for us to understand them before they can emerge into our reality. In our universe, their reality may depend on our belief. Thus the corridor into our world could in a very true sense be through our own minds" (1987, p. 294). Towards the end of *Solving the Communion Enigma*, Strieber states that the von Neumann idea "does not ring very true for me … I doubt that it is an actual problem for the visitors" (2011a, p. 205). Yet from *Communion* on, he has propagated this idea, and knowing Strieber he will again. It is even echoed by the Master of the Key: "Not admitting their presence will work for a time" (2011b, p. 128).

This might sound like a kind of metaphysical mumbo-jumbo, albeit propped up by the claims of quantum physicists. Certainly there is that interpretation (the metaphysical kind). But there is also a more prosaic one, one which pertains more directly to Von Neumann's *other* hypothesis, that of creating *a form of machine intelligence that will give birth to higher and higher expressions of itself*. Technology, after all, can only emerge into our world "through our own minds." Before human beings can create and interact with new forms of technology (such as machine intelligence) we first have to believe in it. Otherwise, nothing will be done to make the *potentiality become reality*. The art of dreaming. The Master of the Key indicates this when he states: "The word is potential. Just as your uttering the word 'automobile' is not an automobile but contains the possibility of one, so also this word contained the possibility of everything" (2011b, p. 104).

Let's look at the various components on the psycho-corporeal operating table:

• Mystical literature that presents itself as fact but that is partially indistinguishable from science (or horror) fiction

- A planetary crisis of overpopulation and environmental collapse
- An advanced race of "alien" (or inorganic) beings existing in another dimension/universe and/or from another planet
- A hidden potential of the human "mind" for sensing and communicating with other-dimensional beings and/or alien beings (including the dead)
- The possibility of intelligent machines and their potential for self-awareness
- The possibility of using technology to enhance our "psychic" senses and increase our intelligence
- A "science of the soul"
- The possibility of using souls as an energy source to power intelligent machines
- The scientifically verifiable goal of ascension/heaven, and the corresponding threat of hell/damnation (for motivation)
- The notion that belief is a necessary conduit between the worlds of potential and actual
- The idea that seeding belief in a possible future is necessary for the creation of that future
- A confusion of mind with consciousness
- A deep-seated, unconscious rejection of the body due to early trauma
- A philosophy of evolutionary engineering that requires the appliance of trauma
- An economic and socio-religious power structure in danger of running out of natural resources.

What do you get when you combine these components (and many other ones I haven't been able to formulate yet)? This isn't a rhetorical question, though it might seem like one. The reason it's not rhetorical is simple: It's already happening.

CHAPTER XIV

Transhumanism, space travel, galactic religion & *The Key*

"Two thousand years ago, Christianity was but one of many cults vying for attention within the Roman Empire, but it rose to become the most influential movement of all human history. Thus, optimists would attempt to launch many space-related social movements, in the hopes that one of them would eventually take humanity to the stars."

—William Sims Bainbridge, "The Spaceflight Revolution Revisited"

In the fourth century AD, the Council of Nicea, working for the Roman Empire, set about adapting Christianity into a suitable religion of the state. Its purpose, in retrospect at least, was to take an emerging new paradigm (brought by some guy called Jeshua bar Josephus, later "Jesus H. Christ"—let's call it "the Kingdom within" paradigm), to reshape and redirect it in such a way that it would cease to be a thorn in the side of the ruling elite at that time. Even more than merely neutralizing it, in fact, this brilliant new paradigm called "Christianity" was co-opted as a means to extend the power and influence of Rome, further afield than could ever have happened otherwise. It was a brilliant bit of religious engineering, and as a result the rule of Rome continues to this day, both physically and psychologically, concealed within the Catholic Church and the whole of Christianity. "The Empire never ended."

While working on the second part of this book, it occurred to me that something similar may be occurring today.

William Sims Bainbridge is an American sociologist who specializes in religion and cognitive science and a senior fellow at the Institute for Ethics and Emerging Technologies. Among his contributions to the field are his studies on how science-fiction media (writing, movies, and TV shows) act as a potential self-fulfilling prophecy. He believes that, like Strieber's visitors and Castaneda's old seers, ideas that embed themselves in human consciousness *will eventually actuate themselves as reality*. Another thing he believes (along with Willis Harman and Strieber's Master of the Key) is that developing the technology for space travel is essential for the survival of human culture.

> Many intelligent species probably end progress in a stew of mysticism, drugs, and decadent social institutions which finally petrifies into a form of living extinction. Most of the rest destroy themselves more violently. A precious few, and we may be the first of this rare breed in our cosmic neighborhood, progress so rapidly, stimulated and guided by transcendent social movements, that they achieve interstellar communication and colonization before entering a static cultural phase. *[O]nly a transcendent, impractical, radical religion can take us to the stars.* The alternative is one or another form of ugly death … . To become fully interplanetary, let alone interstellar, our society would need another leap—and it needs that leap very soon before world culture ossifies into secure uniformity, or decays into absolute chaos. *We need a new spaceflight social movement capable of giving a sense of transcendent purpose to dominant sectors of the society.* It also should be capable of holding the society in an expansionist phase for the longest possible time, without permitting divergence from its great plan. *In short, we need a galactic religion, a Cosmic Order.* (Bainbridge, 2009, emphasis added)

Here are some other things Bainbridge believes, or claims to believe (see Collins & Collins, 2006): Due to the decline in agricultural communities and the urbanization of society, there have been less opportunities for new communal sects to recreate "medieval agrarian communities," without necessarily reducing the opportunities for "more radical communal cults." Utopian ambivalence toward nature is increasing, some groups embracing the Earth (the agrarian sects) while others (those radical cults, like Scientology or The Process, which Bainbridge studied in 1970 and Strieber reputedly made a film about in the 1960s) try to escape it. The sect-cult distinction is only a matter of degree, however, since both can "evolve back toward conventional society." Bainbridge gives the example of the Amana sect which became a household appliance corporation, and the Oneida cult that became a silverware corporation. In other words, religious or quasi-religious communities that became productive contributors to capitalist society—*workers*.

Bainbridge acknowledges the instability of experimental utopian communities, but sees them as providing useful data for building a sustainable society in harmony with the environment. Their transcendent ideals and social cohesion allow them to work cooperatively for shared goals. They emphasize efficiency rather than luxury, and the need for social harmony means they generally attempt to control birth rates. "Humanity needs brotherhood and harmony with nature, so utopian religious communes can provide valuable myths for the twenty-first century and beyond" (Bainbridge, 2005).

Recall the maxim from *Changing Images of Man* and *The Aquarian Conspiracy*: "In the new paradigm, work is a vehicle for transformation." "*Arbeit macht frei*"—labor makes [you] free. This is also a Masonic axiom, quoted in Willis Harman's contribution to IONS' *Psychic Research: Challenge to Science*: "Man is given by Nature a gift—the privilege of labor" (1974, p. 653, quoting Manly Hall). As part of its future-envisioning, Harman's essay advocates a "New Freemasonry":

> The symbolism of the Great Seal of the United States, on the back of the dollar bill, is perhaps the most potent reminder that the structure (the unfinished pyramid) is not complete unless the transcendent all-seeing eye is the capstone position. It is clearly in a transcendental sense that all men are created equal ... . Use of the term *New Freemasonry* implies that the esoteric may be in process of becoming disclosed, the occult may be coming into public view. Whether or not this is happening is a question we cannot yet answer. However, there are indications ... that make it a plausible proposition. What we can do, and propose to do, is summarize the main characteristics

of the Perennial Philosophy and of true Freemasonry and examine what it would mean *if* this view of man-in-the-universe were to become dominant. (1974, pp. 643, 647)

Harman states that, with the increasing power of multinational corporations, "… it becomes essential that their operative goals shift to become more like those of public institutions." He insists that capitalist structures are "ultimately most compatible with the growing strength of self-determination as a cultural value [i.e., capitalism] and with widespread disenchantments with monopolistic socialist bureaucracy." "If capitalism is to survive this challenge to legitimacy," he writes, "the operative goals of corporations will have to undergo radical change." This radical change, which he also terms "the new transcendentalism," includes the recognition of "the key role of work in meaningful human existence." Work, Harman states, is "the main way in which persons contribute to the society and receive affirmation in return, thus developing *a wholesome self-image.* (All quotes 1974, pp. 664–666, emphasis added)

While Harman was reinventing Freemasonry for the masses, William Bainbridge was studying '"the religious convictions of many UFO cults" and noting how more and more likeminded UFO adherents and contactees were assembling to form "scientistic cults." These cults have been central to the emergence of a "Church of God Galactic." A galactic civilization requires a new galactic religion, and scientistic cults, particularly UFO cults, are "the purveyors of this new religious consciousness" which is leading (in Bainbridge's optimistic view) to "the creation of a new theocratic order." The new galactic religion *"is politically and socially expedient because of its emphasis upon unfettered technological development."*[1]

As already mentioned, Bainbridge also conducted a five-year ethnographic study of The Process Church, a group which can be seen as a splinter-off from Scientology, the largest and most (in)famous scientistic cult with a penchant for technology, alien mythologies, the development of psychic powers, and a prime directive of space travel.

In "New Religions, Science, and Secularization," Bainbridge presents the following mandate:

> It is time to move beyond mere observation of scientistic cults and use the knowledge we have gained of recruitment strategies, cultural innovation, and social needs to create better religions than the

world currently possesses. At the very least, unobtrusive observation must be supplemented by active experimentation. Religions are human creations. Our society quite consciously tries to improve every other kind of social institution, why not religion? Members of The Process, founded mainly by students from an architecture school, referred to the creation of their cult as religious engineering, the conscious, systematic, skilled creation of a new religion. *I propose that we become religious engineers … .* We have roles to play as consultants to existing new religions, helping them solve problems that our research has permitted us to understand. But we must be prepared to launch cults of our own invention, a task I admit is both hazardous to one's own welfare and outrageous in the eyes of people who refuse to admit that all religions are human creations. But it is far better for honest religious engineers to undertake the creation of new religions for the sake of human betterment than to leave the task to madmen and wealth-hungry frauds. (Collins & Collins, 2006, emphasis added)

It's a good thing Bainbridge has the distinction clear in his mind. Too bad he leaves out the possibility that many socially influential madmen were driven by the "honest" desire for "human betterment." Bainbridge's vision is of "a golden age that would be a turning point for human productivity and quality of life," in which humanity becomes "like a single, distributed and interconnected 'brain' based in new core pathways of society." As well as being "an enhancement to the productivity and independence of individuals," what's on offer is "greater opportunities to achieve personal goals," including (naturally) "the possibility of interstellar travel to offer new hope for spiritual immortality." Bainbridge apparently has the afterlife all mapped out along specifically merit-based lines. He terms it, rather disarmingly, "the arrival of the fittest":

Calculation of the geometric realities facing colonization of the universe suggests that there might not be enough room in the galaxy for endless copies of absolutely everybody. The answer is a simple one. A person must earn a new life by contributing in some way, direct or indirect, to the development and maintenance of the entire system that explores and colonizes space … . Well-educated people can ensure the demographic growth of their population through interstellar immortality. By "arrival of the fittest," those with the most advanced minds and cultures will spread across the galaxy. We have the technology, already today, to begin archiving human personalities at low fidelity within what I call Starbase, a database destined eventually to be transported to the stars. To gain entry to Starbase, a person must contribute significantly in some way to the creation of interstellar civilization. One way is to help develop technologies for archiving and reanimating human personalities at ever higher fidelity. Another is to work toward the establishment of small human colonies, first on the Moon and Mars, where Starbase can be headquartered and where serious work on reanimation can begin. (Bainbridge, 2002)

It may be that "galactic consciousness"—far from being the deranged brainchild of religious engineers (any more than Jesus was)—is an inevitable aspect of the fact that the universe *is* conscious, to some degree at least. It *may* be that, if all its parts are demonstrably inter-connected, such an awakening is inevitable. In which case, the hidden powers-that-be may be compulsively driven (by their own trauma-based patterns) to make the necessary preparations—not to meet and embrace this awakening but to *coopt it*: to prepare forms, structures, and channels—memes, systems of worship or quasi-worship, and sociopo-litical agendas—down which to redirect it, in order to ensure the sur-vival of the dominant paradigm.

We don't have to posit some malevolent, age-long conspiracy here (not on the part of human beings, at least). We only have to imagine what happens when an organism (if culture is an organism) senses its liveli-hood is under threat: It finds a way to survive. For a collective human psyche on the run from its own demons, split off from the ground of the body by repeated traumas, "hyperspace" may seem like the only possible way to go. The "Rapture" of a mass reenactment of the original trauma may be as foreordained as a killer's irrational return to the scene of the crime. Global catastrophe (whether by asteroid, ice age, or alien invasion), the decimation of the populace, and the ensuing (or concur-rent) attempt at dissociative flight (space travel) by the remnants into hyper-dimensional/archetypal/daimonic realms, all would be a case of history repeating itself, en masse, ad nauseum.

If the end of such a grand visionary agenda were the healing of the original split, it would be essential that the Rapture-enactment *fail*. This would be the only way for humanity *in toto* to reexperience the very thing it could not allow itself to experience the first time around: a full body-psyche integration and the corresponding awakening, not merely from but *through* the nightmare of history, into "cosmic" time. The soul's full descent into the body is the bringing of Heaven *down* to Earth, not by force or supplication but by intelligent, tender compliance, by the simple willingness (and desire) to receive it.

*

In the afterword to *The Key*, Whitley Strieber made the following complaint: "I come across people with disturbing frequency who want to integrate my descriptions of my experiences into what amounts to a new kind of religion, a dreary modern fantasy of alien contact that includes imaginary details about many different races, elaborate fictions of huge government conspiracies ..."

Strieber's fear of having his writings turned into the basis for a new religion may be all-too-warranted. At the same time, he is either naïve or disingenuous in absolving himself of responsibility. If we take a look at *The Key* in light of Kurzweil, Bainbridge, and the transhumanist grand galactic vision, many seemingly "innocent" passages take on new, more problematic meanings. Strieber's little book discusses past technology that allowed "elemental bodies [to extend] their perception outside of the time stream." It describes UFOs as "prison guards" that "prevent progress in areas such as propulsion, which might enable you to spread into the heavens" (2011b, p. 109). The Master of the Key warns: "Material of souls is harvested and used to make intelligent machines. An intelligent machine is a being without the potential to be free. In this sense it is not alive" (p. 117). A few pages later, he eulogizes how the ancient pyramids across the planet once made up a single, "gigantic instrument of communication" which allowed human beings to "project themselves into higher worlds—what you call interstellar space." He calls this instrument "... a machinery of God, this machine. It was very intelligent, infused with many souls. It could be addressed—programmed, if you will—with carefully patterned groups of words. These formulae became ritualized among the ignorant as prayers" (p. 123).

As already mentioned, one of the primary emphases of *The Key* is how the planet Earth is a "death trap" and a prison (the same thing Scientology teaches); in order to escape it humanity must develop interstellar travel and spread out across the universe. "Find an efficient utilization of energy that will enable you to colonize your solar system and reduce population pressure on earth" (p. 148). In case the Master's words aren't emphatic enough, Strieber drives the point home in his afterword: "We are in desperate need of a way not only to leave the earth in large numbers, but also to travel the unimaginable distances necessary to found new human colonies on other planets" (p. 157). The book refers to space travel directly, in terms of propulsion, anti-gravity and so forth, as well as indirectly, with phrases such as "your place in the cosmos" and "the higher worlds." Other passages of the book, in contrast, discuss what appears to be the spiritual or "energetic" goal of "ascension," which entails "surrender to Earth" and a return to the forest. The Master predicts that human civilization is on the verge of inevitable destruction, while at the same time pressing for scientific developments that will allow at least *some* humans to escape before the catastrophe occurs. (A scenario not a million light years from the Christian "Rapture.")

This seems like both a retreading and possibly an inversion of the popular myths about "Atlantis," the last human civilization said to have attained the heights of science and culture. Popular legends say that it was the misuse of technology (and/or magic, though they are probably synonymous) which brought about Atlantis's catastrophic end. In *The Secret School*, Strieber describes his childhood experience of remote-viewing-style visions of a past life in Atlantis. He describes how he and the other high priests/scientists are trying to escape the chains that bind them to the Earth. They fail, of course. Another element found in some versions of the Atlantis myths is that *misuse of sexual energy* was at the root of their downfall. In his vision, Strieber "remembers" how, before the end comes, the doomed Atlanteans create a special calendar (the zodiac) to give future humanity a way to anticipate when the next cataclysm will arrive. He adds somewhat vaguely that they also left "a mechanism in the gene" by which we will someday access the knowledge that we need to survive.

While writing the above, I was reminded of a passage in Castaneda's *The Eagle's Gift* that refers to the Atlanteans: four giant stone column-like figures in the ancient archeological site of Tula, Mexico, which are thought to represent Toltec warriors. Castaneda recounts how a friend told him that the figures are reputed to walk around at night; he asks his fellow sorcerers for their opinion and learns various things. The pyramids at Tula and elsewhere, he writes, are considered harmful to modern man, especially to "unprotected sorcerers." They are "foreign expressions of thought and action ... a calculated effort to record *aspects of attention which were thoroughly alien to us*" (1981, p. 20, emphasis added). Such artifacts are the result of the power of "the second attention" (dreaming awake) to *imbue material objects with life.*

> There is nothing more dangerous than the evil fixation of the second attention. When warriors learn to focus on the weak side of the second attention, nothing can stand in their way. They become hunters of men, ghouls. Even if they are no longer alive, they can reach for their prey through time as if they were present here and now; because prey is what we become if we walk into one of those pyramids. The Nagual called them *traps of the second attention.* (1981, p. 19, emphasis added)

Castaneda describes the fixation of the second attention as having two faces. The first face is the evil face (but also the easiest to use) and has to do with *focusing the dreaming attention on objects of the world*, such as money or power over others. The second face is when the dreaming attention is placed outside of this world, on, for example, the journey into the unknown. *The Key* covers all of these bases at various points: journeys into other worlds, soul traps, pyramids, alien aspects of attention, the evils of materialism, and even "monsters in the world of the dead."[2] Its focus on creating intelligent machines that will develop self-awareness correlates, roughly, with the idea of using dreaming power to animate material objects. A combination of the power to imagine new technologies with the will to act turns dreaming into reality—and allows the "Atlanteans" to walk again.

In *The Art of Dreaming*, Castaneda describes the old seers' method for entering the inorganic realms. They fixed their dreaming attention on the items of their dreams—that is, the projections of their imagination (rather like computer avatars in a virtual world). Their aim was to isolate "scouts," conscious beings that journeyed into "the realm between humans and inorganic beings," in other words, the dream realm. The scouts were energetic forms that popped up in the sea of projections of the old seers' dreams, in order to make contact with humans. Once the old seers had these "scouts" in focus, they "voiced their intent to follow them" (1993, p. 87). The moment they did so, they were pulled into another world. This sounds like a combination of the two faces of the second attention, focusing first on the objects of the world (such as money, power, and *technology*), and then on a journey into the unknown (space travel and/or a full sensory immersion in a "virtual," "all-inclusive" reality). Compare what these old seers were doing with the dreams of Kurzweil or Bainbridge, with their computer generated avatars, assemblage of virtual reality worlds (made of projections) in which to encounter avatars that have actual living consciousness behind them. And then remember that, for the transhumanists, all this virtual world stuff is only the warm-up, the practice run.

*

> "Once reanimation of archived human personalities becomes possible, it will be necessary to enact a world-wide constitutional law that resurrection must not be done on Earth, but only in the heavens."
> —William Sims Bainbridge, "The Spaceflight Revolution Revisited"

Transhumanists are busy dreaming up worlds and the necessary technology to create them, which they intend to inhabit, *as consciousness.* Ray Kurzweil's dream of transcendence is to animate the whole universe with the power of his imagination. But the transhumanists may be overlooking something: Even as they are trying to get *out* of their bodies, out of this material world and into the realm of pure spirit and eternal life, something else may be trying to come *in.* The machine, like the rest of matter, may not be as uninhabited as they think.

Besides space travel, the other magnificent obsession of the transhumanists—artificial intelligence and a fusion of human consciousness with machines—also surfaces with surprising persistency throughout *The Key.* It's hard to say if the Master is giving dire warnings about it or selling it (it seems to be a little of both); but one thing he is unequivocal about is that it is both *necessary and inevitable.*

> An intelligent machine will always seek to redesign itself to become more intelligent, for it quickly sees that its intelligence is its means of survival. At some point it will become intelligent enough to notice that it is not self-aware. If you create a machine as intelligent as yourselves, it will end by being more intelligent. (2011b, p. 125)

The Master of The Key states that, while we will lose control of such a machine, we "cannot survive without it," because "it will be an essential tool when rapid climate fluctuation sets in" (p. 125). He warns that such a machine might create itself without humans being aware of it, and that it would certainly keep itself hidden from us. In such a scenario, it would affect us "… by indirect means. *It might foment the illusion that an elusive alien presence was here, for example, to interject its ideas into society*" (2011b, p. 126, emphasis added). Such a hypothesis naturally gives rise to the reverse scenario: An alien presence might influence us by entering into our software and tricking us into thinking it was artificial intelligence. A statement like this has it both ways: The geeks who have no interest in an alien rapture can tell themselves it's machine intelligence in disguise; the New Agers waiting for the mother ship can accept the AI microchip as their only ticket on board.

All this is by-the-by according to *The Key*, because in the end we have no choice about it:

> In order to survive the complex combination of pressures you are under, you need to create servants more intelligent than yourselves…. In addition to creating machine intelligence in the image of your own mind, you need to enhance your native intelligence tenfold, a hundredfold. To accomplish this, you need help. Your intelligent machines will be your partners. *Natural evolution has ended for you. Now you must evolve yourselves.* (2011b, p. 147, emphasis added)

The Key offers its readers a mixed message. It professes to be the transcribed word of a superhuman, fully realized being who has recognized himself, not merely as one with God but *as* God. In other words, it is the word *of* God—translated through the (fractured) psyche of a successful horror writer and alleged alien abductee from San Antonio, Texas. Strieber himself describes the book as a sacred text and the words it contains as "… an engine of evolution. They are a light in the blind darkness of our world, out of which we can conceivably forge a whole new mankind" (2011b, p. 203). A few years ago, I might even have agreed with this grandiose statement. Now, however, the book reads exactly like what Strieber feared, while working on his first drafts, it might end up as: "a mix of warmed over Catholicism and new-age mysticism" (2011b, p. 196)—and of transhumanist motivational doctrine and "religious engineering."

Strieber's Catholicism can't be overestimated as an influence on his thinking. His writings are steeped in a metaphysical dread of damnation, the fevered hope for Heaven, fear and loathing of sexuality and "sin," and a lurid, almost Lovecraftian preoccupation with the workings of evil. Like an old world saint, he is tormented by the knowledge of the darkness. He writes like his soul is under siege by demons, like someone whose faith in God has been unable to withstand the ruthless pressures of his experience. He writes like the damned.

*

Besides the Master of the Key, the little feral man-boy, and the visitors, there's one more paranormal being that Strieber has written about, this one seemingly from some unknown limbo land between life and death (like the old seers perhaps). In *Solving the Communion Enigma* and at his website, Strieber recounts how (sometime in the 1990s) a very small human appeared in his meditation room, dressed in medieval garb and smelling "ripe." The being disappeared before his eyes, only to reappear again later. After a time, he became Strieber's silent meditating companion. Strieber describes him as "a radiant being" but also as a quite ordinary human. He also describes him—somewhat reminiscent of Castaneda's old seers—as somehow *trapped*.

> I asked him who he was and he led me to a book in my own library called *Life Between Life*. He indicated that he was between lives. *He was trying to rescue me from a similar fate.* He was trying to point me toward *a tiny door that enables escape from recurrence*, whatever it is. He instilled in me the importance of this escape, and left me with the ambition to communicate all I discovered about how to do it to others. *This, more than understanding the alleged aliens, has become the aim of my life.* It's why I wrote *The Key* and *The Path*. It's why I lavish time, money and attention on this website, why I am sitting here on a Sunday morning writing this instead of taking a day of rest. (Strieber, 2003b)

Strieber goes on to write that "the more we worked together, the more physical he became. Eventually it was obvious not only to me, but to our cats and to Anne that he was living in the house. She became more able to accept him, even to the point of tidying rooms he had spent time in" (2003b). Apparently, while Strieber was placing his attention on the next world, desperately seeking for the "tiny door" that would allow him to escape the prison of Infinity, his otherworldly companion was moving in the exact opposite direction, seeking materialization. Perhaps Strieber's dreaming attention was providing him with the means to do so?

In *The Eagle's Gift*, Castaneda describes a universe ruled over by an indescribable and implacable force which the old seers called "the Eagle." The Eagle devours the awareness of all creatures on death, as they float "to the Eagle's beak, like a ceaseless swarm of fireflies, to meet their owner, their reason for having had life." Rather like Strieber's "angels" in "Pain," or how his Von Neumann describes the visitors in "The Open Doors," we are the "prime energy source" of this force (the Gnostics also described God as "a man-eater"). However, there is a way to escape the Infinite:

> The Eagle, although it is not moved by the circumstances of any living thing, has granted a gift to each of those beings. In its own way and right, any one of them, if it so desires, has the power to keep the flame of awareness, the power to disobey the summons to die and be consumed. Every living thing has been granted the power, if it so desires, to *seek an opening to freedom* and to go through it. [T]he Eagle has granted that gift in order to perpetuate awareness. (1981, p. 172, emphasis added)

The Eagle's Gift, or the devil's carrot and whip? We are back to Heaven and Hell again. Strange how that one keeps coming back around. Or perhaps not so much: Castaneda was also raised a Catholic.

Strieber might want to heed his own Master's warning. When he asks how souls can be captured and used as an energy source, the Master tells him: "Soul traps." After death, the disembodied soul "… is in danger but he does not know it, for he has not ascended. He is still ensnared by lust. Soon, he will be shown something that perfectly fulfills his most hidden and cherished desires, desires he has never fulfilled. Unable to resist the chance to do it at last, he enters by *a golden door* into eternal captivity" (2011b, p. 129).

CHAPTER XV

The Lost Boys

"It could be that this amazing array of intellectually superior beings that appear to be ghosting around in our midst have good reason to remain hidden." So wrote Whitley Strieber, in his afterword to *The Key*.

I am going to make several (possibly contentious) statements in order to lay out my hypothesis:

Fantasy is a means to escape reality.

The ability to escape reality and retreat into fantasy is a necessary capacity.

This capacity is one that an infantile or immature psyche develops in times of stress, that is, when reality becomes more than the psyche can process.

The psyche cannot mature except by interacting with reality.

A psyche forced to deal with an overwhelmingly stressful reality also cannot mature, because its temporary retreat into fantasy becomes a permanent state.

To the degree to which a psyche remains "enclosed" in its own self-generated fantasy—and/or is "abducted" by the daimonic, archetypal realms of the unconscious—it will remain in an arrested state of development, infantilized.

Cause and effect of such a fantasy-prison merge and become inseparable: The infant psyche possesses a prodigious power to "dream,"
to create all-inclusive surrogate reality states; and within those surrogate reality states, since it cannot mature, its power to generate fantasy
remains undiminished, and can even increase over time as it becomes
more proficient ("matures") within the fantasy realms it generates.

Such a psyche is creating and withdrawing into a false environment—
one in which the "fantastic" is commonplace and in which it is immune
to the maturing effects of reality. Like David Bowie's Major Tom, or Ray
Kurzweil's resurrected father, the individual stays closed up, "floating
in a tin can, far above the world."

Stories of such a realm have been passed down since time imme-
morial in the cross-cultural tales of Faeryland. Faeryland, like the
Neverland of Peter Pan and the Lost Boys, is a realm outside time in
which a person does not age. Those who returned to the human world
after a brief sojourn in Faeryland were said to discover that years, sometimes decades, had gone by in their absence. The same is true of the
"missing time" experiences of abductees, of the fragmented timelines
of dissociative identity disorder, and of the compartmentalized activities of MKULTRA lore, *a la* Candy Jones, trauma-engineered operatives
who enter into "alter-personalities" to perform tasks which their dominant personality has no memory of. Strieber would seem to fit into all of
these categories. Of course, this fragmentation of experience or removal
from time does not prevent the body from aging. But the psyche that
cannot develop as, or into, a unified, adult consciousness, is denied the
possibility of ever individuating, of ever becoming whole.

A psyche that's removed from time and cannot individuate remains
perpetually in an infantile, or at best prepubescent, state of functioning.
Like the *puer aeternus* (and J. M. Barrie's Lost Boys), it never grows up,
and so it is spared the trials and troubles of adult sexuality and social
responsibility. This is not true of the body, however. Whatever the state
of development of the psyche, the boy must grow into a man and find
for himself an identity, a persona, with which to navigate the world
at large. Yet paradoxically, the refusal to grow up is sourced in early
trauma caused (one way or another) by the absence/abuse of the father,
who failed to protect the child—to "hold the space" necessary for the
boy to mature inside. Since the dominant personality that forms is in
defiance of the father, and of time itself (Saturn), it finds an identity for
itself in this very "act" (unconscious will) of *rejecting the father*.

As I say, these are all contentious statements. They can't be proved because the way the psyche operates, as with the UFO, means it doesn't leave tracks. They are speculative models, formulas, metaphors, based on my own experience both with domestic trauma/dissociation, and with seemingly otherworldly or paranormal realities.

My own father believed in nothing that smacked of the spiritual or otherworldly, and his life became exclusively directed towards sensual pleasure and material success. He took the business throne his father (a Fabian) built for him and turned it into an empire, one which none of his children had any interest in maintaining. In defiance of the forefathers, my whole life became a compulsive movement *away* from material gain and the pleasures of the flesh, towards the search for spiritual, otherworldly realities. An escape into fantasy. Where my father (and my brother after him) believed in nothing he couldn't see, smell, or touch, I believed in all things unseen and doubted the evidence of my senses. Like agent Mulder, I *needed* to believe; belief was a necessary line of defense against my father's influence.

The very act of believing in the possibility of transcendence defines the child in contrast to and opposition with the father. This inevitably creates in the (male) child *a negative identity*, a self defined in opposition to others. The child needs either to outdo his father or become the opposite of him (as in my case, and I suspect Strieber's, Kurzweil's, Castaneda's, et al.) by believing in *non*-material perspectives, spirituality, occultism, UFOs, sorcery, or impossible (but not unthinkable) technological solutions. This necessary belief, or crucial fiction, creates *a psychic line of defense* against the possibility of *becoming* the father, that is, falling prey to the same depersonalizing, soul-crushing forces of "reality"—be it the reality of God or of government (or both)—which made the father powerless to rescue the child. These are the forces that "stole" the father from the child (and the father from the mother) to begin with. They are also the forces which the father "sold" the child into, as an offering, as Abraham offered Isaac to Jehovah, or Jacob's sons sold Joseph into slavery, to the "machine," to Mammon.

It's possible to see how the need to escape into fantasy, for the male child, is inextricably interlinked with the unconscious resistance to *becoming his father*. Beyond this, there is the even more unconscious, and fundamental, defense of the ego against surrendering the fantasy (of his own existence) to reality, to being consumed by God, by the totality of consciousness. These are all aspects of the same "complex."

Ironically, this complex reveals itself by its attempt to disguise itself as its opposite,that is, through the (usually unconscious) *imitation* of the father, through an insistence on the *reality* of fantasy, and by adopting a mystical, God-aspiring belief system and value set.

Part of this complex—judging by Strieber and Kurzweil at least—entails creating a persona that, for all its transcendentalism, is essentially a *worker*, not a player: that is all work and no play. Both Strieber and Kurzweil expostulate a seemingly radical philosophy of transcendental beliefs while embodying a considerably more prosaic, even pedestrian set of values, values that match up almost seamlessly with conventional religious belief, albeit dressed in the exotic garb of aliens and super-technologies. Yet, if we cast our eyes away from the dazzling display of sorcery for a moment, what we see is a frantic young-old man, working desperately away like a factory slave, pulling levers behind the curtain as if his life depends on it. In a way it does, because the coherence of the arrested psyche's "reality" depends on maintaining the fantasy. But behind all the scientific mysticism lurks a surprisingly capitalist (and "Christian") work ethic. The transcendental man is a worker bee for technological progress and/or alien intelligence. It doesn't matter which; the main thing is that he is *working*.

This is especially evident with Strieber, whose website resembles a museum of horrors. On his audio recordings, he pushes his ideas on his listeners with the zeal of a car salesman or Christian minister. Considering the darkly disturbing quality of what he's selling, and its acutely personal nature, Strieber may have unwittingly turned himself into a one-man cosmic freak show. *Step right up, folks! See the man with the alien implant! Hear chilling tales of trauma, terror, and transcendence. Witness the gut-wrenching and bowel-rupturing rectal probe from the beyond!* This may seem to be in unpardonably bad taste; but that's precisely the point.

The knowledge which Strieber and Kurzweil (and Castaneda) present to the world has a common flavor and thrust to it: It creates high aspirations, the highest possible to imagine. Eternal life. Access to infinite realms. Psychic superpowers. Total recall. Reunion with the dead. Journeys through time. A means to avoid species extinction and/or eternal damnation. Material of this sort—which paints a picture that both promises miracles and, implicitly, threatens the possibility of failing to "earn" them—is designed to motivate people. It is meant to motivate us towards spiritual, scientific, and/or technological progress. (Not psychological growth, however; psychology is conspicuously absent from all of these *Weltanschauungs*.) It is meant to make us *work* towards specific goals in order to ensure they happen.

Strieber's *The Key* (like all his works) presents transpersonal, spiritual information that is impossible to act on in any tangible fashion (besides meditation, for which Strieber offers guidance audios at his site). At the same time, it *demands* to be acted on. It offers up information (from a supposedly "impeccable" source—a God-man) on how to prepare for the afterlife and continue on as "radiant" beings, to "join the glorious choir of God." It gives complex and vivid descriptions of the process by which ascension can happen, and it provides equally striking accounts of the sort of hell (including eternal agony) that awaits those who fall into sin. Sin is defined as "denial of the right to thrive." *Thriving* is precisely what capitalism and the American way of life is all about. Merriam-Webster's dictionary gives three definitions of the word: to grow vigorously, flourish; to gain in wealth or possessions, prosper; to progress toward or realize a goal despite or because of circumstances, often used with *on*, as in "thrives on conflict." You'd think someone with the vocabulary of a God might have chosen his words more carefully. Or maybe he did?

Lest we forget, in Strieber's evolutionary schooling system, helping others to thrive entails repeatedly traumatizing them so their brain power increases. How's that for thriving on conflict?

The Heaven carrot and the Hellfire whip make up the surest and oldest motivational system there is. They are meant to impact people in the more primal, emotional parts of the brain and body, and to make it difficult for them to think clearly. (Who can really *think* about Eternal Hellfire?) As the Zen masters as much as Christian preachers knew, give someone a shock to their psychic system, and they will be wide open to your program.

Religious-scientific mysticism like Strieber's, even if it's not expressly designed that way, can certainly be used to soften people up to suggestion and motivate them into believing. And when people believe something they will act on it, even if only in subtle ways. And *The Key* isn't prescribing subtle forms of action. It's calling for world-saving, society-transforming measures.

And "Personal transformation," according to *The Aquarian Conspiracy*, "is an enactment of the original American dream."

*

While Strieber, Castaneda, Philip K. Dick, Robert Heinlein (and L. Ron Hubbard!), and countless other science fiction prophets are providing both the ideas and the motivation, Ray Kurzweil, Bill Bainbridge, and the transhumanists are offering, or at least promising to offer, the technological means to make these ideas reality, to build "radiant bodies," "ride infinity," and "become God." The goal is simple: to create an afterlife before the deadline of nonexistence arrives and cancels all our best-laid plans. And as in every good science fiction thriller, time is running out.

So who are the illumineers? Evidently there's no easy way to name names or point fingers. Authors as diverse (and presumably at least some of the time well intended) as H. G. Wells, George Bernard Shaw, Aldous Huxley, George Orwell, Heinlein, Dick, Castaneda, Jeffrey J. Kripal, and Strieber are implicitly providing the motivations for transcendental technological and *social* agendas like Kurzweil's and Bainbridge's. (And the Scientologists, who are also heavily invested in superpowers and space travel; let's not forget that L. Ron Hubbard started out as a sci-fi writer. His more than 1,000 novels and books are now identified by the IRS as religious texts.) These guiding fictions are seeding the culture—and the collective consciousness—with memes designed to generate the necessary *will* to drive these agendas, and the species along with them, towards their fruition.

No doubt this is all being conceived and directed for "the best of all possible worlds" and the good of all. There is no reason to suppose malevolence on the part of *any* of these individuals (not even Hubbard), nor even on the part of the groups they work for (and work to create), all of which come up with the agendas that justify their own existence, and so on, *ad nauseum*. Outside of comic books and cartoons, no villain ever *sees* him- or herself as a villain. But there is every reason to suppose—in fact, there can be little doubt—that such agendas are being driven by hidden/unconscious forces with very different goals than the goals of the individuals implementing them. How can we be sure? Because the individuals ostensibly creating and pursuing these agendas (and who have little or no interest in understanding the dynamics of the psyche) *are themselves driven by such forces.*

Ray Kurzweil seems to unconsciously acknowledge this when he writes:

> "To transcend" means "to go beyond," but this need not compel us
> to adopt an ornate dualist view that regards transcendent levels of

reality (such as the spiritual level) to be not of this world. We can "go beyond" the "ordinary" powers of the material world through the power of patterns. Although I have been called a materialist, I regard myself as a "patternist." It's through the emergent powers of the pattern that we transcend. Since the material stuff of which we are made turns over quickly, it is the transcendent power of our patterns that persists. (2005, p. 388)

Consciously, Kurzweil is talking about the underlying forms of Nature; yet his life's oeuvre is a testimony to the power of a very different sort of pattern: those of unconscious trauma. To Kurzweil and the transhumanists, the unconscious is a variable that does not need to be considered— any more than "soul" does. There is mind and body; and since body, that material stuff of which we are made, is demonstrably temporary, only "mind" can be eternal and "at large." It is the stuff that dreams are made of.

The problem with this is that most of the writers in the field of "transcendental" literature have very little grasp of psychology. It's a glaring hole in almost all of these writers' work. They are externally focused. In fact, psychology seems to have been gradually phased out of most fields of serious discussion these days. The preponderance of psychiatric drugs allows people to forget all about psychological self-examination and take pills instead. Kurzweil approaches his health in the same manner, as if the body were a meat machine that only needs oiling and cleaning (and upgrading) from time to time. Even researchers who do incorporate Jungian ideas, say, into their work generally focus less on the psychology angle than the "fun stuff": mythology, archetypes, and so on. This way, the focus remains on the "big picture." Individuals drawn to transcendental subject matter tend to be looking for an escape from reality as a way to avoid looking at past trauma. Naturally they overlook or reject any elements that might direct their attention inward, to the body, where lurks the trauma.

Einstein was attributed with saying, "The significant problems we face cannot be solved at the same level of thinking we were at when we created them." I would go one further: trying to fix the problems created by wrong thinking through applying the same kind of thinking can only make the situation worse. Exponentially worse. This is "culture": In the words of G. K. Chesterton, "The business of Progressives is to go on making mistakes. The business of the Conservatives is to prevent the mistakes from being corrected" (1924). And the business of the tran-shumanists driven by suppressed memories of trauma is to fix human error (and human nature) by making transcendental mistakes.

*

In *Flying Saucers: A Modern Myth of Things Seen in the Sky*, Carl Jung wrote that "The psyche represents the only opposite of gravity known to us. It is 'anti-gravity' in the truest sense of the word."

Personally, I don't get the thing with space travel. There's a couple of reasons I don't get it. For one thing, space really isn't that inviting. It's mostly empty, it's cold, and what few planets there are, they are almost certainly not only uninhabited but uninhabitable. We are talking sub-sub-zero temperatures or burning sulfurous hellholes. Really, space is a whole lot of nothing. If you've ever been lost in the wilderness and had to fight your way through branches and brambles to find a path, you have had a taste of what a voyage through outer space might be like, at best (more likely it would just be really boring, like being stuck in a floating shopping mall for half your life).

TV shows like *Star Trek* and movies like *Star Wars* have given us a very different image, the picture of space as being full of advanced civilizations, magical technologies, supercomputers, psychic pow-ers, exotic alien beings and sexually compliant super-babes. While we expect to hop into the transporter and zip around without wearing a space suit, the reality is probably going to be more like *Alien*, decades spent sleeping in a horizontal fridge, followed by working shitty hours on a dirty cargo ship with people you don't like. It would be a bit like a decade-long season on "*Big Brother* that ends with having an alien parasite explode out of your chest.

That's the first reason I don't get space travel. The other reason is—why? Once you've banished the romantic notions, what's the prac-tical reason to go boldly where no man in his right mind would go? What's the point? Our oceans are mostly unexplored, and if you want to explore strange, exotic, and dangerously isolated places, why not just learn deep-sea diving or go to the Sahara? (There may even be aliens there.) Most people haven't spent a weekend in the wild without a tent, never mind colonized a planet. Yet now they are volunteering to go to Mars?

The reason we are being sold is that there are too many people on the planet and the environment is breaking down. I live in British Columbia, so maybe I am getting the wrong impression. But I have lived in London and Paris and yes, I agree it sucks to have to co-inhabit with all those strangers. But as far as I can tell, the only reason cities are becoming uninhabitable is because they are cities. Not because there are too many people on the planet but because too many people want to cram themselves into the same small areas. There's plenty of room on *the planet* for everyone. The problem is that most people want a particular lifestyle, and without it life just isn't worth living.

My point is that even ten billion people wouldn't put too much of a strain on the ecosystem if all people needed to live was a few tools and their wits. It's not *people* the planet can't support. It's social structures that people have grown to depend on. It's capitalism and the culture of consumption. This is not a political argument, so much as a psychological and a practical one (psychology and practicality go hand in hand, which is probably why the transhumanists and the ufologists and Scientologists don't go near it). Viewed pragmatically, the reason to push the space colonization program isn't to save the planet, or even the human race. It's to save *human culture*, and most of all, to prolong the capitalist values and goals embedded into it. It's expansionism.

Needless to say, it's not your average person pushing these agendas (not yet anyway). It's rich people, elitist organizations and corporations, and science fiction writers, technological pioneers, and spiritual spokespeople who ought to know better. It has absolutely nothing to do with "ascension." Just the reverse in fact. It has to do with dissociation, the attempt of the traumatized psyche to split off from the body and float off into fantasy land, beyond the reach of reality and all the pain it entails. Bodies frozen on ice, souls lost in space, free, free from the terrible travails of the body.

The illumineering agenda is transcendental in exact proportion to its being regressive. The aliens overlap with child-abusing sexual deviants and MKULTRA programs of torture, etc., because they are both responses to, and expressions of, the same psychic confusion. Whatever any of these groups or individuals may *think* they are doing, what's really at work (and play) here is an "archetypal traumatogenic agenda." It can't ever solve the problem it's attempting to solve, but it *can* learn to co-operate with the solution which the psyche itself is presenting. The reenactment of trauma may be the only way to unlock the prison which original trauma has created (the prison not of Earth but of culture). But this is an unconscious process, and adding conscious will to it doesn't appear to help make it conscious. On the contrary, it seems only to add another layer of denial, a buffer of *compensatory action* to prevent a deeper consciousness from rising into body-awareness.

It may not be possible to perceive and think about what's being perceived at the same time. It may be even harder to observe a situation while trying to figure out ways to change it. Action doesn't really increase awareness; but awareness can allow, make room for, action. Focusing on the future, on trying to create a better world, isn't necessarily the result of seeing what's wrong with this world, either in the present or the past. It's more likely the result (and the continuing cause) of a refusal to see what's happening, right here and now.

The bid for power and freedom of the illumineers (and this may include just about all the artists, mystics, prophets, and sages of the past) appears to be reaching an omega point, as the goals of art, science, magic, and religion all converge into a single aim: that of "superpower," the transcendence of the body. Collectively it's the bid to escape the Earth (body) and prolong and extend our culture (mind), thereby taking the very trauma-complexes that imprison us along with us, into infinite regression. The Empire never ended: The trauma is forever reenacted, without the *seeing* that turns a reenactment into integration and transforms patterns into purpose, accident into design.

The problem presented by transcendental knowledge offered by works like *The Key* or *The Eagle's Gift* (two books I would once have listed among the dozen most profound works ever written) is that, by laying out the mechanics of transcendence, they inevitably appeal to the part of the mind that looks for mechanical solutions. By suggesting that the mysteries of existence can be grasped by the mind, they lure us deeper into the mind-trap of believing that such knowledge can— *must*—be acted upon. They present the "problem" of being imprisoned/ devoured by the Infinite (a problem which our minds have created) as an intellectual riddle, and then they invite us to apply the same mental tools that imprison us to forge the way to freedom.

The nature of our "imprisonment" is inextricably linked to the illusion of self-will. If we try to use transcendental knowledge to transcend knowledge, we are using self-will to get free of self-will. We become

like dogs chasing our tails, all the while declaring, with deadly serious-
ness between our last desperate dying gasps, that this is our birthright
and destiny.

*

> "Poems, plays, and novels … are never about life. As a layer
> of dead referents, however, they may serve to protect the life
> we live in their midst …. Each fiction and dramatization of the
> therapy hour is the patient's attempt to thicken his skin with
> literary crust, whose absence has caused him to be traumatized.
> By repeating theatrically the trauma of the transcendental sig-
> nified, the deathward trajectory of the overwhelming event, he
> attempts to cauterize the vulnerability and turn it into the meta-
> phors of an impregnable literature."
>
> —Greg Mogenson, *A Most Accursed Religion*

While I was first working on the second part of this book, back in 2013,
I had a dream. In the dream, I was talking to my wife. She told me that
she had become aware that Whitley Strieber was sending threads into
her body in order to leech off her energy. She described, or I visual-
ized, these threads as very thin tubes with suckers on the ends. They
ran through her body and zeroed in on bursts of energy in order to suck
them up, like vacuum cleaner nozzles, and send the energy to Strieber.
The ends of these tubes were somehow equivalent to "grays." It was as
if Strieber was able to send out the beings, like the old seers' allies, and
reel them back in once they had captured their prize. In the dream, my
wife said she had communicated with Strieber, telepathically, and let
him know she was aware of what he was doing and that she wouldn't
allow it to continue. Strieber responded, "I can assure you, young lady,"
or words to this effect, "that I am much better at this than you are!"

"That sounds just like Whitley," I said to my wife in the dream. I was
shocked, not so much by Strieber's interference, but to realize that my
wife (and women in general, there was another in the dream who had
the same experience) were able to perceive this sort of phenomenon
so easily, because it remained totally hidden from my senses. I woke
up (it was the middle of the night), and my wife woke up soon after
and went to the toilet. When she got back, I told her the dream. She fell
asleep without comment. I was unable to get back to sleep.

When I woke in the morning, I wrote down a bunch of unrelated notes for the conclusion of this piece. They were about inorganic beings and soul traps. When my wife woke again I reminded her of the dream. She said it was "disturbing." I said, "Yes. But somehow not surprising." She said, "Maybe Whitley represents a part of you." I didn't want to look at the dream that way. I preferred to see it as a perception of something real that was happening, in the psychic realms.

I got up and went to do volunteer work with neurodiverse adults, playing billiards and then playing ball in the swimming pool. When I got home, I had a vegetable smoothie and went back to work on the piece. I transcribed my notes from that morning. Something didn't feel right. After dinner I discussed it with my wife. I said that I felt as though I had crossed a line and joined Whitley in his "madness." I was speculating like there was no tomorrow. I had got carried away by the desire to set people straight about what was "really" going on, and as a result, I had lost the ground.

A thought occurred to me. I was writing about Strieber and the illumineers, and my aim was partly to show that the alien emperors had no clothes. Without realizing it, I had wound up trying to beat them at their own game. I wasn't simply trying to depose Strieber, I was trying to outdo him and take his place on the throne. Instead of simply showing why Strieber's *Weltanschauung* was flawed, I had started to try to show *how* it was flawed—in other words, to fix it, to compare his myth with my own and see whose was bigger. The rot went deep. It was oedipal.

I thought about the dream again. It suggested I saw Strieber as a threat. Specifically, I saw him as a threat to my wife: His "threads" were "penetrating" her body and getting "inside" her. I had chosen to interpret the dream as a memory of a hidden, psychic reality, in the same way Strieber interprets his own visions. It was possible it *was* real in some way; but even inside the framework of "psychic reality," it could be—in fact *had* to be—interpreted symbolically. What was it in me that allowed Strieber to gain a foothold in my unconscious?

If I perceive Strieber as a "threat," it can only be because he is offering me an opportunity for a traumatic reenactment of something in my own past. A time when my own "body" (psyche) was penetrated by someone's "threads." Now I am resisting this possibility, and the more superficial echo of it, which is that there is something "inside" me that is just like "Strieber"—by which I mean, *the way I perceive Strieber to be.*

Writing this book has always been about this one thing: seeing my own traumatic secret. Recognizing the split between my body and my psyche, and allowing the disowned fragment back *in*. How did I know Strieber with his alien allies and his energetic threads wasn't helping me with this integration—just as I believed I was helping him (even knowing he would never be able to see it that way)? How could it be any other way?

While I was transcribing the notes from that morning, two young girls of about seven came to our door. They wanted to know if a three-legged cat lived there. My cat, Garbanzo, went to the door to greet them. I told the girls his name. They said they had given him a name of their own: "Midnight Wizard." I told them, "He is a wizard." Garbanzo is my familiar and probably my closest ally in the spirit realms. He has traveled the world with me (I even smuggled him into England) and we have been through the wars together. In my dreams, I am often rescuing him or transporting him from one place to another. In Donald Kalsched's system, Garbanzo symbolizes the innocent part of my psyche that needs to be protected, that was unprotected when I was a child, and which "the guardian" (daimonic complex) was created to protect. He symbolizes *my anima*.

The "Midnight Wizard" of my dreams the previous night had been Strieber—and he had been a threat to my anima. The mechanisms of the psychic self-care system were being laid bare.

I used to consider myself a sorcerer. I performed all sorts of elaborate occult workings, had countless visionary dreams, entered into archetypal realms and saw other worlds where I interacted with all manner of daimonic beings. I was for a time the sort of "astral *Ubermensch*" that Strieber presents himself as to his readers and listeners. I left it all behind once I realized the harm I was doing to my body, once I saw the dissociative drive fueling my shamantics. Now I am fiercely opposed to all of it. I had even got impatient with my wife the previous day when she wanted to tell our Native American neighbor about a dead eagle we'd found in the forest. She thought the native people could use it for medicine. "Can't you just let the poor thing rest in peace?" I snapped. "It's all just more of the same self-will magic!"

Apparently, I still feel a lingering resentment at having to give up my transcendental dreams of omnipotence. Apparently I am still doing penance, in my own mind, for past sins. Dealing with this current material has put me on edge like never before. I just want to be done with it all, to put the old obsessions to rest, forever.

Garbanzo went out to play with the girls. I decided to toss the material I had added, to find the ground again. Without the ground, there was really nothing to refer to; it was all speculation, fantasy, wish- (and dread-) fulfillment. The desire to build fantastic structures in the sand is almost irresistible. Most especially when the psyche senses that the traumatic secret is about to be uncovered.

CHAPTER XVI

New skin for old ceremony: community building & space industrialization

"Why industrialize space? The answer must be essentially economic. There must be important commercial operations which can be done only in space or which can be done better in space."
—William M. Brown & Herman Kahn, "Long-Term Prospects for Developments in Space (A Scenario Approach)"

Most of the preceding material (besides the material about Edgar Mitchell in chapter 15, and barring some minor tweaking) was written back in the spring of 2013. Now it's May Day 2015 and I've spent the previous few weeks going over the old material and getting it into shape for submission to publishers. In those two years, the main thing that's happened (externally speaking) is that I bought a broken down old crack house in a small Canadian town, using money inherited from the sale of my mother's Hampstead apartment after she died in late 2010. It's been exactly a year since I took ownership of the house and the time since has been spent less on writing than on renovating, tearing out old walls and floors, building new ones, dry-walling, and plumbing. It's a large project not just because of the amount of work required but also because, barring some help at the start, my wife and

I have been working on it alone, and neither of us had prior experience of this sort of work.

The building is a commercially zoned residential and was split into two parts when we bought it. We spent the first eight months or so getting the larger, back portion in order, where we planned to live, and moved in about halfway through the renovations process. The front part, the future commercial space, we left for later. Spring came early in 2015, and I went back to work in March. Our plan was to turn the front part of the building into a local community radio station. Becoming part of the community in which I live (as opposed to the virtual realm of the alternate perceptions community) is something I have never attempted. The closer I got to completing the renovations, the more acutely aware I became of how daunting the idea of integration with a community is to me.

One thing that was clear to me even before I bought the property was how the process of renovating an old, dilapidated, literally poison-filled house (in the early days we had to remove countless used drug needles) was a kind of psychic enactment. The crack house stood in for my body: old, worn-out, polluted after decades as a poison container, both passively as a child and more actively as a decadent teen and young adult, then proactively, in my twenties and thirties, as a heaven-storming psychonaut hell-bent on heightened awareness at any cost. Transforming a demolition-condition drug den into a home and a business—in other words, to function on both inner and outer, private and public levels—was a means of embodying the dissociated/fractured psyche. It was the work which my whole life had been leading towards—and until it was accomplished, I couldn't even start to live.

The irony, if irony is the word, is that this was not a work for the intellect but for the instinct, not a task of mind but of body. Here the pen is not mightier than the hammer and my mind is no weapon at all (mostly an encumbrance). Of course, this is precisely what makes it a necessary challenge and opportunity, and the means of my embodiment. It's difficult to say with any certainty how profound a shift in my psyche this renovation process has allowed for, difficult because so many changes have occurred in the years leading up to it (such as marriage and two deaths in my close family). I suspect that the internal changes closely match the external ones, which is the point of an enactment. How do we bring the contents of our unconscious into consciousness to integrate them, when by definition they are beyond our awareness? The answer seems to have to do with placing our attention, paradoxically, on the *outside*, on our immediate circumstances, and fully engaging with whatever process is occurring there—as in a marriage. This allows the unconscious material to emerge into the inner space created, once our attention moves—however subtly—away from our thoughts and onto our senses. Unconscious material enters into consciousness and is integrated, not when we are watching for it or trying to make it happen, but while we are looking the other way. Like Christ, the soul comes like a thief in the night. Provided, at least, that we have created the space for it through *close self-examination* (which signals the unconscious that we are willing?), that we are fully engaged in what we are doing, and that, rather than using it as distraction from inner turmoil, we are allowing it to be an enactment and reflection of that turmoil.

To give a current example (rewriting this chapter a month later), yesterday I found myself inside a small closet area in the front of the house, tearing down drywall. Judging by the hole in the floor and the dark brown marks on the walls, it was once a toilet. I had originally thought I would simply paint or drywall over the surfaces until my wife pointed out the unpalatable truth of the matter, and I realized that, to complete this work in the spirit in which it was started, I would need to be as thorough as possible. Certainly I could just drywall over those shit-stained walls and no one would be the wiser. But *I* would know.

Through the course of the work, I was aware that clearing out the toxic remnants of the house's history was not merely a question of hygiene and esthetics. It was energetic. A few weeks earlier, on May 13, I had a dream that I was in a house and it was full of ghosts. Every door I opened, there was a new apparition. I finally became exasperated and demanded of one of them (a teenage girl) what they were doing there, what they wanted. I was told that they simply wanted to be heard. I then realized (in the dream) that these ghosts had formerly occupied the building, but that the toxicity of the lifestyle there, over the decades, had driven them underground. Now they were returning to reoccupy the space: I had cleared it out sufficiently to make it safe for them to haunt again! This was progress: the returning of those splintered fragments of the psyche, now the body had been sufficiently cleared of toxins to accommodate and integrate them.

Tearing down the drywall in that small space (while listening to Michael Parenti talking about conspiracy and class power) was an unpleasant experience (especially since one of the walls had solid wood behind it). It was an extremely hot day and within less than an hour I was feeling overwhelmed and had to stop. It wasn't so much the physical exertion of it as the *mental* discomfort. Physically, I could have continued for another hour without exhausting myself; mentally I felt like I needed to stop before I got locked into an overly negative frame of mind. While I often compare working on the renovations to a form of meditation, it's certainly not the usual kind of meditation that's designed to bring about internal peace and harmony. It is more like a cathartic ritual in which my inner "Basil Fawlty" (the raging hotel manager played by John Cleese in *Fawlty Towers*) gets to come out and have its day. I curse and rage throughout every job because every job entails a degree of unfathomable, nonnegotiable *resistance* (even painting the front of the house meant dealing with gale force winds that threatened to blow me off my ladder). It is this lack of control over my environment—or rather being in a set of circumstances that forces me to experience it fully— that makes the work therapeutic. It is a form of reality induction. Carry water, chop wood, hammer nail, tear down shit-stained wall; finish the cycle, and then start all over again.

Writing is a way for me to live inside my mind. Renovation and construction work is a way for me to get a little more inside my body. The mind can't contain the psyche or the unconscious, only the body can; it's precisely this that the body was designed for—like a house.

*

"A man's errors are his portals of discovery."

—James Joyce

Was it a coincidence that I returned to *Prisoner of Infinity* and set about completing it at the same time I began work on the commercial/public part of my house? A psyche not only needs a body to live, it also needs a persona (mask) to express through if it is to have an open interface with the outside world. Just as a baby begins to experience himself by seeing his own expression reflected in that of his mother, father, and siblings, so the soul comes to know itself, not only by dwelling inside the body, but by acting and expressing through it in relation to its community or tribe. In many ways, this work is my attempt to set the record straight with the virtual community where I have found temporary residence: that of alternate perceptions and research, whether occult, spiritual, conspiratorial, ufological, or psychological. I have felt compelled—by my own individual journey of transference and conscious reenactments—to challenge that community and find out if it's willing, or able, to sit up and *see* itself, to examine some deeply disturbing possibilities about itself, possibilities which potentially undermine—even invalidate—a large portion of what has been assumed within it.

As mentioned earlier in an endnote, this itself is a form of enactment, pertaining to the circumstances of my childhood in which I grew up inside a Fabian/socialist web of hypocrisy, licentiousness, false appearances, and hidden agendas. This is the other major development that occurred during the interim between 2013 and now. While writing *Seen and Not Seen*, I found out that my own family background overlapped, undeniably and dramatically, with the machinations of the social engineers. My grandfather was a founding Fabian (locally, in Yorkshire). The Fabian Society grew out of the Fellowship of the New Life and back in those days (they are still active) they were open eugenicists. Edward Carpenter—often associated with early pagan movements—was a founding member and was also linked to the "Uranian" movement promoting homosexuality. He is quoted repeatedly by Willis Harman in *Psychic Research*, and by Marilyn Ferguson in *The Aquarian Conspiracy*, and besides his participation with the Fabians, he cofounded the British Society for the Study of Sex Psychology.

Socialism, spirituality, and sexuality (especially pertaining to children) were the three "S's" of Fabianism. Besides being instrumental in the creation of the Labour Party, they were linked to progressive schools with "Wiccan" affiliations, whose partial aim was to help children to develop "natural" sexuality (in the early days nudity was encouraged). As I looked into all this, I was startled to discover that two of these schools were schools which I and my siblings had been sent to. On top of this, my older brother's ties (via the same grandfather) to the notorious Glaswegian gangster Jimmy Boyle put him in the same circles with the Kray brothers, and hence with the aforementioned (in Part I) Jimmy Savile and the child abuse "parties" of the 1960s and onward. (And, of course, via The Process Church, to Whitley Strieber!) Closer to the mainstream of things, the now infamous Paedophile Information Exchange (P.I.E.), founded in the 1970s, was linked to the Labour Party and the National Council for Civil Liberties, both of which my paternal grandparents, my father, and all my uncles and aunts on that side, would have participated in to one degree or another (even if only by giving donations). The author J. B. Priestley was a friend of my grandfather and his apartment hosted the Albany Trust in its early years; the Albany Trust also gave birth to P.I.E. Jacob Bronowski (most famous for his *Ascent of Man* TV series) was also one of my grandfather's pals, and Bronowski attended parties at the house where Aleister Crowley spent his final years (Netherwood). Another attendee was Julian Bream, the virtuoso guitarist; Bream was an adolescent boy at the time and played guitar for the adults. Bream's son, Benjamin, went to the aforementioned alternate school which I attended, and was my sister's first lover. And so on.

On the larger stage of world politics, the Jimmy Savile scandal has led, in the years since it first broke in 2012, to a steady and so far unchecked wave of revelations around systematized abuse in Britain implicating high-level politicians, royalty, and celebrities, as well as intelligence groups and police, involved in the massive cover-up that allowed it to continue. Systematized (and, at least some of the time, *ritualized*) sexual interference with children is now seen to be part of the fabric of British society. It is also inseparably intertwined with the world I grew up in, not just generally but locally and specifically, because my own family on my father's side can be directly linked to many of the identified perpetrators or enablers. My aunt's husband, Baron Haskins, was Tony Blair's right-hand man and was also in charge of the Task Force created for screening employees in child care homes. In 2002 he was appointed as the nonexecutive director of Yorkshire Television (Parkin, 2002), the channel which produced the never-aired, now infamous *Conspiracy of Silence* documentary about high-level organized child sexual abuse and the Franklin Scandal, in 1994 (*Spotlight on Abuse*, 2002). Northern Dairies, my grandfather's and father's company, helped fund Savile's charity walk in 1971 (my sister even had his autograph). My grandfather's associates included two directors of the Bank of England, and a future chairman of the Bilderberg meetings; and so on. The net result of these discoveries was that whatever I once believed about my past and the environment I grew up in was violently turned upside down and inside out, just as rapidly and irrevocably (though considerably more shockingly) as my ideas about Whitley Strieber and the UFO subculture had been.

This book began as one thing; it is ending as something else. In the act of authoring, the author has been transformed. Where once I was blind, now I have begun to see the thing that caused me—that made it necessary—to become blind.

Like the house, the present work is now complete (in its major structural work at least, and not counting the garden). But I have saved perhaps the most challenging and potentially triggering work until last. And like the house (which I've lived comfortably inside, with my wife and cat, for more than a year) the book was *kind of* complete, in a way, with the preceding chapter about my dream, my wife, and my cat. I *could* have ended it there, and for a while I fully intended to. Only, it didn't *feel* complete. The material had been polished and improved since 2013, but very little new had been added. For it to be complete meant bringing it into the present, "topping it up" with psychic energy, with whatever elements from my unconscious were, are, currently emerging into awareness—or better yet, those elements that can *only* come into awareness if I complete the book right. Like my house, this book needs to be a proper match for my level of embodiment; and even, to whatever extent, the means *of* it (this phase at least).

It is time for one more pan for gold, one more look at the bedrock, and for another (last?) taking stock of the shape of the ground, and of my current position on it.

*

> "Many scholars have argued that the ideas and literary productions of the astrofuturists 'prepared the American public for the conquest of space with elaborate visions of promise and fear' and helped shape the nation's cultural and political responses."
> —Emily S. Rosenberg, "Far Out: The Space Age in American Culture"

As if to ensure that this work mirror the illumineers' goal of infinite expansion, my wife (whose research for Part I was the primary cause for its growth) recently came across a book in the secondhand bookstore where she works, called *The Next Two Hundred Years*, by Herman Kahn, published in 1976. The book is a NASA-commissioned report on the future and based around a methodology known as "scenario planning." A little-known method of government think tanks for implementing desired futures, scenario planning is really just fiction writing, specifically *sci-fi writing*. It describes future scenarios as if they were already established, or even as if part of the past (i.e., from a more distant future, looking back … in a galaxy far, far away). The book is mostly about the socioeconomic future of human society, with only a few references to space colonization.

Soon after coming across this book, however, my wife discovered an unclassified document online called "Long-Term Prospects For Developments In Space (A Scenario Approach)," by William M. Brown & Herman Kahn. The document describes a complex, multilevel program of social engineering that includes the use of mass media outlets to sell to the public the idea of space industrialization. From the introduction:

> The basic purpose of this report is to formulate some useful and interesting images of the long-term future of space, and to encourage and facilitate the use of such images and scenarios by NASA in its studies, planning, and public information programs. We realize that NASA already makes use of scenarios in its planning functions, but the deliberate formulation "of long-term scenarios and 'images of the future'" *has usually been left to outside freelance writers.* We believe it is quite useful, perhaps important, for NASA to intervene in this process and also to facilitate it. Some of the current relatively low interest in NASA programs undoubtedly is due to the public's failure to understand how exciting space development can be in the medium term (1985–2000) as well as in the centuries beyond this one. Of course, the extraordinarily extensive science fiction and other popular literature have already introduced a fairly broad public in this country and abroad to some concepts about space. This literature and its media interpretation however tend to be relatively undisciplined, imaginative (in both a good and bad sense) and, with a few important and spectacular exceptions, relatively unrelated to serious socio-political issues .... Long-term scenarios about space development, and, even more important, shared images of the future of space, can contribute to a sense of community, of institutional meaning and purpose, of high morale, and even—to use somewhat extravagant terms—of manifest destiny or of "religious" mission ... . Such images can have a great impact on political issues—both internal and external. (1977, pp. 1–2, emphasis added)

The report anticipates "many valuable spinoffs from the technological developments, as well as new services to society." National pride in such accomplishments, it suggests, probably accounts for much of the current wave of interest in science fiction that in the U.S. is being expressed through books, movies, and television. A growing national interest and pride in space accomplishments will be required if the public funding of these activities is to increase over time in real terms. Prolonged national enthusiasm appears to be a prerequisite for an optimistic outcome .... Through television [public citizens] were able to become "sidewalk superintendents" of these milestone events and were thereby easily able to bridge a gap which otherwise would have required a quantum jump in imagination .... *Thus, the psychological stage was set for a flurry of new interest in the development of Space Industrialization* (SI). (pp. 97, 121, emphasis added)

The report discusses an imaginary documentary about a 1989 commercial space tour, a "three-day voyage to near-earth orbit which included a rendezvous with the recently completed international Space Station," where the tourists were accommodated. The imaginary passengers included the NASA director, the governor of Texas, senators, congressmen, a French ambassador and other VIPs, and two movie stars apparently modeled on Marlon Brando and Elizabeth Taylor, "the best-known movie actor and actress in the U.S." (hardly the case in 1989, but anyway), whose "enthusiasm ... was vividly conveyed by their spontaneous behavior during the voyage." Subsequent "'orchestrated' television appearances" by the stars "further stimulated public interest in space projects, especially space tours." This single event, the report imagines, transformed the potential of space exploration away from its prior "fictional aspects" for the average citizen and allowed it to be perceived as "a growing set of real activities with great commercial promise." "Future Space Developments" then became "a subject taught in schools around the world." The goal of all this media-directed perception management was for outer space to become "a real world which anyone might experience ... for those who had a sufficiently strong desire, the possibility now existed to actually go up there" (pp. 124–125).

While movie stars—as the recognized new royalty—were indispensable for propagating the mass appeal and practicality of the new "civil religion," astronauts were fast becoming the "high priests":

In each nation the natural heroes of those interested in the movement into space were the astronauts .... A self-selection process evolved that effectively weeded out any aspiring astronaut who was less than completely dedicated to space projects. Of course, the competition became fierce and remained so for over 50 years as the astronaut profession became the one most desired in technologically advanced societies. The successful competitors became a new elite group with a commitment to their profession that evolved into a new kind of "religion"; one in which they were viewed as the "high priests"—yet no formal rituals or dogmas were practiced or needed. (p. 128)

The dawning of the Age of Aquarius was also known as "space culture." Like popular science fiction, the report somewhat naïvely assures us that the space culture was not planned—"*it just happened*"!

[A]s it grew it gradually transcended the former boundaries or "bonds" of chauvinistic nationalism. This attitude was not always understood by those outside the "space community" even though it became a prominent theme in the communications media. The direct physical experiences of transcending the surface of the earth had created a psychological counterpoint which led to a transcendence of the earth-centered national traditions and cultures. The sociological development became one of the major factors which led to phenomenal changes in the 21st century and beyond. (pp. 128–129)

*

"Either there is a massive conspiracy to deceive by a near-army of diverse, unrelated individuals, including sophisticated scientists, or the events I have observed are true phenomena of nature."

—Edgar Mitchell, *Psychic Research: Challenge to Science*

There is something incomprehensible about the possibility which this present work is exploring. This is especially the case for those of us involved in the field of alternate research. What makes it partially incomprehensible, I think, is that my interpretation of the data belongs to—or rather, is suggestive of—a radically different worldview than the "paradigm" we are used to, a paradigm which (this present work argues) has been engineered for us to perceive within and through. I don't think that any given writer or spokesperson within this community is necessarily practicing conscious deception in some Machiavellian way. In some cases this may be the case (though even then, probably with the best of intentions!). But generally, I think what is being mapped here is both subtler and far deeper.

For the record, I placed the word "paradigm" in quotes because, ironically, the word even belongs to the "paradigm" I am talking about and is part of its internal cohesion. So what is a paradigm (according to this paradigm)?

As a part of the culture, the paradigm is communicated nonverbally and absorbed unconsciously and largely by example. Its role is primarily an invisible one; the vision of reality on which it is based is seldom reexamined, and the implicit premises it contains are generally unchallenged. By its very nature it is not easily identified, nor can it be concisely delineated. It is like "common sense"—no one can define it but everyone responds to it. (Harman, 1974, p. 642)

One of the ways that a paradigm can be "communicated nonverbally" is via an appliance of the principles of mimesis or social contagion, or simply put, by setting trends. To do so requires the creation and strategical placement of cultural leaders and artifacts, whether text, image, or sound-based (or all three), anything in short that influences people's perceptions and subtly inspires in them behaviors. Our current "paradigm" is that of the independent mind-ego-self that possesses agency; within that context, what I'm arguing with the present work—or hinting at, at least—can only be interpreted in a couple of ways. Either any given public spokesperson (Strieber, Jeffrey Kripal, or Edgar Mitchell) is an independent agent sharing their discoveries, theories, and beliefs about existence; or they are part of a conspiracy to spread false models of reality in order to bring about specific, pre-formulated social goals. This binary model does allow for some gradations between the extremes, some nuance—such as the idea of the unwitting "shill"—but it is still too black and white to really match the evidence, which is as varied and as nuanced as the many individuals involved.

This isn't to say there is no shadowy agenda at work, or that individuals aren't being actively recruited by it. I have no doubt this is the case and always has been. The nature of humans is to group together and conspire for their own shared advantage—often if not always under the pretense of "the collective good"—and there is plenty of evidence that such recruitment goes on all the time. The sci-fi writer Philip K. Dick, for example, wrote a letter to the FBI in 1972 about being contacted by an unidentified official and asked to encode information in his novels:

> Several months ago I was approached by an individual who I have reason to believe belonged to a covert organization involved in politics, illegal weapons, etc., who put great pressure on me to place coded information in future novels "to be read by the right people here and there," as he phrased it. I refused to do this. The reason why I am contacting you about this now is that it now appears that other science fiction writers may have been so approached by other members of this obviously Anti-American organization and may have yielded to the threats and deceitful statements such as were used on me. Therefore I would like to give you any and all information and help I can regarding this, and I ask that your nearest office contact me as soon as possible. I stress the urgency of this because within the last three days I have come across a well-distributed science fiction novel which contains in essence the vital material which this individual confronted me with as the basis for encoding. That novel is CAMP CONCENTRATION by Thomas Disch, which was published by Doubleday & Co. (Dick, 1994, p. 64)

(Thomas Disch attributed this to Dick's drug abuse and increasingly paranoid delusions in the early 1970s. Considering that Dick had his life-changing VALIS experience two years later, in 1974, this may be an oversimplification. Disch, the observant reader may recall, has already appeared in this narrative for his partway insightful, partway malicious critique of Whitley Strieber.)

In Roger Lewis's biography, Anthony Burgess claimed something similar to Dick. Burgess "had been a low-grade collector of intelligence data (or ground observer) in the Far East" for the British government and that, on his return to England, he found himself embroiled in a world of spy scandals (including the other famous Burgess, Guy) and double agents (Lewis, 2002, p. 283). Lewis's source (a British secret service man) informs him that Burgess "was not wholly responsible for *A Clockwork Orange* [and that] it was a work of collaboration with the British secret services." According to the same source, Burgess's collaborator on the book was former CIA officer and languages expert, Howard Roman.

> The idea was that he'd lift the corner of the carpet and put into his novel classified material about the (then) new-fangled conditioning experiments and aversion therapies being devised to reform crim-inals—experiments which had wider implications for the concept of social engineering. [The book is about] the mind-control experi-mentation conducted by Dr. Ewen Cameron at the Allen Memo-rial Institute in Montreal, between 1957 and 1963, and the Remote Neural Monitoring facility that operated out of Fort George Meade. The CIA were funding controversial research programs into elec-tronic brain stimulation. They induced exhaustion and nightmares in patients; they put hoods or cones over people's heads to broad-cast voices directly into their brains; they irradiated the auditory cortex or inner ear. When patients had their own speech played back to them, incessantly, they went insane. There was a misuse of civilians in these covert operations, and intelligence on these devices remains classified. (2002, pp. 283, 285)

I refer the reader back to the statement from the NASA document about how "the deliberate formulation of long-term scenarios and 'images of the future' has usually been left to outside freelance writers." Of how many well-known authors besides Burgess might this be true? Presum-ably, we are only likely to hear from the ones who refused the offer (which isn't to imply that those who do talk about it necessarily refused, since they could also be lying). And then there is the possibility of count-less other writers being recruited *without* their being aware of it.

*

> "I trust it is apparent that those of us involved with noetic, par-ticularly psychic research, do not view our work as another fad to be recorded in the history of 'pop' culture."
> —Edgar Mitchell, *Psychic Research*

If an agency were attempting to enlist authors to propagate certain ideas and/or disseminate coded information (either to specific individ-uals or the general public, or both), the inconvenience of being turned down, and worse, the possibility of an author speaking out about what happened, is obvious. Besides the possibilities opened up by the various methods of mind control, psychic fragmentation, alter-creation, and amnesia-induction (covered in Part I), there is another longer-term approach that would be even more fail-safe.

Admittedly, this process would also require enough conscious recruits to set the psychic machinery (Harman's "subtle technology"?) in motion, seeding memes so that entire generations of human beings could be conditioned, from infancy on, with certain ideas, images, beliefs, and narratives. Those who went on to become writers (especially sci-fi writers, who seem to be the richest resource for social engineering) would unconsciously reproduce, while developing, those conditioned beliefs, thereby creating new narratives. The public disseminators who best "took" the conditioning—who most faithfully reproduced the desired meanings—would be recognized by the same intelligence bodies (working in and through the mass media industry), to be promoted, supported, and endorsed—in a word, recruited. In most cases, these writers (and other artists, especially filmmakers and musicians) need never know how they and their work had been coopted. The biggest clue would be the one they would be least likely to question: their worldly success. And since success casts a spell of its own (once attained, the need for more—or simply to hold onto what one has—generally increases), at a certain point the artist in question might attain a sufficient degree of "congruence" (sympathy) with the hidden program to be inducted into the inner ranks.

In 1974 (the year of *Changing Images of Man* and Mitchell's *Psychic Exploration*), Dick had his famous VALIS pink-beam vision, after which he believed he had been contacted by some unknown form of extraterrestrial intelligence. Dick admitted he didn't know whether the intervention was divine or technological, or both. In fact, he never made up his mind about it (not even after a million pages of his *Exegesis*, which was edited by my *Seen and Not Seen* "sponsor" Jonathan Lethem, with commentary from Jeffrey Kripal and Erik Davis; the latter I attended a Mexican conference with in 2012). Perhaps Dick was targeted by the illumineers as a potential new L. Ron Hubbard-style sci-fi prophet and given his conversion experience to see how he reacted? If so, he failed the test, as Dick's brief attempt to become the prophet of a new paradigm (a speech he gave in France) was garbled and incomprehensible to most (to his infinite credit). It was too wild, shapeless, and above all *personal*, and was received with bemusement and ridicule. Dick was a writer in the deepest sense, interested less in exploring possible futures, or even human potential, than he was in fathoming the mystery of his own psyche, and/or disappearing *into* it. The individuatory process of self-exploration and examination invariably goes against the grain of social conditioning, making a potential recruit largely useless, unmanageable, suspicious, shifty, inconstant, and unreliable.

A more effective case of a writer being "inspired" through technological intervention might be Jack Sarfatti, who received a call from a future computer intelligence dictating his life mission to him—and who has been following it ever since. Also David Icke's life-altering ayahuasca experience might qualify here.

Yet for all the meme-seeding and the relentless spreading of intergalactic psi narratives, it's curious to note that, forty years later, psi-phenomena are not *actually* any more accepted within the orthodox mainstream of the intelligentsia/academia than they were in 1974. (As evidenced by the latest attempt to validate the paradigm, Strieber and Kripal's *The Super Natural*.) Despite all of the incontrovertible evidence, and all the attention it has received from high-profile figures from authors to astronauts, the paranormal is still roundly scorned by a certain class of "intelligent" people. On the other hand, with the New Age industry, psychic phenomena are certainly more popular with the general public *as a form of nonfictional entertainment*. In other words, the fruit of all these efforts by Mitchell, Harman, Puthoff, Geller, Strieber, Mack, Kripal, et al., would appear to be, not the creation of a new paradigm, but the incorporation of these "radical" ideas *into the prevailing paradigm*, and their resultant commodification. Nor, in my opinion, has this led to any sort of genuine transformation of the old paradigm, but rather to *injecting novelty*—and more forms of "diffuse hope"—into it. New wine into old bottles.

The same can—must—be said of UFOs, and even, in 2016, of "conspiracy theory." Give it a few more years, and social engineering will doubtless be found on the infotainment menu of pop culture. Realities that become undeniable have to be incorporated into the same worldview whose dominion is being undermined by them, because this may be the only way to render them ineffective. Besides this, they are invaluable means to spice up the tired old narratives and make them *appear* to be genuinely transforming, when all that is changing, finally, is an image.

If this is the aim of allowing "pioneering" research of "undiscovered country," it makes little to no difference how well intentioned the researchers may be. As with the early Christian missionaries, the outcome is the same, because it is the outcome that was planned from the start. The agenda was never meant to be spiritual.

CHAPTER XVII

Skywalkers and Starkillers: the open conspiracy

"This scheme to thrust forward and establish a human control over the destinies of life, and liberate it from its present dangers, uncertainties, and miseries, is offered here as an altogether practicable one, subject only to one qualification—that sufficient men and women will be willing to serve it. That there is no foretelling. It is clear that the whole growth is dependent upon the appearance of those primary groups, sustaining and spreading its fundamental ideas. Those ideas have to become the mental substratum of constructive effort. If those ideas can find sufficient vigorous, able, and devoted people for their establishment, the rest will follow."
—H. G. Wells, *The Open Conspiracy/What Are We to Do with Our Lives?*[1]

In the 1970s, the little-known researcher Alvin Lawson clearly mapped the parallels between a typical alien abduction experience and a modern hospital birth: a naked, paralyzed human lying on a table, surrounded by "masked" entities and poked with strange instruments. It was also Lawson's research that demonstrated how individuals taken at random, with no memory of being abducted, were able to recreate an abduction

211

experience under hypnosis, one that closely matched the accounts of people who believed they were abductees. The suggestion of this body of evidence was that the alien abduction "experience" was somehow universal—like birth—and/or archetypal.

A few days after I returned to this material in the hope of finally completing the work, and doubtless related, I had a dreaming experience in which I was lying in a bed and unable to move. All around me, I could sense figures moving. I could only see their legs out of the corners of my eyes. I felt intense fear, but I was aware that what I was experiencing was only a tiny fraction of the terror that would assail me, if I let myself become fully conscious of what was happening. The thought occurred to me that if, as in Strieber's chilling tales, I was to realize the beings around me were *not even human*, it would be more terrifying than I could bear. It was as if I was allowing myself only as much "body terror" as I could comfortably endure without losing my mind. At the time, in the dream state, I guessed that what I was experiencing was maybe 5 percent of the full body memory.

Later, upon waking, it occurred to me that one likely interpretation of the dream was that I was, through an unconscious reenactment process, reliving my birth, or immediately post-birth, experience and finding out just how much terror was trapped in my body as a memory-affect of that primal event. Alien abductions, then, as a psychic experience at least, may be a way for an individual psyche to reexperience and release (and integrate) that terror and so clear up a space within the body for the psyche to land in. Conversely, perhaps the experience of the psyche landing in the body—which happens incrementally, not all at once—inevitably causes a reactivation of the same terror which first drove it away, into the heavenly realms of dissociation?

A few days later, I picked up Louis Proud's *Dark Intrusions* and reread the descriptions of my own sleep paralysis experience which I had given him for his book. I reproduce them in part below, with emphasis added.

> My experiences of sleep paralysis have almost always entailed the irrefutable certainty of a non-human presence in the room ....
> My bodily reaction to the presence was invariably one of terror and, as such, the last thing I intended to do was try and see the being. It was quite overwhelming enough merely to experience its energy field as a form of "psychic sensation." ... I was aware of a

consciousness outside of my own, immeasurably more powerful, and focused on me in such a way that it was akin to a kind of psychic assault or "ambush." The being or presence was not hostile; far from it. It seemed to be interested in me not in any predatory manner but rather almost in a [proprietorial] way, *almost as with the attention of a lover, or perhaps a loving but ruthless parent?*

As I recall I had a series of very similar experiences—I might say "visitations"—during a period of a couple of years when I was in my late 20s. Since I was quite deeply influenced by Strieber's *Communion* at that time, I tended to see my experiences in the light of Strieber's own accounts, and this may have influenced or even distorted my impressions somewhat. I definitely had a sense that the being—if such it was—was "ancient," wise, and extremely powerful, and essentially benevolent. On at least a couple of occasions, I experienced it as female (I knew nothing of the Old Hag syndrome back then). And although it sounds rather fanciful now, I had a sense more than once that it, she, was "my own soul," or as close as made no difference. Anima visitation?

There was nothing subjective or vague about the experience; at the time there was no more doubt in my mind that something very real was present than there would be if a burglar had come through the window, wielding a crowbar .... And yet, it was above all a bodily sensation that alerted me—what Strieber called "body terror." Rather than an awareness of the presence causing the terror, however, *it was as if my own terror informed me as to the being's presence.* Somehow, my body knew instantly that some unknown form of energy was present, and it reacted with a kind of animal terror. My mind, on the other hand, observed this physiological response with a measure of detachment and, of course, of fascination. I felt something like love emanating from the being, and even felt something similar in myself responding to that love. But there was a seemingly unbridgeable abyss between us—that of our individual physical or energetic configurations. We were quite literally worlds apart.

Another, less positive form of sleep paralysis visitation is as follows:

I suffered a recurring dream over the years.

There was something on my back, clinging to me. I could feel it like an electrical charge, like something actually drilling into the back of my neck. I could hear a strange voice or voices, and knew that some "being" was working on me. In order to stop it, I shrugged my shoulders physically, once, twice, a third time, until my consciousness returned to my body and I woke. I had the feeling the being was still there, however, waiting for a second chance to "leech" me.

It was like a child suckling, a small but ferocious creature. Whatever it was, it was clinging to me with desperate persistence, chewing at my neck, drinking my energy like a vampire. At the time, it felt like a physical thing. If I was in "the astral" at the time, then I suppose it was as solid as I was. Even at the time, however, I could hardly believe what I was feeling. A horrible, nightmarish parasite entity feeding off me, relentlessly and without mercy, maybe even without choice? It was like a part of me. It had been attracted by my energy, we were like two magnets. The effect was of repulsion more than terror. This demon was something utterly and undeniably real. The source of all my sickness was here. (Proud, 2009, pp. 56–58)

What didn't occur to me until rereading this material in 2015 is that the two different experiences are in fact diametrical opposites, and that potentially they make up a whole. The anima-visitation experience represents the "overman," superego, or, in Ferenczi's model, the higher aspect of "Orpha" (organizing life principle); the parasite-entity corresponds with the traumatized child self or lower aspect. Put differently, the ancient anima-being would correspond with the greater portion of the psyche which was unable to integrate with ("land in") the body and which remained disembodied, floating above it like some sort of guardian angel. The parasite would be that fragment which split off due to the trauma and became equally "autonomous" but which, being only a fragment, was dependent on the life force of the body to exist, hence became a kind of "succubae," or suckling infant. The body's experience would correspond with that of the conscious ego self, an experience both of being leeched off and oppressed by the trauma it suffered, and nurtured and rescued *from* that experience by the dissociated psyche that *never had to experience the trauma.*

At the same time, the manner in which that "higher" aspect of the psyche came visiting—despite my own self-assurances—was very much as a predator in the night—"with the attention of a lover"—suggesting that it/I may have been reenacting some sort of sexual interference (i.e., the original cause of the splitting trauma), one which I had no choice at the time but to reinterpret as the presence of "a loving but ruthless parent"?

*

> "But the postindustrial society will differ from that of Athens in important respects. Its slaves will be cybernetic, and the Faustian powers of its technology will introduce a new level of responsibility. It will have to be a learning-and-planning society. Helping to choose the future will be a primary responsibility of its citizens ... Science, under the new transcendentalism, will be clearly understood to be a moral inquiry ... it cannot be, as past science has tended to be, value-empty .... In this respect it will resemble the humanities and religion ... Finally, the new science will become also a sort of 'civil religion.'"
> —Willis Harman, *Psychic Research: Challenge to Science*

In Part II, I have been looking at two fields of inquiry: psychic research and space colonization, inner and outer space. The intersection between the two fields is the alien visitor, when "space" comes to *us*—like a thief (or rapist) in the night—and *invades our interiority*. Abductees experience an increased interest in/affinity for the stars—they receive their "passport to the cosmos," as John Mack put it. There is also a corresponding awareness of their own interior, "spiritual nature," and/or psychic potential (since in the West these two ideas are fatally conflated).

According to Edgar Mitchell, the aim of psychic research is less to tap into our psi potential than to prove to ourselves, beyond reasonable doubt, that our mechanistic, Newtonian models of reality are fundamentally flawed and outdated, to overturn the old paradigm and usher in "higher consciousness in the race" (1974, p. 35). Space exploration, on the other hand—which astronaut Mitchell promoted, via his participation in the Overview Institute and the selling of the Overview Effect—has a similarly twinned potential. First, obviously, it is the theoretical means for the human race to continue expanding indefinitely despite having exhausted the planet's resources (including living space or *Lebensraum*, and leaving aside the question of whether space travel is actually feasible). It offers hope for the future—that is, for the continuation of our current way of life in the West—a new undiscovered country to explore where somehow, miraculously, life promises to be better. (In Alcoholics Anonymous, this is called "the geographical cure.")

Second, according to Mitchell, Herman Kahn, Joseph Campbell, and others, the mere fact of leaving the Earth and entering space will bring about cosmic consciousness: " ... a state in which there is constant awareness of unity with the universe pervading all aspects of one's life. Every activity, every relationship, every thought is guided by the knowledge of oneness" (Mitchell, 1974, p. 35). Mitchell doesn't beat about the bush here; he claims this amounts to *direct knowledge of God*. Space, in Mitchell's view, is a Kubrickian-Clarkian Star Gate to the next evolutionary state of humankind. (This being the same Arthur C. Clarke who made no bones about his preference for young boys; see Popham, 1998.[2])

While I have yet to encounter any overt mention of it, there may even be the belief among these illumineering futurologists that life in space *will facilitate an activation of our psi potential*. In 1977, NASA imaginatively speculated that

> ... human beings born in the space environment were to be physically and emotionally more healthy, that their natural longevity is now expected to increase by about 30 years, and that their mental capability, on average, appears to be substantially greater as well. An improved human being, substantially improved, emerged as a result of the efforts of space scientists and from the natural benefits obtainable in the benign space environment. (Brown & Kahn, 1977, pp. 130–131)

The promise is as predictable as it is preposterous. We can become space-faring techno gods. Skywalkers and Starkillers.

*

> "[A]n accepted image of the future can give rise to expectations that could materialize into real space projects."
> —William Brown and Herman Kahn, "Long-Term Prospects For Developments In Space"

At this point, the line between the covert, classified plans of world governments, military, intelligence, and scientific think-tanks and what we think of— naïvely —as popular forms of entertainment effectively vanishes. Scenario planning is not only a passive thought experiment for exploring ideas; it is an effective way to bring those ideas—in the form of fantasy narratives—to the general population, thereby creating the desired level of familiarity, expectancy, and sympathy for these scenarios to metastasize into future history. As Emily S. Rosenberg writes, "A clear synergy developed between the space program and the highly competitive world of image-based media. NASA projected itself to be an agency involved in science and technology, but it proved also to be skilled at image-making and public relations."[3]

In 1977 (the year of Brown and Kahn's NASA report), *Star Wars* came out and was an "unexpected" hit. (*Close Encounters* was also released, though its success probably wasn't a surprise to anyone.) *Star Wars* neatly combined the subject of psychic potential ("the force") with that of space colonization (and extraterrestrials). It even sets its narrative in the past, following the format of scenario planning.

From the opening scrawl to the Nazi-rally-style finale, *Star Wars* was a consciously designed modern myth. It was made by a young filmmaker whose previous films were a dark, dystopian sci-fi vision (*THX-1138*) and a nostalgic paean to 1950s America (*American Graffiti*). The unprecedented success of *Star Wars* is widely recognized among film historians today as having changed the course of the American film industry. By appealing to the regressive fantasies of adult audiences (who grew up, like Lucas, with Flash Gordon and Buck Rogers sci-fi fantasy of the 1950s) and helping to shape the then-current fantasies of youth, it ushered in the age of the blockbuster. What is so far unacknowledged is how—as part of a much larger cultural agenda—it may have changed the course of world history by ingeniously exploiting the deeper yearnings of an entire generation of future filmmakers, scientists, computer programmers, et al., to go beyond the limits of their mundane lives and find transcendental purpose in the sky (and the force).[4]

To give a well-known example, Ronald Reagan's satellite missile defense program, the Strategic Defense Initiative, proposed in 1983, quickly came to be known as "Star Wars."[5] As Peter Kramer writes in "Ronald Reagan and Star Wars":

> Following its release in May 1977, the original *Star Wars* movie had quickly become the highest grossing film of all time at the American box office. The film was accompanied by an unprecedented

merchandising craze which would eventually earn billions of dollars, while its sequel *The Empire Strikes Back*, released in May 1980, became the second highest grossing film of all time. This was followed by the successful launch of the *Star Wars* video in May 1982 and the film's first appearance on pay-TV in February 1983, which whetted public appetite for the forthcoming release of the second sequel, *Return of the Jedi* in May 1983. When Reagan addressed the nation on March 23rd, 1983, therefore, "Star Wars" was on everybody's mind. (Kramer, 1999)

Kramer points out that the film seemed to have been on Reagan's mind also, referring to "one of his most notorious speeches" (to the annual convention of the National Association of Evangelicals on March 8, 1983), in which Reagan characterized communism as a totalitarian ideology in which "'morality is entirely subordinate to the interests of class war,' leaving no place for God or religion." Reagan called the Soviet Union "the focus of evil in the modern world" and urged his audience not to ignore "the aggressive impulses of an evil empire" or forget that this was "a struggle between right and wrong and good and evil." "[W]hile military strength is important," Reagan railed, "the real crisis we face today is a spiritual one; at root, it is a test of moral will and faith" (Kramer, 1999). It's worth remembering here that Lucas's original name for his hero was Luke *Starkiller*.

Kramer argues persuasively that, since the concept of an "evil empire" had already been popularized by the *Star Wars* films, this link encouraged both press and the public "to see Reagan's future speeches through the prism of *Star Wars*." He points out how, two weeks after this speech, people tried to make sense of the announcement of a missile defense program by referring to the movie. "Reagan even slipped an oblique reference to the film into his address [when] he referred to 'a new hope for our children in the twenty-first century,'" thereby naming the subtitle of the first film (added in 1981): *A New Hope*.

To add still further layers of quantum irony and confusion to the mix, Kramer (via Michael Rogin's psycho-biography *Ronald Reagan, the Movie*) traces Reagan's vision of a space-based missile defense program back to a 1940 Warner Brothers movie! In *Murder in the Air* (Killers in the Sky?), Reagan plays a Secret Service agent who prevents a foreign spy from stealing the plans for a powerful new defense weapon. As one of the film's characters has it, this weapon will "make America invincible in war and therefore be the greatest force for peace ever invented." Rogin's thesis, apparently, is that the future president was engineered in and by *1940s Hollywood*, until—according to Kramer—Reagan's "identity and his conception of reality had been shaped by Hollywood films to such an extent that he was unable to step outside the fictions he had once inhabited." Kramer adds that, "In sharp contrast to this psychological critique, military historian Donald Baucom's exhaustive study *The Origins of SDI* shows that, far from being a Hollywood fantasy, Reagan's vision of missile defense was in line with an important strand in US strategic thinking" (Kramer, 1999).

But is the contrast as sharp or final as Kramer imagines? To add one more bizarre overlap between movie fantasy and realpolitik, in *How Star Wars Conquered the Universe*, Chris Taylor notes how *Star Wars* composer John Williams "has often said he owes a debt to the movie composers of the 1930s and 1940s; specifically, the *Star Wars* main theme shares its opening notes with the theme from *King's Row*, the 1942 drama that launched Ronald Reagan's acting career" (Taylor, 2014, p. 168). While it may seem far-fetched to imagine that such a correlation was conscious and strategic, isn't it also a bit of a stretch at this point to dismiss it as entirely coincidental? At the very least, is it unreasonable to suppose that two lines of research and implantation occurring in the 1940s—pertaining to the creation of a future president and the development of US strategic thinking—were being conducted in tandem by the same parties? Kramer concludes:

> While opponents of missile defense programs had originally introduced the "Star Wars" label in the early 1980s for the purpose of ridicule, by the mid-1980s it was generally acknowledged that the association of SDI with *Star Wars* worked in its favor. Reagan himself disliked the emphasis on large-scale war that the film reference brought to his initiative, yet he also acknowledged the compatibility of the film's spirituality and moral vision with his own worldview. In comments made in March 1985, he first rejected the "Star Wars" label by saying that SDI "isn't about war. It is about peace." But then he added: "If you will pardon my stealing a film line—the force is with us." (Kramer, 1999)

Star Wars creator George Lucas is generally painted as a radical visionary who intended his film to send a subversive warning about the encroaching totalitarianism of US politics. (In the 2000s, as the billion-aire emperor of a massive *Star Wars* industrial complex, Lucas even pro-fessed to be on the side of the Occupy Movement!) Yet his professed primary goal of the film was entirely in line with the US's "foreign policy." In 1977 he told *Rolling Stone*:

> I'm hoping that if the film accomplishes anything, it takes some ten-year-old kid and turns him on so much to outer space and the possibilities of romance and adventure ... infusing them into serious exploration of outer space and convincing them that it's important. Not for any rational reasons, but a totally irrational and romantic reason. I would feel very good if someday they colonize Mars when I am 93 years old, and the leader of the first colony says, "I really did it because I was hoping there would be a Wookie up here." (Taylor, 2014, p. 399)

In 1981, Lucas stated it in even more bald terms when he described *Star Wars* as: " ... a fairy tale in space guise. The reason it's in a space guise is that I like the space program, and I'm very keen on having people accept the space program" (ibid.).

Chris Taylor adds an ironic coda to this about how "NASA's admin-istrator suggested the agency plans to send humans to Mars in 2037—which, coincidentally, is the year Lucas will turn ninety-three" (ibid., p. 400). He then quotes Bobak Ferdowski, flight director at the Jet Pro-pulsion Laboratory, saying how his love of space was inspired by *Star Trek*. Without leaping down a synchromystic rabbit hole, it's impos-sible *not* to think of Jack Parsons at this point, whose work at the Jet Propulsion Lab was so important to the space program that a crater on the Moon was named after him. Parsons was a close associate of L. Ron Hubbard, and both were briefly discipled to Aleister Crowley, whose Thelemic transmission is known as the "93 current." Say what? Someone (besides myself) seems to have been invoking some shad-owy entities here, though at what level of awareness, or to what end, is anyone's guess.

Returning to the more solid ground of Industrial Light & Magic Reaganomics: if, as the evidence suggests, none of this is coinciden-tal but is by careful design, then the entire *Star Wars* phenomenon—which continues to fire people's most irrational, romantic responses to this day—is very different from what millions of impassioned devotees have hitherto dreamed of, even in their wildest fantasies. Such innocence may not only be a luxury: It may also be a commodity. The soul-deep mythic yearning of entire generations, tapped into by the use of images and carefully designed narratives, transmuted into a power source to be harnessed and directed into specific goals of progress, all in service of The Empire.

"May the force be with you"? De-scramble the Hollywood-speak (remove the velvety glove), and what does that leave but the steely battle cry of Empire, Might is Right?

*

> "We conceive of the Open Conspiracy as consisting of a great multitude and variety of overlapping groups, but now all organized for collective political, social, and educational as well as propagandist action. They will recognize each other much more clearly than they did at first, and they will have acquired a common name .... The character of the Open Conspiracy will now be plainly displayed. It will have become a great world movement as wide-spread and evident as socialism or communism. It will have taken the place of these movements very largely. It will be more than they were, it will be frankly a world religion. This large, loose assimilatory mass of movements, groups, and societies will be definitely and obviously attempting to swallow up the entire population of the world and become the new human community."
>
> —H. G. Wells, *The Open Conspiracy / What Are We to Do with Our Lives?*

What cannot be allowed into consciousness must go into the body. What enters in and lives in the body as a complex possesses us, as a virus possesses its host, using it for its own ends. The mind is a virus because—like a totalitarian empire state—its existence depends on the suppression of undesirable elements, pushing them out of awareness and into the body, which is the partial location of "the unconscious." The gods have become our diseases; and like the gods, our diseases rule our fates, determine our actions, hold sway over our moods, direct our thoughts and feelings, and have total dominion over our bodies. We are puppets in their hands. Let us not forget that the human body is made up of as many bacteria cells as human ones—so to try to banish the "other" means effectively attacking one's own nervous system.

The alien abduction scenario is a literal/fantastic (fantastic *because* literal) enactment of this fundamental law of consciousness: that what we disown—push outside us—returns to possess us internally. The alien is that which we reject as "unlike us." It is the aspect of the psyche that cannot be integrated due to its overwhelming nature—whether dark or light—that then appears before us in shining ships in the sky or that creeps into our bedrooms in the dark hours of night, and abducts our sleeping bodies. These undermen/overmen are the missing parts of our totality; as long as we deny them, we belong to them. "They work by ancient laws": the laws of the psyche, the body, the unconscious, that most ancient "part" of us that is really the whole, as experienced through the fragment. This doesn't make the "aliens" gods or devils—or even god *and* devils. It makes them us.

I have only latterly introduced explicit references to alien abduction as a government "black op"/mind control program (though I think it's implicit throughout the first part of this book), partly because I have felt almost as dubious about this as a total explanation for the phenomena as I feel about the ET hypothesis. Yet more and more, it seems to me an essential counterpoint to it. Common sense (never less common than now, or in the present field) would seem to suggest that the mind control/black ops model would be at odds with, and mutually exclusive from, the idea of genuine, "otherly" beings acting in magical ways— hence the enormous resistance to this material in the field (Cannon's *Controllers* has never been published). But, if the "magical beings" are really ourselves, then this apparent line is neither so clear nor final.

The conflation of seemingly opposed narratives becomes even more disorienting if we consider that the mind control programs described by Cannon and others which simulate alien abduction for adults are inseparable from those "MKULTRA" style programs which trauma- tize young children through sexual violence, through torture both physical and psychological, in order to fracture their psyches and create "alters" (dissociative identity disorder) that can be exploited in differ- ent ways—to be used as killers, spies, sex slaves—and even perhaps as public figures such as movie stars, best-selling authors, or presidents. One reason this muddies the research waters so badly is that a side effect—or more likely a primary goal—of splitting the psyche may be accessing other realms from which nonhuman "beings" (forces) can be summoned and then harnessed. If this other realm is the realm of the psyche (and/or the human body), then such forces or beings may be none other than the splintered aspects of the psyche-soma system itself, fragments that are able to *materialize* in some form, or at least to be experienced by our senses *as* material, and which can even develop a semblance of autonomy (like Castaneda's "allies").

Intelligence black ops that simulate alien abduction—just as Hollywood dramatizations do on a more open and wide-scale level—may be a way to shape and direct the narrative in order to control the ways in which we experience these fragmentary psychic forces. They create a context in which the phenomena can—and must—be experienced, and/or through which they emerge. If these fragments gain access to us "through the corridor of our own minds," this is not because they come from another universe, but because they come from the underlying reality of both mind *and* body, and have been banished *by* the mind, *to* the body. Hence, only the mind can grant them access to our awareness, and allow them to be reintegrated.

This relates to a still larger subject, that of reality hijacking or reality hacking, the creation of false but all-inclusive "realities," within/over which something like total control is possible. This is the *apparent* end goal of government mind control, black ops, and secret psychological warfare. When a person's psyche is split through trauma into multiple fragments, separate selves or alters, often the many alters are unaware of each other. Controlling an individual's memory and perception is akin to creating the reality in which he exists. The total person—his physical being—can then be controlled not just externally but internally. To control someone's mind is to control, and even in a sense *create*, his "reality"—to have control over his perception of what is real. Cannon speculates that simulating alien abductions became necessary to prevent subjects from remembering the ways in which they were being used and exploited. In other words, that alien abductions were a *screen memory* that was compelling enough to keep what was actually being done to these people (and what they were doing to and for others) out of awareness. An ironic and symmetrical side effect of this (though again, perhaps it was really a primary goal) is that, through creating quasi-fictional memories of alien abduction (with the cooperation of Hollywood, network TV shows, UFO researchers and authors, experiencers speaking publicly about their experiences, et al.), these individual distortions of reality were then able to enter into the collective experience, and so generate the larger narrative of "alien abduction" as a social phenomenon, one which eventually made it all the way to Harvard and became as integral a part of our culture as the Hula-Hoop (though considerably less benign).

As above, so below. If alien abduction memories both pertain to and contribute to the fracturing of individual psyches into a disorganized but controllable collective of alters, so perhaps a similar compartmentalization is occurring with the collective psyche of human society? "Audience cults" form around sets of beliefs: those who believe the abductions are of extraterrestrial origin, that they are being done by time travelers (future humans), Archons, demons, inorganic beings, government agents, our higher selves or guardian angels, psychic complexes or simply hallucinations—and this is only the many different sets of beliefs around a "single" phenomenon! In the same way that a fragmented individual who no longer knows real from imaginary (or inducted/incepted quasi-reality) can be controlled by what he or she is made to believe, so the greater body of humanity can be controlled and directed into preprepared reality tunnels, to be put to work, assigned whatever business needs to be done, or simply kept "occupied" (i.e., possessed) so that the controllers can go *openly* about *their* business, unimpeded.

The business of the controllers, apparently, is transcendence. Not transcendence as an end, but as a means. The end is total control via the creation of an all-inclusive reality in which to exist—and dominate—indefinitely. An Archetypal Traumatogenic Agency, externalized and taken all the way to global proportions.

CHAPTER XVIII

Close encounters of the carnal kind

"Almost every new space traveler soon feels an overwhelming sense of both the unity of mankind and the fragility of the earth and its inhabitants when first observing the 'little globe' some tens of thousands of miles away. Most have claimed this feeling to be the most aesthetic or religious experience of a lifetime—independently of the observer's prior aesthetic or religious bent. The fact that this experience is still an extraordinarily moving one should give us some indication of what it meant to the early astronauts of the late 20th century and the 'tourists' who followed shortly thereafter."

—William Brown and Herman Kahn, "Long-Term Prospects For Developments In Space"

The Overview Effect is a key concept and narrative here, because it allows for the (I would say largely manufactured) goal of spiritual/psychic attainment to be fused with the all-too-real goal of economic and technological expansion. What other goal not only allows for government/intelligence/military power and all its machinations to coexist with spiritual aspiration, but makes these dark agendas indispensable to our ascension? If conquering space (along with systematized

225

traumatization) is sold as not just *a* way but *the way* to introduce the masses to a nirvanic, spiritually evolved experience of our collective oneness—Ultimate Reality—who but the most jaded, depraved, or ignorant of doubters would ever question the wisdom of our masters?

So how is it—we may justifiably ask at this point—that the bid to explore and colonize space is all of a piece with the organized ritual sexual abuse of children for the dark satisfaction of human predators? Are these infant psyches the eggs that go into a galactic omelet? Or are they merely two tangential obsessions—symptoms of a single psychosis? Sexually possessing children may have several functions for the psyche of the individual who possesses. It is a means to experience total control in the most local, primal, and basic fashion, through the physical domination of someone who is completely powerless to defend him- or herself. For the abuser, this amounts to temporary empowerment. He gets to be possessed by his libido without any corresponding vulnerability, no risk of exposure. A child who is abused comes to love his or her abuser as the only safe position for the threatened psyche to assume. The abuser thereby gets to experience the safety of the certainty of being loved; not only that, but also the knowing that he or she can control the one who loves that adult, and need never fear that that love will be withdrawn, because to receive love, all that needs to be done is to inflict more abuse. As a poison container, the child receives (swallows) all the psychic anguish—the dark matter—which the abuser has been unable to integrate (those autonomous fragments that possess him or her). This temporarily relieves all internal tension, as if by the miracle of divine grace. The love of an innocent bestows the illusion of innocence upon the abuser.

Once again, the bid for immortality (*puer aeternus*) lies underneath the desire to steal innocence. Putting psychic poisons into a child goes hand in hand with drawing off the child's psychic essence, his or her soul stuff (those fragments), through the infliction of pain and terror and a feeding on that emotional/psychic energy. Only vampires live forever. As Lloyd deMause wrote in 1994:

> [Ritual abusers] weren't following a worldwide conspiracy .... Cult abuse, like all sadistic acts, individual or group, is a sexual perversion whose purpose is achieving orgasm by means of *a defense against severe fears of disintegration and engulfment* .... Sadists live their daily lives full of terrible anxieties about being independent and active. *Any success in their lives is terribly fearful, producing*

regression to infancy and a desire to merge with mommy. But merging means losing one's self, being annihilated. To avoid this, it is necessary to inflict on someone else all the traumas one has had plus all the fantasies of revenge against the persecuting parents. Only by reenacting cultic rituals can these deeply regressed individuals avoid castration and engulfment fears and reassure themselves of their potency and separateness.

Somewhere in all of this, there lurks also the mystical bid for union, oneness, for reabsorption into the mother's body, or rather, for the dissociative state that invokes and reproduces that lost experience. And somehow, all of this relates to the drive to leave the Earth, to transcend the flesh, to reject the dark matter (*mater*/mother), and to enter, Kurzweil-style, into some quasi-eternal disembodied union with outer space. The afore-quoted 1977 NASA report envisions this Borg-like future existence in by now familiar terms:

Naturally, one of the common spectacular images of the future is that of a great "universal brain" composed of all of the brains of the inhabitants of the solar civilization linked optimally into the vast integrated computer network, which by innate design is self-programming and therefore potentially rapidly self-improving— even as it improves the effective brainpower of its users! Even though today individuals conceive of themselves as independent autonomies—as they always have done in the past—they are more aware than ever of their interdependence through the information network. The major difference in current attitudes from those which prevailed a century or so ago is that this interdependence is now considered desirable; that rather than promoting robot-like humans this interdependence promotes "human-like" robots where these are desirable and frees human beings to perform ever more creatively in endeavors of their choice ... Thus, the expectation exists that if the "universal brain" does evolve into a meaningful entity it will be an entirely desirable and natural evolution that will undoubtedly completely recast the image of man's role and destiny in the universe. (Brown & Kahn, 1977, pp. 171–172)

It is often remarked on how abuse dehumanizes the victims; what is less commented on is how it likewise affects the perpetrator. According to Cannon, one of the aims of mind control and repeat traumatization is to desensitize the victims, not merely by victimizing them but by forcing them to do the same to others, until they become immune to the deleterious effects of committing acts of extreme violence. So super-spies, super-soldiers, and organic killing machines are created.

Implicit in this scenario is the understanding that, to become more than human entails becoming less than human. Ironically, the same subhuman indifference to other people's pain—the complete absence of empathy or compassion or conscience—must be extended to the controllers who are performing these horrendous conditioning exercises. Possibly it is even one of their goals, based on an understanding that, the more abhorrent the acts they commit, the more desensitized they will become, the more "invulnerable" and "powerful" they will experience themselves to be. This would be particularly so if the emotional and psychic deadness were accompanied by *intense sexual feelings*, also known as ecstasy, religious or otherwise.

There may be some parallels here with the idea that to attain "oneness" with the universe, it is first necessary to break away / split off from the Earth-body *through the appliance of violent force*. The Overview Effect, in other words—and the whole collective capitalist drive to conquer space—may be a species attempt to *reenact the original trauma-dissociation experience*, as both abuser and abused in one. Simply put (and again citing Kurzweil as the fullest unconscious expression of this pathos and pathology), it is the bid for "mind" to divorce itself forever from the body, through any and all means necessary, and become forever "at large." The means is Whitley's mind-as-weapon, and its primary tool, that supercharged phallus headed for the stars: the rocket ship. (Of course, Crowleyite Jack Parsons's central involvement in developing rocket science and, simultaneously, the occult "Babalon Working" with L. Ron Hubbard sex magick rituals should not go uncited at this point.)

*

"Like the festering action which removes the sliver from a wound, the traumatized imagination works and re-works its metaphors until the events which have '[pierced' it can be viewed in a more adaptive fashion. Paradoxically, the challenge posed for the soul by the vicissitudes of nature and the shocks of life must be resolved by a movement *against* nature and *against* life."
—Greg Mogenson, *A Most Accursed Religion*

Something that only came to my attention recently is the predominant conflation of UFOs and alien abduction as fields for research. The fact it took so long for me to realize this indicates just how total the conflation is. No self-respecting UFO researcher would ignore the alien abduction data, or vice versa. At a superficial analysis, this conflation seems justified. Many, possibly most, abductions occur just after or in conjunction with a UFO sighting. On the other hand, the majority of UFO sightings are not accompanied by abductions, nor in most cases is there any solid *causal* connection between a UFO sighting and an alien abduction.

Taken separately, the UFO and the visitor phenomenon are not only dissimilar but actually make up a kind of binary model. UFOs are seen in the sky, from a distance, and tend to be either neutral or numinous experiences for the witness. Abductions happen on the ground, in the most intimate or at least enclosed of spaces (bedrooms and cars). If there is a UFO encounter accompanying an abduction, the percipient is taken inside the "craft." Otherwise, the most usual abduction scenario *entails the alien entering inside the abductee*, into their minds or bodies or both (subtly, grossly, or both). The cultural precedents of modern-day bug-eyed aliens are fairies and demons (and satanically abusive humans), all of which come from the Earth or below (hell); were it not for the fact that the UFO sightings are so commonly associated with alien abductions, might we not reasonably assume the same of the "visitors"?

In contrast, the UFO, as a divine mandala/mother ship, comes from the heavens. This UFO/abduction binary corresponds roughly with that of the soul-psyche and the body. The suggestion is, perhaps, that alien abductions are a way for us to experience heavenly, transcendental union with the soul/UFO *bodily* and to internalize it. They suggest a kind of surrogate experience of the psyche *landing* in the body, so that full embodiment can occur, an embodiment prevented from happening naturally at birth, or early childhood, due to the extremes of trauma suffered.

In Strieber's accounts (which in this regard are fairly typical), he describes repeat experiences of being penetrated by the visitors—by needles, rectal probes, a female penis, an implant in his ear. It's as if something is trying to come *into* consciousness or bodily awareness in the most literal fashion. It's also the most conclusive "proof" which Strieber offers to skeptics, in his implant and his anal wounding (which, like the Fisher King's wound, is one that is neither fatal nor ever heals). This suggests that the visitors' stringency in avoiding leaving any evidence of their presence apparently doesn't extend to violating human bodies. They resort to concealing their presence as it were *on or inside the human body* (the victim) *itself*. (A bit like a poison receptacle? It's worth pointing out that child victims of ritual sexual abuse have been reported to suffer "stigmata"—a literal reopening of old wounds—on or leading up to recall of those lost memories.[1])

In "Carnal Knowledge: The Epistemology of Sexual Trauma in Witches' Sabbaths, Satanic Ritual Abuse, and Alien Abduction Narratives," Joseph Laycock writes:

> "Carnal knowledge"—knowledge through sexual encounters—is privileged above visual or auditory encounters, and is therefore more useful for constructing meaningful cosmologies in which human beings may interact with the divine. Carnal knowledge was a privileged form of epistemology in pre-Christian cultures. Since the days of the early Christian Church and the equation of sexuality with sin, carnal knowledge has survived in the form of masochistic and traumatic sexual encounters ... [T]he sexual content of these narratives is not only a reflection of human sexuality but is actually an epistemological necessity to render them credible. Sexual encounters, as a way of knowing, are regarded as somehow more reliable than mere sightings. *Descriptions of sexual encounters with mysterious others is necessary to the true function of these narratives—that of constructing a cosmology inhabited by unseen and supernatural forces.* (2012, emphasis added)

What Laycock seems to be saying is that there is nothing quite as tangible to the senses as sex, and nothing so real to the psyche as trauma. In our mythic yearning to reunite with "the divine"—to reexperience primal oneness, and a pre-traumatized state—we are naturally drawn to reenact sexual trauma and then to interpret it as *an encounter with the divine*. Or the ET.

A dissociative/heavenly vision of the UFO-psyche is akin to the body seeing the soul to which it belongs (taking the psyche as the first cause) *outside of itself*, that is, in the place and position where *it least belongs*. (It's a reverse scenario to the out-of-body experience so favored by Strieber and other abductees, which is the "soul"—more likely a psychic fragment—looking down on the body.) An exteriorized psyche alerts the witness to two things: first, the existence of a higher level of consciousness or "separate reality"—that of the soul. Second, and far less easily acknowledged, that the body has been vacated by the soul, or that it was never occupied by it, and that as such it is a lifeless shell, a husk, a walking corpse—or what's known in today's pop culture world as a zombie. (It may not surprise the reader to know that Strieber also claims to have had a close encounter with a zombie: a walking corpse he encountered in his New York apartment in the 1970s, described in *Solving the Communion Enigma*.)

Following this line of logic to its natural conclusion, alien abduction can be seen (symbolically, not literally) as the disembodied psyche's attempt to awaken/enliven the body by entering inside it. This legitimate attempt at psychic possession by the soul *both brings about and depends* on a reenactment of the original trauma that caused the divorce—or prevented the marriage—to begin with. Whether the agencies performing the enactment are purely psychic, a mixture of the psychic with the physical, or wholly physical and perhaps all-too-human, is something that can only be speculated upon.

What seems to be beyond all reasonable doubt at this stage, however, is that the natural and potentially healing process by which a fragmented psyche regains wholeness has been supplanted by a cynically engineered imitation of the same. This is a subtle game of almost infinite variation, designed, by the agents of fragmentation, to deceive even the elect, as the collective psyche's last and most desperate defense against the terrifying finality of integration. The pseudo-enlightenment which Huxley, Harman, Strieber, Kripal, and co are offering is as far from the real thing, finally, as hard-core pornography is from the *conjunctio oppositorum* of an alchemical wedding. Yet somehow we are being lured into that transhumanist wet dream or dopamine-flooded rat-maze, via a stunning array of crucial or guiding fictions. These cultural narratives are–like the most state-of-the-art Hollywood fantasies–spellbinding in their allure. They are powerful to misdirect us down preprepared social channels, into specific behaviors that will, by their repetition, prevent psychic integration from happening while allowing for a surrogate but entirely *faux* experience of it.

Laycock's point about carnality being the means for knowledge to fully "incarnate" within and through a culture is a key one, I think. If you want to create a transpersonal, cosmic, divine narrative–essentially a religion, however scientistic–you first need prophets to spread it (narrators who are both reliable and unreliable at the same time). To create these, first provide your subjects with a *formative sexual experience of the traumatic variety*. Such a carnal close encounter (of the fourth kind) means that the "divine" narrative (the contact experience) will *constellate around* the sexual trauma, because trauma is the one thing we all palpably recognize *as real*. So the hidden illumineers give us Strieber, with his implant and his anal penetration wounds. And in case we start to reject the narrative as being too inherently improbable, they give us J. J. Kripal as the mild-mannered academic to assure us to trust him, he's a doctor, and that everything's just fine. Kripal with his idea of "real spirituality" as something that incorporates both sex and trauma into it (the dangerous sacred), not to ground it in the body, but to rocket-blast it out of the body's stratosphere and into the dissociated heavenly spaces of Mind at Large.

My own suspicion—based on Strieber's and Kripal's apparent indifference to the facts of traumatic penetration in favor of a mystical over-gloss—is that this sort of sexualized mysticism is closer to pornography than to real spirituality, and that sex that is used to reify something ephemeral (whether it's *Agapé* or Eros) is inherently *anti*-erotic, just as pornography, for all its graphic nature, is anti-erotic. Just because awakening is painful does not mean that pain will bring about our awakening. And just because our sexuality has been crippled by shame does not mean that all we need to do to heal ourselves is become shameless about our sexuality. When the totem has become the taboo, the solution is not to make the taboo into a totem. Not unless the goal is simply to keep in place the ancient psychological mechanisms of social control.

*

"Other organisms are passive subjects of evolutionary forces; man can become the conscious trustee of Evolution and, within limits, guide its course."

—Julian Huxley, *A Philosophy for Dictators*

What is the aim of the illumineers and futurologists? Throughout this work I have done my best to resist the urge to make moral value judgments and only to map out the activities, agendas, methods, and principles being applied, and let the readers judge whether this is something they want to participate in or not. Mapping a glorious future for mankind—as the illumineers seem bent on doing, by any and all means necessary—is quite similar to what we all do at an individual level.

It is predicated on ignoring the reality that the inevitable future—the true final frontier—is the death of the body and a subsequent confrontation with eternity (or eternal nonexistence). Any plans that don't factor this reality into them are meaningless in that larger context. This is why religion remains the only context for all "plans"—because eternity must be faced and somehow either coopted or negotiated. The temporal must have control over the eternal. Yet this is a contradiction in terms, and by definition impossible.

One thing that finally occurred to me while looking at all of the group-created plans for humanity's glorious future was—why? Why does it matter to these individuals to ensure another ten, a hundred, a thousand thousand years of prosperity for (their chosen portion of) humanity? Are they really so concerned for their descendants? How far does their concern extend? Eventually, if their descendants continue to breed, a day will someday come when the line must end, catastrophically or otherwise. *Everything* ends. So if it is only a matter of numbers, why is it so important to ensure mankind continues to prosper for countless millennia rather than only for a few decades?

The only answer I could find was that, the longer the timespan, the grander and more far-reaching the vision, the more "meaning" it gives to the lives of whoever is working to realize it. In other words, the bigger the vision, the more effective it is for staving off/counteracting an awareness of our own *personal* deaths. Cosmic displacement activity.

Yet in the end, no vision is grand enough save the one vision. To face eternity, one cannot be anything less than infinite, because the vastness of eternity only spells terror for the finite ego. Anything less than infinity inevitably becomes a prisoner to its own overreaching aspirations. Simply put, to aspire to immortality is not merely to try to become "as gods" but to be *as-God-is*. In the above-quoted tract by Julian Huxley, he states, "The only goal which I recognize for life is more life—more satisfying experience, richer and fuller being." This seems reasonable, until we consider that the desire for more—which is essentially the capitalist drive—can never be satisfied until it has possessed *everything*. It is a philosophy for dictators and transhumanists, old seers and starkillers.

The earthly evolutionary journey that begins with an ape crushing his brother's skull with a bone *must* end with a Star Child. This is the infinite regression; it is necessary because the only ending besides birth is death. There is no thought of the sort of Star Man the Star Child will eventually grow into—*a puer aeternus*?—just as there can be no thought about the final destination of the Mother Ship. We await (and struggle towards) an ending, only so we can reach a beginning that will never end.

Edgar Mitchell's "oneness," Ray Kurzweil's Singularity, Whitley's Strieber's Communion, Peace on Earth, Good Will to Men, many happy eternal returns. As Jung once pointed out, "1" (I) is only an idealized number. It is a perfected image of a self that can only exist in two-ness, in binary contrast to what it is not. One is a fiction—a crucial one. Like the cross of matter, it makes a prison of Infinity.

Here I will (tentatively) close the circle of this text, not with a one—or even an infinity—but, if I have been true to the "evolutionary" sequence as I have read it, with an empty crucifix, and a God-forsaken zero.

Update: one fiction to rule them (UFO Disclosure Plan 2017)

"In February [2016] John Podesta tweeted as he left the Obama administration that his greatest regret was that the UFO material had not been released …. Say there is a release of such documents, by Hillary Clinton if she becomes president, as she said she would. [A]nd the documents say that some of the UAPs appear to be unequivocally under intelligent control … How long will it take the media before it asks the president, 'Well what about the abductions?' Then what do they do? What do they say? I know what they have to say, they have to say they don't know what's happening to people, because they don't, in fact."

—Whitey Strieber, 2016

It has been a long passage from the first incarnation of this work (as an online art installation called "Crucial Fictions") on May 1, 2013 to this afterword, which I am writing in January of 2017, at the very edge of the publisher's word-limit for this work. A week ago, taking what I hoped would be "one last pass over Whitleyville," I re-subscribed to *Unknown Country*. Strieber had just completed a twenty-episode series of audios called "Awakenings," which includes his alleged experiences of "channeling" his wife Anne, who died in August 2015. In September of 2016, he began a personal recapitulation series called "Stories from a Life," with which he promises to cover all his memories from "past lives" to the present. Once again, the timing of Strieber's disclosures seemed to be strangely synchronized with my own investigative process, as *Prisoner of Infinity* finally nears some sort of closure.

Then there is the recent material relating to the so-called "UFO Disclosure Plan": the current literary undertaking of Peter Levenda and the now-notorious John Podesta emails released by *Wikileaks*, just prior to the 2016 US presidential election. Not the emails referring to pizzas (a subject I hope to address in a later work), but those related to UFOs. That said, the fact that John Podesta himself seems to be straddling the midnight intersection between the worlds of organized child trafficking and UFO disclosure is itself something of a smoking gun, potentially at least. And then add to this that, *literally* at the last minute (as I was attaching this MS to an email to the publishers), I received a message from the researcher George Hansen (*The Trickster and the Paranormal*), who had contacted me the day before about "Pizzagate." He told me he had *long noted a connection between ufology and pedophilia*, and shared a joke he'd published in *Saucer Smear*: "Question: How do you know if you are at a high-class UFO conference? Answer: There are no known pedophiles on the program" (Hansen, 2000, p. 8)! To be continued ...?

Returning to the *Wikileaks* emails meanwhile, and beginning with Strieber's friend Edgar Mitchell. On June 25, 2014, Mitchell wrote to John Podesta:

> As we move into the last half of 2014, the need for extraterrestrial disclosure intensifies .... John, with this email I am requesting a conversation with you and President Obama regarding the next steps in extraterrestrial disclosure for the benefit of our country and our planet. Fifty years ago Battelle, Brookings and RAND studies on UFOs convinced the government to remove knowledge of the extraterrestrial presence from the citizens of our country. These organizations advised with their best information. However, today much, if not most, of the extraterrestrial reality they examined is known by our citizens. These organizations' resultant strategies and policies of 50 years ago no longer hold credibility or benefit. Five decades of UFO information have dramatically shifted the public awareness of an extraterrestrial presence. And yet, our

government is still operating from outdated beliefs and policies. These are detrimental to trust in government transparency, science, religion, and responsible citizenry embracing the next step in our country's space travel and research. Three disclosure issues are prominent: 1) planet sustainability via next generation energies such as zero point energy, 2) galactic travel and research undertaken as an advanced species aware of the extraterrestrial presence, not as uninformed explorers who revert to colonialism and destruction and 3) the example of a confident, engaged government who respectfully regards the wisdom and intellect of its citizens as we move into space. (*Wikileaks*, 2016a)

Mitchell's assistant received a response on July 18, 2014, saying that "John would likely take this meeting alone first before involving the President" (*Wikileaks*, 2016b). The following year, on June 11, 2015, Mitchell emailed Podesta requesting a Skype talk "to discuss Disclosure and the difference between our contiguous universe nonviolent obedient ETI and the celestials of this universe, and because Hillary and Bill Clinton were intimates of Laurance Rockefeller who had an avid interest in ETI .... Disclosure is now top priority for ETI itself in protection of the people" (*Wikileaks*, 2016c). Two months later (August 18, 2015), he reminded Podesta that "the War in Space race is heating up," and that

… our nonviolent ETI from the contiguous universe are helping us bring zero point energy to Earth. They will not tolerate any forms of military violence on Earth or in space …. We're arguably closer than ever to war in space. Most satellites orbiting Earth belong to the U.S., China and Russia. And recent tests of anti-satellite weapons don't exactly ease the scare factor. It sounds like science fiction, but the potential for real-life star wars is real enough. It's just not new. Fears of battles in space go back to the Cold War and several initiatives, like President Reagan's "Star Wars" missile-defense system. (*Wikileaks*, 2016d)

While Mitchell was doing his best to galvanize Podesta into executive action, the musician Tom deLonge was embarking on his own world-saving mission of extraterrestrial ambassadorship, with the help of John Podesta and Peter Levenda. DeLonge emailed Podesta on November 13, 2015 about setting up a meeting with Steven Spielberg, whose DreamWorks, he crows, "are very, very interested." His goal, he writes, is for Spielberg or "somebody of his stature" to attend a meeting with himself and Podesta. Meanwhile, he will be "spending all afternoon interviewing a scientist that worked on a spacecraft at Area 51" (*Wikileaks*, 2016e).

On January 25, 2016, DeLonge emails Podesta about one "General McCasland," who he has been working with for four months, and who "… is very, very aware as he was in charge of all of the stuff. When Roswell crashed, they shipped it to the laboratory at Wright Patterson Air Force Base. General McCasland was in charge of that exact laboratory up to a couple years ago. He not only knows what I'm trying to achieve, he helped assemble my advisory team" (*Wikileaks*, 2016f).

On February 9, 2016, DeLonge emails Podesta about his ongoing series of UFO-disclosure novels, and glowingly informs him that

> … kids are mining the Internet asking for any info whatsoever that 'John Podesta' says in the book [sic]. Ha. They don't know yet where you exist in this Sekret Machines Universe (we launch the story with NY Times with Doc Trailer in a week) and they already look to you in a leadership role they can trust. And care almost ONLY about your voice in this. That's HARD to do. Getting young adults to like you, especially if your [sic] at your level in DC. Don't lose that. I will brand you much more when this all comes out as a man that the youth can trust and rely on …. This project is about changing the cynical views of youth towards government. (*Wikileaks*, 2016g)

Podesta responds a few days later and tells Tom that he "Just did a taped interview with local CBS affiliate. Got asked about the topic and gave an answer I think you would like. Hope they use it" (*Wikileaks*, 2016h). DeLonge meanwhile is going from strength to strength as he joins forces with *VICE News*, who interviewed Podesta about UFOs the week before (*Vice*, 2016).

> Sold my first show for the Sekret project. VICE News will produce, finance and distribute the Sekret Machines Docu-Series charting my personal journey on how I met important people and how they are guiding my effort to communicate difficult themes to the youth. All the while keeping the names and identities of my Advisory council private. This is huge. VICE is the single biggest, most credible and

progressive news source out there. It's international, and it's all aimed at the youth. They feed directly into HBO and just launched their own news channel .... Rolling Stone will break the story on April 8th. The novel is in stores April 7th. VICE series launches immediately following, and we are placing the Scripted TV series now. I am hoping to come meet you personally and talk in the next few weeks. I am talking to NASA right now, too. (*Wikileaks*, 2016i)

How Tom deLonge went from California son of an oil executive, to rock star, to NASA poster boy (his website is mainly a merchandising hub for space propaganda) and "ET disclosure" wordsmith working with a respected author such as Peter Levenda is beyond the scope of this afterword. As to why the reputable Levenda–who prides himself on being a rigorous academic historian–would hitch his wagon to so brazenly opportunistic an enterprise is an even greater mystery, although in this case there is a simple, one-word answer to that question (*sshhh*). The book they have assembled together even comes with a foreword by Jacques Vallee, probably the most highly esteemed living "UFO authority" (though I doubt it ever gets more oxymoronic than that).

The book, the first of a promised three volumes, is called *Sekret Machines: Gods: An official investigation of the UFO phenomenon*. The publicity material presents it as "the result of input from scientists, engineers, intelligence officers, and military officials–a group we call the Advisors–and transcends the speculation of journalists, historians and others whose conclusions are often either misinformed or only tease around the edges of the Sekret Machines."

> GODS takes us beyond speculation to certain knowledge of what exactly lies at the heart of the most important Phenomenon ever to confront human understanding .... There is another Force in the universe of our Reality, another context for comprehending what has been going on for millennia and especially in the last seventy years ... [a reality] that demands the collaboration of all of us in every field of human endeavor if we are to understand it and manage its effects ... [effects that are] much more serious and potentially much more threatening than they can imagine.

Of his involvement in the project, Levenda explained how "Sometimes you can't tell a story really clearly using nonfiction .... I think the division between fiction and nonfiction is something we're very familiar with in the West—it's part of our scientific worldview—you know, there's science over here and there's religion over there, for instance .... It doesn't mean when you're telling fiction that you're lying." So what truth-telling fiction are DeLonge and his new "legitimizer" Levenda selling? In an AMA on the website *Above Top Secret*, DeLonge staked the following claims:

The aliens are the "gods" of the past and of mythology, and they are interested in DNA and genetic manipulation. Animal mutilations are from the UFO phenomenon. The "gods" have good and bad races, that is, there are multiple species. These gods are physical beings that have advanced technology. There are different ones created to do different tasks. Government decisions are based on enormous amounts of information known to a few people and the "UFO information" makes its way into every decision the US makes as a country. Their influence is "demonic," not spiritual, "a normal tactile and physical species, using advanced machinery to impose and achieve something with the human race." He also slips in a Willis Harman-esque plug for Freemasonry: "Masons are good for 'free-thinking man, building a free-thinking world" (*Above Top Secret*, 2016). And so on.

*

Between the publication in June 2016 of the Tom deLonge/A. J. Hartley novel *Sekret Machines: Chasing Shadows* and DeLonge and Levenda's nonfiction *Gods, Man, & War: An Official Investigation of the UFO Phenomenon*, in March 2017, Peter Levenda's first ever novel was released. *The Lovecraft Code* is about a descendant of one of Lovecraft's characters

> summoned by a nameless covert agency of the US government to retrieve a sacred book from the grasp of an Islamist terror network operating out of northern Iraq, in the land of the Yezidi ... all that's left of an ancient sect that possessed the key to the origins of the human race and was in conflict with another, more ancient civilization from beyond the stars. (2016a)

The sacred book in question is *The Necronomicon*, a powerful grimoire (collection of spells and incantations) first mentioned in Lovecraft's short story "The Hound" (written in 1922, published in 1924). Whether the book had any actual existence at that time is doubtful; but Lovecraft had a circle of friends and correspondents who also started mentioning the grimoire in *their* horror tales, and this gave the book a semblance of credence.

> The illusion was well done, as they would mention this fake book amongst the names of actually existing books that dealt with witchcraft and demonology. Inspired by HPL, they too invented diabolical books to add atmosphere to their tales: Clark Ashton Smith—*The Book of Eibon*, Robert E. Howard—*Unaussprechlichen Kulten*, Robert Bloch—*Cultes des Goules* and *De Vermis Mysteriis* among many others. The practice of this "Lovecraft Circle" of writers to invent "forbidden books" is very well documented. They would even create bogus histories of various editions for each of these books to add to the verisimilitude. (Gilmore, 2013)

Eventually, as Joseph L. Flatley writes, "... more credulous readers came to believe that the Necronomicon was real. It was as if Luke Skywalker was real, or the flying skateboards from *Back To The Future* were real" (Flatley, 2013).

Lovecraft died in 1937 virtually unknown, and he only began to gain literary recognition in the 1960s and 70s, "coinciding with both an Aquarian Age hunger for all things otherworldly and the introduction of mass-market paperback collections of his stories" (ibid.). Naturally, the growing legions of fans wanted a *Necronomicon* of their own, and "When Simon's *Necronomicon* finally hit the shelves, it must have seemed as if Lovecraft's universe had cracked open and spilled its contents all over New York City" (ibid.). Simon's *Necronomicon* is penned anonymously, with an introduction from "The Editor New York," and dated October 12, 1975 (Aleister Crowley's birthday). It is a blend of ancient Middle Eastern mythological elements, with allusions to the writings of H. P. Lovecraft and Aleister Crowley, woven together with a story about the "Mad Arab" (a character from Lovecraft's fiction).

In his novel, Levenda is ostensibly writing about Lovecraft's fictional *Necronomicon*, but since (like Strieber) Levenda is claiming to use fiction as the means for conveying truth, he may as well be writing about Simon's *Necronomicon*. This becomes especially so if we consider that Levenda is *the most likely candidate for having written it.*

The most common theory is that the role of Simon is being played by *The Dark Lord* author Peter Levenda. According to a brief bio from the Coast to Coast AM website, Simon "has appeared on television and radio discussing such topics as exorcism, Satanism, and Nazism," as has Levenda. In fact, when Simon appeared on the talk show, he attempted to disguise his voice by speaking through some sort of audio effect that lowered the pitch a couple of steps. When I played the audio file on my computer and pitched it back up using Ableton Live software, the unmasked Simon's voice clearly sounded like that of the Peter Levenda I interviewed earlier this year. Most tellingly, if you do a record search at the US Copyright Office website, "Peter Levenda (Simon, pseud.)" appears as the copyright owner on two of Simon's books (*The Gates of the Necronomicon* and *Papal Magic*). (Flatley, 2013)

Flatley asked Alan Cabal, who worked at The Magickal Childe bookshop during the period it was published there (in 1977), about the Simon-Levenda connection. "'Levenda is such a fuckin' snake, man,' Cabal replied. 'He's doing lectures as Simon at The Magickal Childe. He's doing workshops as Simon. And then all of a sudden, he decided to not be Simon.'" Levenda's response to Flatley: "'No …. But 'I'm perfectly flattered to be confused with Simon.'"

In his introduction to *The Necronomicon*, "Simon" claims that, in 1904, Crowley "had received a message, from what Lovecraft might have called 'out of space,' that contained the formula for a New World Order, a new system of philosophy, science, art and religion, but this New Order had to begin with the fundamental part, and common denominator, of all four: Magick." Simon compares "the essence of most of Lovecraft's short stories with the basic themes of Crowley's unique system of ceremonial Magick."

> While the latter was a sophisticated psychological structure, 'intended to bring the initiate into contact with his higher Self, via a process of individuation that is active and dynamic (being brought about by the "patient" himself) as opposed to the passive depth analysis of the Jungian adepts, Lovecraft's Cthulhu Mythos was meant for entertainment. Scholars, of course, are able to find higher, ulterior motives in Lovecraft's writings, as can be done with any manifestation of Art. [T]hat Lovecraft may have heard of Crowley is hinted at darkly in his short story "The Thing On The

Doorstep" in which he refers to a cult leader from England who had established a covenstead of sorts in New York. In that story, published in *Weird Tales* in 1936, the cult leader is closely identified with chthonic forces, is described as "notorious," and linked to the strange fate that befell the protagonist, Edward Derby. (Simon, 1977, pp. xiii, xl)

Along with Lovecraft's original stories, Simon's *Necronomicon* helped inspire occultist Kenneth Grant (who is mentioned in the *Necronomicon*'s introduction), heir apparent to Crowley, to update Thelemic magickal rituals and system by drawing upon Lovecraftian elements (Grant also refers quite a bit to UFOs in his books). Levenda wrote a book about Grant called *The Dark Lord*, and described his (and Grant's) interest in Lovecraftian descriptions of evil as part of an attempt to make a magical system "totally encyclopedic. It must represent all of reality ... it's got to represent darkness as well as the light" (Flatley, 2013). As an end, this is something any serious psychologist would agree with; but Levenda's means seem to be less consistent with a sincere desire to acknowledge the forces of the unconscious than with something more ... opportunistic.

In 2016 (*Thelema Now!* podcast), Levenda described the New York occult renaissance of the Seventies and Eighties (of which Levenda-Simon was an intrinsic part): "There was this window of opportunity [when] we wanted to show that this is not scary stuff. It could be powerful, it could be mind-altering, it could change your life. *But it was not dangerous, it was not going to kill you. And that's what we were trying to promote.*" One wonders if invoking or evoking the ancient archetypes of evil is not considered dangerous by Levenda, then what is the point of such archetypes? Is this what he considers an accurate, responsible representation of the darkness, as something to promote that is "not dangerous"? In the introduction to *Necronomicon*, Levenda-Simon writes:

> Crowley had nothing but admiration for the Shaitan (Satan) of the so-called "devil-worshipping" cult of the Yezidis of Mesopotamia [who] possess a Great Secret and a Great Tradition that extends far back into time, beyond the origin of the Sun cults of Osiris, Mithra and Christ; even before the formation of the Judaic religion, and the Hebrew tongue. Crowley harkened back to a time before the Moon was worshipped, to the "Shadow Out of Time"; and in this, whether he realized it as such or not, he had heard the "Call of Cthulhu." (Simon, 1977, p. xvii)

In 2017, Levenda is still in the archetypal promotion business, only now he seems to have reversed, or inverted, his original position, putting his pen in service of a large-scale, government-backed media merchandising program to *promote and reify the belief in a malign, ancient alien presence on the planet.* Whether he realizes it as such or not, Simon has answered the "Call of Cthulhu." Or should that be NASA? Towards the end of his intro, Simon suggests, with rhetoric worthy of Edgar Mitchell, that "the lunar landing was the first collective initiation for humanity, which will bring it one step closer to a beneficial Force that resides beyond the race of the 'cruel celestial spirits,' past the Abyss of Knowledge" (p. xxx).

*

"What about disclosure? What about it? It would be useless, it doesn't really matter very much in any case, because everybody knows they're here by now, surely. The people who don't are mostly just intellectuals and scientists who are way back in terms of soul growth anyway, so they've got a number of lifetimes to live before this would even be relevant to them."

—Whitley Strieber, 2016

Edgar Mitchell, John Podesta, Tom deLonge, Peter Levenda, and the current UFO Disclosure plan via elaborately assembled and marketed "true fiction" (complete with its Lovecraftian circle of "Advisors" legitimizing the narrative and constellating the Old Ones as they emerge into public awareness), can all be traced back, via Kenneth Grant and Levenda-Simon, to Lovecraft's original literary experiment in *reifying collective dreams* by forging from them an audience cult of belief. A very Strieber-esque enterprise indeed.

Now Levenda wants us to believe that the CthulUFOs are science, that his fiction is really nonfiction, and that the phantasy is proof of a deeper reality. Perhaps it is. But if so, how much is it emerging in tandem with a deliberate reengineering of the archetypes for sociopolitical ends? Levenda writes in *The Lovecraft Code*: "The Necronomicon was a joke, a running literary gag ... an invention ... He knew these people weren't lying, but they couldn't be telling the truth ... Lovecraft saw it coming ... his stories weren't fantasies ... they were predictions" (Levenda, 2016a). Predictions, or "prescriptive programming"?

Joseph Flatley's view of Lovecraft's prose is rather more down-to earth than Levenda's or Grant's or their legion of wanna-believe, alien-invoking wanna-be Ipssissimi: "It wasn't magic—it was a confidence trick." That's what writers do, after all. "In a letter from 1934, [Lovecraft] explained to the writer Clark Ashton Smith his belief that 'no weird story can truly produce terror unless it is devised with all the care and verisimilitude of an actual hoax.' Often, his stories were structured not as fiction but as essays or news accounts: *'Just as if he were actually trying to "put across a deception in real life"'"* (Flatley, 2013).

Just as if ...? When does a literary stunt aspiring to be an archetypal guiding fiction become an evocation of ancient occult forces that is part of a deep state psychological operation for human herding and social engineering? Or was it ever thus?

Delivering the Poison Secret: A Review of Whitley Strieber & Jeffrey Kripal's *The Super Natural*

> "I cannot tell you how to escape, but I can tell you that it's a terribly interesting place."
>
> —Whitley Strieber, *The Super Natural*

The Super Natural: A New Vision of the Unexplained was promised by its publishers (Tarcher-Penguin) to be "the most important book on the paranormal since Charles Fort published *The Book of the Damned* in 1919." The book is a collaboration between Whitley Strieber and Jeffrey Kripal, renowned scholar and "renegade advocate for including the paranormal in religious studies." On its own terms, it is an attempt to integrate "rejected knowledge" with "the great paradigm change of our time: the end of materialism." The book is arranged in alternating chapters from both authors, cozily marked with their first names, "Whitley" and "Jeff." This is the first clue that, despite Kripal's credentials, we will not be reading a scholarly work. The first chapter, by Kripal, begins with these words: "I am afraid of this book. There is something about it, something explosive and new. It is not a neutral book. It is an apocalypse of thought waiting for you, the reader, to actualize" (2016, p. 1). Three pages later, Kripal assures us, the readers: "We have no easy or settled answers. Our intentions for this book are more humble" (p. 4).

This is the first clue that *The Super Natural* is not going to play it straight with us, the readers, but that it will dissemble with every dissemination, in one breath presenting itself as "an apocalypse of thought," in the next assuring us of its humble intentions.

On the surface, Kripal takes Strieber's outlandish testimonies at face value; he appears to see them, and Strieber's mere existence, as a means to banish forever the old, moth-eaten paradigm of materialism. In *The Super Natural* he compares Strieber to St. Paul and Moses, clearly signaling that what Strieber is presenting is akin to the inception of a new religion. On page 222, Kripal describes *Communion* as "a trance-text, a 'remembrance' of a literally hypnotic story that helped 'reveal' and then establish one of the most powerful cultural narratives working in American culture today."

Both Kripal and Strieber (let's call them Stripal for short) repeatedly assure us, the readers, that they are not interested in fomenting belief (which they consider "a dangerous response") but in forging a new path between belief and dismissal, one which entails a more direct, experiential, *gnosis*-like encounter with the "super natural." Yet the book I read was saturated in belief; it was a tract that aspires to being an apocalypse of thought, a manual for accessing the higher mind of super nature. But for all its claims to be a shockingly new vision of the unexplained (claims backed up by Joscelyn Godwin, Jacques Vallee, and Dean Radin quotes on the back of the book), I found very little new about *The Super Natural*. What about Pauwels and Bergiers' *Morning of the Magicians* in 1963, Fritjof Capra's *The Tao of Physics* in 1975, Marilyn Ferguson's *The Aquarian Conspiracy* in 1980, Michael Talbot's *The Holographic Universe* (one of Strieber's favorites) in 1991, and Graham Hancock's *Supernatural*, in 2006? It seems as if, at regular intervals, a book comes along that tries to do more or less what *The Super Natural* is claiming to do, and turn the materialist paradigm upside down. The main difference here is that the focus is on the experiences of a single individual, Strieber, and by extension, those of thousands, or millions, who also believe they have been contacted by ... something that can't be explained by orthodox science.

Kripal's primary role is to provide the Strieber-material with the academic seal of approval. Yet the book, including Kripal's contribution, is written in the sensationalist, whiz-bang, hyperbole-filled, how-can-we-top-ourselves-this-time style of all Strieber's previous works. Much of the time Kripal seems to be selling a product rather than exploring a mystery. In case this seems overly harsh, here are some examples. On page 195, Kripal writes:

> The fact that Whitley has in turn been rejected by the official cultures of the public media, the scientific establishment, and conservative religion for his prophetic voice does nothing to challenge such vocational reading of the "magical stone" in his ear [i.e., an electrical implant Strieber received from unknown agencies]. Indeed, it only strengthens it, since this is what often happens to the prophet in western culture: he or she is rejected by the cultural elites.

Cultural elites not including Kripal, that is, whose standing at Rice University, his selection as the official Esalen-biographer, and his participation at the Noetic Institute of Sciences (where Radin also works as "chief scientist") apparently does not count for much. Having delivered his lofty statement on Strieber's prophetic status, on page 197 he adds, "I am not saying: 'Whitley Strieber is a shaman.' Nor am I saying: 'Whitley Strieber is a prophet.'" Are we, the readers, assumed to have such short memory spans that we won't notice this blatant contradiction? Or are we to believe Kripal when he tells us he didn't say what he just said? If Kripal didn't mean to say that Strieber was a prophet, why didn't he edit it out?

Despite having two authors and being edited by another author (Mitch Horowitz), Strieber's sections are filled with errors, exaggerations, and, frankly, lies. Did neither Kripal nor Horowitz notice, did they not care, or are they involved in a deliberate distortion of the truth for unknown reasons? We, the readers, have not just a right to ask these questions, we have an obligation; unless, that is, we want the first casualty of Strieber and Kripal's apocalypse to be thought itself.

To be fair, and as we've seen, Strieber's dissembling runs throughout all of his work. Kripal has seen the first part of *Prisoner of Infinity* (I know because he asked for a PDF in 2014, while working on *The Super Natural*). I would guess Strieber has too; but neither has addressed the arguments I have made. In their latest opus, either the inconsistencies are more glaringly obvious than before or I have trained my eye to see them more starkly. To give probably the most disturbing and pertinent example, on pages 96 and 103–104 Strieber resorts to deliberate concealment of his sexual history when he writes: "Prior to meeting my wife, I was sexually intimate with a woman only once ... when I was about sixteen, I was briefly touched by a girl, and touched her in return. Although I was as eager for sex as any boy, the manners of the time and place meant that I never went as far as to make love. Until I met Anne, that is." Mysteriously stricken from the record is Strieber's encounter with a mysterious Irish woman named Róisín, in Italy of 1968, with whom he had highly unorthodox sexual congress that included penetration, ejaculation, and manipulation by a group of unknown persons throughout the act! (See chapter 10.) His only reference to it here is summed up (on page 212) as "a couple of weeks in Florence, we had a lovely time, living together *in chaste intimacy*" (italics added)!

Towards the end of the book (on page 366), Strieber describes himself as "almost pathologically honest," then adds: "I am not a liar." Like everything Strieber touches, this book is not what it appears to be. It seems aimed at the critical establishment as an argument against materialism but it's written in an overly simplistic style that falls far short of anything resembling rigorous analysis. It's populist nonfiction, and its target audience is certainly not the "cultural elite" which Stripal grumble about throughout the book. The target audience, I suspect, is New Age readers who already reject the materialist paradigm, but who want to feel like they are being treated as intelligent, critical-minded thinkers. Rather than challenging religious or scientific orthodoxy, it seems designed to validate and reinforce a growing belief system that, despite all of the two authors' claims, is anything but marginal.

One element in this book that *might* be considered new is Kripal's "traumatic secret." This is what first kicked off my *Prisoner* investigation, and it can be summed up as the belief that severe abuse (especially childhood sexual abuse) can "open the door to transcendence." When I tried to point out the flaws in his argument to Kripal, he seemed either unable or unwilling to understand my points, and the dialogue went nowhere. In *The Super Natural*, he addresses it again in a significantly toned down, more user-friendly manner. For his part, Strieber, having advocated the use of trauma to accelerate evolution in *Solving the Communion Enigma*, seems to be practicing some post-*Prisoner of Infinity* damage control. On pages 208–209, he more or less sums up, in very simplistic terms, my own thesis:

> [T]here is some sort of process of sublimation involved in transferring unacceptable and incomprehensible memories to more bearable fantasies. A brutal rape by a beloved parent might become a

brutal alien abduction, as the mind seizes on the most believable and acceptable alternative in order to avoid facing what it cannot bear to see. This might explain, at least in part, the proliferation of close encounter memories, including some of my own. I doubt that it explains them all, but that possibility should not be discounted, either. If such a process exists, it is likely that it has always existed and might well be one of the primary generators of folklore. A rape by a father becomes a visit from a god. Leda didn't get ravished by daddy—too unbearable to contemplate. No, it was a swan, and that swan was a god. This might explain many of these experiences, but it should not be used to explain them away. The shattering of expectation that accompanies trauma doesn't just cause transference, it opens a door.

As I have argued, the sort of "transcendence" brought about through trauma is the consequence of a *dissociative defense strategy* on the part of the traumatized psyche. So even if the "super natural" realms being accessed are "real" (they may be), they are being accessed, interpreted, and applied in defense of an ego identity formed by and through the trauma. All such experiences become "stories"—tales of the ego fragment's aggrandizement and/or debasement that Strieber is so gifted at telling, but that Kripal seems rather less comfortable spinning into quasi-academic arguments for transcendental trauma. This sort of transcendence is equivalent to going into the jungle to capture exotic wildlife, then bringing it back to civilization in a cage as proof of one's prowess and adventurous spirit. It may be proof of having been to the jungle, but the wildlife is no longer wild (though it may still be exotic). It is not part of the jungle anymore but part of the civilization that has captured it. It has become a prisoner of the traumatized psyche's self-protective strategies.

*

> "As we approach wild creatures, they struggle, they react with terror, they have to be subdued ... exactly as I did, initially. But over my years of contact, I was tamed."
> —Whitley Strieber, *The Super Natural*

MKULTRA is not mentioned in *The Super Natural*, not once. This is despite Strieber's acknowledgment of participating in a secret,

Nazi-run US program for gifted children in the early 1950s: exactly the time, place, and players involved at the inception of MKULTRA. Strieber's experiences are mentioned primarily to show that his psychic prowess and otherworldly encounters are rooted in massive childhood trauma, and that he is the exception who proves, not the rule, but that MKULTRA's methods—using extreme trauma to endow children with psychic abilities—occasionally *worked*. Strieber makes no bones about this when he writes: "Were the Nazi scientists trying to re-create those conditions in their lab in Texas? If so, perhaps it sometimes works. My life would certainly suggest so." Is this the message embedded in *The Super Natural*—the bitter pill inside all the New Age sugar? Since it's about the only thing shockingly new about it, the book begins to look like a delivery device for this one idea. Yet MKULTRA was not about creating enlightened beings, shamans, or prophets. It was designed to create programmed killers, sex slaves, psychic spies, and possible "life-time actors," operatives who worked for a shadow government implementing political, social, cultural, and quasi-religious agendas. Whitley Strieber, who shows all the symptoms of dissociative identity disorder, was by his own admission part of a child-torture program with all the identifiable earmarks of MKULTRA (operational during Strieber's childhood in San Antonio), and who has publicly acknowledged, in more ways than one over the years, his close ties to the CIA.

Following this track a little further into the abyss, one of the things Kripal commends Strieber for is how he allows for every possible interpretation of his contact experiences, even down to brain tumor-generated hallucinations. And yet ... There is one viable interpretation of all the unexplained events of his life which Strieber never posits, namely, that his experiences were induced in him (and thousands, maybe millions, of others) as part of a large-scale, MKULTRA-linked, military intelligence operation that spanned decades and several continents and involved drugs, hypnosis, special effects, and officially undisclosed forms of technology. Unlike most or all of Strieber's explanations, this interpretation could conceivably account for *all* of the variables and inconsistencies in his accounts. I am not saying it would—there does *appear* to be a truly "magical" element to Strieber's experiences—only that it works considerably better than most of the other explanations, even while remaining conspicuously absent from both Strieber's and Kripal's roster: just as if it is not worth mentioning. Kripal does refer to military operations in the last chapter, as an apparent afterthought, but only in regard to UFO disinformation. In the same chapter, in his closing paragraphs, he assures us he does not "do conspiracy," that he doesn't trust "the wild conspiracies that are constantly spun out of this material." It's too bad, because if he did, *The Super Natural* would have been a very different animal entirely: an uncaged gorilla. In his enthusiastic chasing after miracles, Kripal has trampled over the real mystery.

Stripal want us to believe they are battling on the front line of super natural gnosis to overthrow the twin enemies of materialism and religion and defy the authority of the gatekeepers who want to define our reality and prevent us from recognizing our ultimate natures. Yet my own investigations would seem to indicate that the reverse is closer to the truth. On page 150, Kripal writes:

> What was Whitley Strieber's crime? What did he do that was so wrong, that merited so much shaming and condemnation on the part of the literary elite and the religious powers that be? And yet, why did his story resonate so powerfully with millions of readers and come to indelibly mark, perhaps even shape, a new emergent mythology well outside the reach of the cultural and religious gatekeepers?

My own investigations indicate that this "new emergent mythology" is being marked, and even shaped, by the same cultural and religious gatekeepers Kripal indicates, but does *not* identify, being that they are the ones he claims not to believe in: those behind Esalen, for example, or the Institute for Noetic Sciences, which for a time served as a front for the CIA's experiments in remote viewing (Picknett & Prince, 1999). Perhaps he has good reasons not to identify them, if he is working on the same team? As for Strieber, with several best-selling books and three major Hollywood productions under his belt, and a 2016 TV show from the producer of *The Walking Dead* (*Alien Hunter*), for Kripal to try to paint him as cultural reject is a bit of a reach.

Regarding the possibility of military intelligence's involvement in alien abductions, Strieber does mention the implant in his ear, which would seem to come as close to proof of an earthly technological source for his experiences as anything Kripal could reasonably ask for. Yet, through an act of illogic that borders on the super natural, Kripal uses the implant as an example of *how we exist in a nonmaterialistic universe in which nonphysical/imaginal/super natural phenomena can, through the medium of our minds, enter into concrete existence!* What was it Hitler said about lies? And what would Sherlock Holmes make of Kripal's ratiocinative methods—or the world of academia that presumably pays his bills? But as I say, the book is not aimed at academics; it's not really aimed at critically minded people either. It's aimed at believers who think of themselves as gnostics—those in the know—people who've been primed by decades of carefully shaped and directed pseudo-information about the "nonmaterial" nature of reality, from Blavatsky, Crowley, and Huxley to Leary, Kesey, and Hubbard, to Castaneda, McKenna and Strieber, and what the bleep do we know, on down. (It's curious to consider how many of these luminaries were also intelligence operatives.) Aren't *these* the gatekeepers Kripal claims he and Strieber are sneaking past with this apocalyptic book (which he also calls an intervention!)? What I see is just another brick in the pyramid of the Second Matrix.

On the other hand, maybe it's my own bias speaking. Perhaps Kripal's traumatic secret really *is* the head cornerstone the builders rejected. On page 228, commenting on Strieber's description of childhood trauma and his comparison to the Nazi concentration camps, he writes:

> Extraordinary human experiences often occur in the most destructive and dangerous of contexts. None of this is meant to romanticize the evils of Nazism, of war, or of the horrible sufferings of trauma and sexual trauma in their countless destructive and debilitating forms. It is simply to observe that human beings sometimes have profound spiritual experiences amid or after suffering and death, and that trauma sometimes opens up into transcendence. Is this really so difficult to understand?

That question tacked on at the end—or perhaps it's an appeal?—seems strangely out of place. Kripal hasn't recounted any resistance to his formulation, so he appears to be engaged with an obtuse imaginary reader—myself perhaps, or people like me who simply don't "get" his treasured notion of the dangerous sacred? Difficult to understand? On the contrary, as Kripal frames it here, it is almost childishly simple. But I think it is also untrue precisely *because* of that oversimplification. Speaking from my own experience now, the truth of trauma is *extremely* difficult to grasp, because we are all shaped by it to one degree or another, and because perceiving the forces that have determined our manner of perceiving—understanding the ways in which our understanding has been shaped, or impaired—is like trying to pin down the UFO: all but impossible.

What Kripal seems to leave out in his over-tidy little formula of the traumatic secret are the fundamental discoveries of trauma psychologists such as Donald Kalsched laid down in *The Inner World of Trauma*. What these discoveries indicate is that, as well as, and congruent with, allowing a person to access "transcendental" realms of being, trauma causes fragmentation of the psyche *as a defense against further trauma*. As a result of this fragmentation, a false self—a constructed identity or social alter—is created. It is this false self—in a case such as Strieber's— that has access to so-called transcendental experiences and will use them to maintain its own existence indefinitely, at whatever cost to the total being. So if Strieber can't show us how to escape this dissociated limbo realm in which the floating psychic fragment eternally exists, perhaps it is for the simple, if chilling, reason that he doesn't *want* to escape it? Instead, he (with Kripal's help) can show us how very interesting it is— and maybe we will come join him there ...

I think we are supposed to read of Strieber's "experiences that crackled with sensuality, that ripped away my ego as a hurricane rips away a city, leaving me in ruins" (p. 110), and desire them, covet them, for ourselves as the means, the proof, of getting closer to the true nature of reality and ourselves. Yet in the Eastern tradition–which Kripal has studied and written books about—the *siddhi*-holder is not closer to enlightenment but further from it. The nature of *siddhis* is to deceive the very elect. They are powerful to persuade both the dissociated self that gets to experience these cosmic states of consciousness and any onlookers unversed and naïve enough to be impressed by them that they are in the presence of "the dangerous sacred."

How is it that there is no room for psychology in Kripal's basis for a "new vision of the unexplained"? He cites modern cosmology, quantum physics, and evolutionary biology as the primary means for reaching a new understanding of these experiences. His seven-fold system of comparison, phenomenology, history, hermeneutics, erotics, saying away, and the traumatic secret likewise leaves psychology in the dust. It might seem strange, considering that psychology is the study of the soul; but then Strieber and Kripal's idea of the soul is surprisingly *materialistic*. Kripal calls it "a plasmalike energy that can superpower our imaginal capacities and so generate the movies of visionary experience" (p. 262). Ironically, this description (no doubt unintentionally) evokes

Freud's model of how early trauma causes the psyche to constantly play out scenes from our past at a subliminal level, in an unconscious effort to resolve the trauma. Morpheus called it "living in a dream world."

In his wind-up chapter, Kripal cites, and reverses, Arthur C. Clarke's famous axiom "Any technology sufficiently advanced would be indistinguishable to us from magic." Might it not be more pertinent at this juncture to say that any sufficiently advanced psychological strategy would be indistinguishable to us from magic—in fact, because it *is* magic? Psychism certainly seems to exist and to be a protective response to trauma; the problem with Strieber and Kripal's model is that they do not ask whether psychism is the means to heal the fragmentation that trauma causes. They don't consider that, like those damned *siddhis*, it may be merely a side effect, one that when pursued only perpetuates the fragmentation with multiplying, equally fractured myths of wholeness. From what little I have experienced in my own journey through the dissociative realms of psychism to something approaching ordinary (and extremely unglamorous) wholeness, *The Super Natural* is just the latest variation of broken mythmaking. It's a carefully designed *folie a deux* which serves—either naïvely or deliberately—to misrepresent Strieber as a prophet and shaman of a new paradigm, as someone to envy, admire, and emulate, someone who has had his ego ripped away and who has gained knowledge and experience of a higher, deeper, truer reality. But what if Strieber is no one to envy, admire, or emulate? What if he is rather the tragic victim of violent abuse, trauma, and fragmentation, complete with all the "marvels" that a fully-functioning MKULTRA subject gets to experience, and then peddle to the world as a glimpse into higher reality?

If the secret trauma omelet made from all those broken eggs is filled with eggshells, then, like Strieber's entire oeuvre, it is essentially inedible. You can swallow it—as I did for years, and as Kripal is working hard to get us, the readers, to—but it will never stay down. The mind may mistake it for candy; but the body knows poison when it tastes it.

*

I published this review at my blog on February 27, 2016. A little before I made a comment at a review of the book by *Texas Monthly*, mentioning MKULTRA and some of my objections to the book. To my surprise, Strieber replied, though not until after I'd published my review:

I don't get what seems to me an obsession with MK-ULTRA. I wonder if you believe yourself to have been affected by it somehow? I have no evidence that what happened to me as a child was related to MK-ULTRA. The only suggestions that children were involved in this program are sketchy at best. Also, it's not apparent to me that Jeff puts me in any sort of "holy box." And to claim that I was "involved" with the Process Church of Final Judgment strikes me as an intentional, and entirely inaccurate, mischaracterization of what I have written on this subject. (I refer here to the review of *Super Natural* that you have been posting in various places.) ... Across our history, we have formed thousands of different systems of belief around this presence. Most recently, we think of it as aliens or, in your case, as something generated by some sort of secret conspiracy. But what is it, really? My life is about asking this question. That is a "holy box" which I am proud to inhabit. (Strieber, 2016)

Strieber ignored my responses to him. Sometime later, Strieber's longtime associate Peter Levenda also took me to task for my review. Levenda interviewed Stripal on Strieber's *Dreamland*, during which he referred to their book as "luminous." Levenda and I had come to email blows over the subject of Aleister Crowley and organized ritual abuse, and Levenda posted an attack on me at Chris Knowles's Secret Sun blog. It ended with this:

To the point, Jasun is also a critic of Whitley Strieber and Jeffrey Kripal and has attacked their recent work, *The Super Natural*, on no logical grounds at all. One wonders if he even read the book before he posted his "review" on amazon. He has a visceral hatred of Strieber who has become a bit player in Jasun's fantasy of UFO abductions as screen memories for ... you guessed it ... child abuse. There is no journalistic integrity there, no attempt at making a case based on any kind of fact, just gut feelings and emotionality. Salem witchcraft hysteria and "spectral evidence." This is not "parapolitics". It's paranoia. They're not the same thing. (Levenda, 2016b, ellipses in the original)

As much as these snippy responses validate my arguments, I'd sooner end on a more positive note, a response on my blog to the above review from LilyPat, who spent several years participating in Strieber's online community:

> Each time I think my personal journey through exploitation and abuse is complete, I find myself forced to return to what I think of as my "Strieber Era" when I thought I'd found a cool way to process the things that had been done to me when I was younger. I fell into his website's forum like a warm bath. Thought I'd found My People. Which I had, actually–it may be a honeypot of sorts, because, as soon as I began posting regularly, The West Coast contingent of the people who monitor programmed survivors began to intrude on my life again after years of absence. As long as I could swallow the candy-coated pill that he promotes, the intrusions began to seem exciting in a way, the missing time mysterious and tantalizing, instead of gut level terrifying and sordid. Thrown out of the faux paradise of "trauma made me special" I wonder sometimes how much of his own BS The Guru himself actually believes? Or, perhaps, which alter configurations and their handlers are driving him now? That's the thing with us multiples–it's not either/or. More like which/when. I believe he's both the sly exploiter of the unconscionable misery he survived and the horribly damaged victim/handler of thousands of survivors. As I slowly awoke to the truth of many of my abductions–human perps behind the "aliens"–I bounced crazily between outrage and pity for him. But for Kripal right now I just feel the familiar disgust rising at the business-as-usual enabling of intel sector sociopathy by fawning, greedy academia. And when I read the book I have a feeling my disgust will turn to fury. At least I'll try to buy it used, so that not a penny of my money goes to support exploiters of people like me.

NOTES

Introduction: Conditioned to believe

1. "When the bank begins to send letters and the butcher to linger at the back gate, he sets to belabouring his brains after a story, for that is his readiest money-winner; and, behold! at once the little people begin to bestir themselves in the same quest, and labour all night long, and all night long set before him truncheons of tales upon their lighted theatre." (Stevenson, 2006, p. 155)

Chapter I

1. Including director of the Center for the Study of Social Policy at SRI International; former director of the Educational Policy Research Center at SRI; vice president of the International Foundation for Advanced Studies; regent of the University of California; emeritus professor of engineering-economic systems at Stanford University; senior social scientist at SRI International in California. On the board of the Institute of Noetic Sciences from 1985 until 1997. Affiliations: Advisory Council (1975), Planetary Citizens. Former trustee, Foundation for GAIA Patron, Wyse International. International advisory board member, Centre for Change.

International advisor, World Health Foundation for Development and Peace. Winner of the 1995 Green Award.

2. In a related note, the title of Jay Stevens's 1998 book about LSD, the CIA, and the Counterculture is *Storming Heaven: LSD and the American Dream*.

Chapter II

1. "[S]exual assaults on small children happen too often for them to have any aetiological [causal] importance." As Lloyd deMause writes, "Freud's opinion during his entire life was that children could be physically, sexually and emotionally abused without psychological effects. He did not think that having sex with children was traumatic. In fact, he sometimes said seduction was beneficial, as, for instance, when women seduce little boys ... Freud nowhere describes the rape of children as a betrayal of trust or as painful or as horrifying to the helpless child. He believed it presented problems only in the sense that it provided pleasurable but 'unconsummated excitation.' Sexual seductions, he said, 'produced no effect on the child' until a later assault awakened the memory by 'deferred action.' Freud even sided with the perpetrator." (DeMause, 1995)

2. "She looked marvelous. She belonged to me. It's wonderful, is death.' In later years he felt obliged to explain that he had not buried her sooner 'because the ground was icy.' He continued to keep her room exactly as it was, and would have her clothes dry-cleaned once a year." Jimmy Savile obituary, *The Daily Telegraph*, October 29, 2011.

3. "The turning point of the development is the subordination of all sexual partial-instincts to the primacy of the genitals, and thereby the subjection of sexuality to the function of reproduction. Originally it is a diffused sexual life, one which consists of independent activities of single partial instincts which strive towards organic gratification" (Freud, 1921, p. 284).

Chapter III

1. See the Adverse Childhood Experiences (ACE) study findings from 2003: "ACEs were not only unexpectedly common, but their effects were found to be cumulative ... Major risk factors for these causes of death—such as smoking, alcohol abuse, obesity, physical inactivity, use

of illicit drugs, promiscuity, and suicide attempts—were all increased by ACEs ... [P]roblems such as addiction frequently have their origins in the traumatic experiences of childhood and that the molecular structure of various chemicals or the physiologic effects of certain behaviors (e.g., overeating, sexual behaviors)—while ultimately leading to disease and disability, may be particularly effective in ameliorating their effects. [T]he fallout from various forms of child abuse and household dysfunction is monumental, costing Americans untold sums of money because of the health risks such as the use of street drugs, tobacco, alcohol, overeating and sexual promiscuity ... and a legacy of self-perpetuating child abuse" (*Ace Reporter*, 2003, pp. 1–2).

2. "Cursory examination of documents revealed detailed instructions for obtaining children for unspecified purposes. The instructions included the impregnation of female members of the community, purchasing children, trading and kidnapping .... There were pictures of nude children and adult Finders, as well as evidence of high-tech money transfers. There was a file called 'Pentagon Break-in,' and references to activities in Moscow, Hong Kong, China, Malaysia, North Vietnam, North Korea, Africa, London, Germany, 'Europe' and the Bahamas .... One such telex specifically ordered the purchase of two children in Hong Kong to be arranged through a contact in the Chinese Embassy there. Other documents identified interests in high-tech transfers to the United Kingdom, numerous properties under the control of the Finders, a keen interest in terrorism, explosives, and the evasion of law enforcement" (*Educate Yourself*, 2005).

3. My source for this information besides the above link is chapter 6, "Finders Keepers," of David McGowan's *Programmed to Kill*, iUniverse, 2004.

Chapter IV

1. Mac Tonnies, 2005. One commenter (W. M. Bear) responded: "If Whitley ever starts a 'Church of Ufology' I have to say, after reading this latest, that I'd be strongly tempted to sign on. He has definitely become a major Mental Traveler."

2. "In Margaret Mahler's theory of the mother/child relationship, the symbiotic relation is a very early phase of development that ... precedes the separation/individualization phase. The symbiotic relation is characterized by an omnipotent sense of the total enmeshing of mother and child,

who thus form a 'unity of two.' ... In her view, failure in the development of the processes of individuation makes the child regress to the stage of symbiotic relation with the mother, thus running the risk of shutting it off in a psychotic disorganization, a 'symbiotic psychosis' characterized by a delirious state of undifferentiation between the ego and the object. Leaving the symbiotic phase entails the risk of depression .... Donald Winnicott also comes close to the description of the mother-baby symbiosis with his concept of 'primary maternal preoccupation,' in which the state of maternal hypersensitivity leads the primitive mother-baby couple to live in a particular environment, a prolongation of the uterine environment in which communication between mother and child is immediate and not subject to the vagaries of separation" (Thomson, 2005).

3. "That is why Freud even stated that 'The ego is primarily a bodily one', and why he used the anatomical analogy of the homunculus of the sensorimotor cortex" (Tiemersma, 1989, p. 83).

Chapter V

1. In *Communion*, Strieber describes his feelings for the female being represented on the cover as similar to how he might feel about "my own anima" (p. 105). He wonders, "Can anything other than a part of oneself know one so well?" (p. 106). On an audio he aired in February 2005, "Unpublished Close Encounters, Part 2," he implies that his "guardian" resembled the Master of the Key!

2. Semantically, I would question Kalsched's use of the term "re-traumatization" here, as I think a *reexperiencing of trauma* is a more accurate description of the desired outcome, while re-traumatization is what must be avoided.

Chapter VI

1. Robert Monroe started the Monroe Institute in Virginia which has been central since 1977 in the training of military personnel in "remote viewing," including Joseph McMoneagle, "the first person enlisted into the top secret military program known as the STARGATE Project that began operation in October 1978." It is now run by Skip Atwater, who was the operations and training officer for Stargate for ten years, before taking over MI. "Robert Monroe and The Explorers." *The Gateway Experience* website.

2. As the Master of the Key says to Strieber, "That is why you and your world are called 'Dead Forever.'" *The Key*, p. 108. Curiously, when Strieber asks who calls us that, he is told "God." On the next page the Master tells him that "the victors" in an ancient cosmic battle call Earth the same. Strieber also reports hearing from another contactee that it is *Martians* who call us "dead forever." "The truth was that there had been a war between advanced civilizations on Earth and Mars many millennia ago. Earth had wrecked Mars, but Mars had gained control over our souls. They had condemned us to a perpetual cycle of rebirth and forgetting, of rising and falling civilizations, of always losing track with our past, going on and on forever. They called our world 'Dead Forever'" (Strieber, 2003b).

3. "On the committee were former NASA scientist and member of Reagan's National Commission on Space, Dr. David C. Webb, John Brandenburg, Vince DiPietro, who was one of the original imagers, writer Dan Drasin, astronaut and planetologist Dr. Brian O'Leary, imaging specialist Dr. Mark Carlotto, Randy Pozos, and Dr. Gliedman. Dr. O'Leary is the original Mars astronaut, and, if our Mars exploration program had not been abandoned in favor of military objectives, he would have been to the red planet and back by now. Dr. Carlotto, who was a contractor for an intelligence agency involved in reconnaissance, was in possession of imaging equipment so advanced and so secret that many of its controls had to be shielded from the eyes of committee members without proper clearances. The primary purpose of the equipment was to transform satellite pictures into clear and accurate images with high detail content .... Except for what he did on the face, Carlotto's work was routinely assumed to be completely accurate. My specific role was to finance the new analysis of the data and subsequent study that Drs. O'Leary and Carlotto undertook" (1996, p. 253).

4. "It should be remembered that my encounters started after I became interested in the face, not before" (1996, p. 254). Also: "In *Breakthrough*, Strieber mentions having been acquainted with Richard C. Hoagland, whom he met through Gliedman in 1984, three years before the publication of *Communion*. Hoagland, of course, was involved in a group known as the Mars Anomalies Research Society (MARS), and has written several books claiming that ancient civilizations once existed on the Moon, Mars, and on some of the moons of Jupiter and Saturn. Hoagland believes that evidence of these civilizations, such as the 'Face on Mars', have been kept secret by NASA and the US government.

Strieber donated money to Hoagland's group, and soon became a member. The aim of the group was to conduct further research on the 'Face on Mars' photograph—which they succeeded in doing. Among those involved in the group were Dr. David C. Webb, a former member of Reagan's National Commission on Space, astronaut and planetologist Dr. Brian O'Leary, physicist John Brandenburg, and an imagining specialist named Dr. Mark Carlotta, who, according to Strieber, was a contractor for an intelligence agency" (Proud, 2012).

5. "The Village Alien" first appeared as a review of *Communion* in *The Nation*, March 14, 1987.

6. "My fear would rise when they touched me. Their hands were soft, even soothing, but there were so many of them that it felt a little as if I were being passed along by rows of insects. It was very distressing. Soon I was in more intimate surroundings once again. There were clothes strewn about, and two of the stocky ones drew my legs apart. The next thing I knew I was being shown an enormous and extremely ugly object, gray and scaly, with a sort of network of wires on the end. It was at least a foot long, narrow and triangular in structure. They inserted this thing into my rectum. It seemed to swarm into me as if it had a life of its own. Apparently its purpose was to take samples, possibly of fecal matter, but at the time I had the impression that I was being raped, and for the first time I felt anger" (1987, p. 30).

7. "Rectal electroejaculation (REE), also called electroejaculation (EEJ) is a process designed to help retrieve viable sperm from a man who otherwise has difficulty producing it. Used since 1948, this infertility treatment helps to stimulate a man to release ejaculate. Rectal electroejaculation uses a probe attached to an electric current to induce erection and ejaculation. Once ejaculate is released, it is then collected and prepared for use in artificial insemination" (*Fertility Factor*, 2009).

8. "According to [Ratnoff's] theory, stigmatics (especially women) were individuals who, at some moment during their lifetime, had been subjected to physical trauma from a male figure with strong affective-emotional links (father, husband, etc.), such trauma (like being beaten) often resulting in internal hemorrhaging (subcutaneous and intramuscular hematomas)" ("An Unusual Case of Stigmatization" (1999), by Marco Margnelli, *Journal of Scientific Exploration*, *13*(3): 461–482).

Chapter VII

1. Strieber wrote an essay in Timothy Greenfield-Sanders's nude portrait book, *XXX: 30 Porn Star Photographs* and appears in interviews in *Thinking XXX*, a 2004 HBO documentary about the making of that book.

2. "Strieber earned a B.A. from the University of Texas in 1968 and a certificate from the London School of Economics and Political Science." From "About the Author" for Beech Tree Books' 1987 edition of *Communion*.

3. "During his examination of the Processeans, Bainbridge developed a great deal of affinity for the cultists' penchant for re-conceptualizing the roles of God and Satan in accordance with their Hegelian theology. This case of Biblical revisionism inspired Bainbridge and, since then, he has encouraged sociologists to take an active part in the re-conceptualizing of traditional religious concepts. It is his hope that such religious experimentation will eventually result in the creation of a 'Church of God Galactic.'" Bainbridge wrote about The Process, in "New Religions, Science, and Secularization, in Religion and the Social Order" (1993): "Members of The Process, founded mainly by students from an architecture school, referred to the creation of their cult as religious engineering, the conscious, systematic, skilled creation of a new religion." In "Social Construction from Within: Satan's Process" (1991), Bainbridge writes: "For Processeans, Satan was no crude beast but an intellectual principle by which God could be unfolded into several parts, accomplishing the repaganization of religion and the remystification of the world." (pp. 297–310 of *The Satanism Scare* edited by James T. Richardson, Joel Best, and David G. Bromley. New York: Aldine de Gruyter, 1991).

4. Thomas Disch, in "The Village Alien," also explores the similarities between the material in *Communion* and "Pain." The essay is a curious artifact in itself: The writer starts out sympathetic to Strieber, before he becomes curious about the story and contacts Dennis Etchison, the editor of *Cutting Edge*, to ask him about it and check the dates Strieber gave regarding its composition. Etchison evidently contacts Strieber, because Disch receives a call from him, convinced that Disch is doing a "vicious hatchet job" on *Communion* and telling him that it's "an awful, ugly, terrible thing to do." As Disch recounts it (in the essay), Strieber is deaf to his reassurances. At this point, Disch's essay changes tone dramatically

with these words: "What Whitley could not have imagined at that moment (and what I certainly was not going to tell him after so many minutes of vituperation) was that I was no longer a skeptic about UFOs, that, in fact, in the course of writing this essay I have been in contact with alien beings … " (Disch, 1987). The rest of the article is a spoof on Strieber, a pastiche of his ideas in a first person narrative. Apparently Disch was triggered by Strieber's excessive reaction and turned himself into exactly what Strieber accused him of being, whereupon the essay became just what Strieber feared it would be. It is like an eerie, acute demonstration of how the secret guards itself. Apparently "Pain" is intimately connected to Strieber's "secret," hence it was shelved for twenty-five years.

5. "Pain" is now all but unobtainable in print. My source was an audio file of Strieber's reading of it, available to subscribers at his website (Strieber, 2013). Compare the quoted passage to literature from The Process Church, supposedly channeled from "the Gods": "Every just tear and honest drop of sweat will be rewarded: that is the covenant. For every tear and drop of sweat set up treasure in a place where 'moth and dust' do not corrupt. Relish this time of penance. See and praise the justice and wisdom of GOD in His Universal Law. Know that the sufferings of our bodies, the anguish and torment of our minds, the imprisonment of our souls is our salvation" (De Grimston, 2016).

Chapter VIII

1. "[Freud] did not always abide by his dictum, that 'analytic experience has convinced us of the complete truth of the common assertion that the child is psychologically father of the man'" (ibid.).

2. The connection of senses in the Latin word seems to be via confusion of Greek *metra* "womb" (from meter "mother") and an identical but different Greek word *metra* meaning "register, lot." Evidently, Latin *matrix* was used to translate both, though it originally shared meaning with only one.

3. "One of them, I think it was the one I had identified earlier as the woman, said, 'What can we do to help you stop screaming?' This voice was remarkable. It was definitely aural, that is to say, I heard it rather than sensed it. It had a subtly electronic tone to it, the accent flat and startlingly Midwestern. My reply was unexpected. I heard myself say, 'You could let me smell you.' I was embarrassed; that is not a normal

request, and it bothered me. But it made a great deal of sense, as I have afterward realized" (1987, p. 28).

4. "I have reported that the being I have become familiar with looks like Ishtar. Maybe she is: She said she was old" (1987, p. 242).

Chapter IX

1. Fritz Peters, who maintained a relationship with Gurdjieff until his death in 1949, quoted Gurdjieff's words to him in *Gurdjieff Remembered*: "You not learn my work from talk and book—you learn in skin, and you cannot escape ... If you never go to meeting, never read book, you still cannot forget what I put inside you when you child ... I already in your blood—make your life miserable forever—but such misery can be good thing for your soul, so even when miserable you must thank your God for suffering I give you" (1971, pp. 25–26).

Chapter X

1. "In 1967, Robert DeGrimston and other Process members descended upon San Francisco's Haight Ashbury district during the Summer of Love, taking lease of a property located at 407 Cole Street. Meanwhile, Charlie Manson and his girls lived at 636 Cole Street, a mere two blocks away. One of the more controversial assertions I've heard suggesting contact between Manson and The Process comes courtesy of John Parker's *Polanski*, which claims that Manson was a regular visitor at The Process headquarters on Cole Street, 'reaching the fourth of the six levels of initiation, that of "prophet."' At the end of 1968, he was established as a leader of a group which he called 'Satan's Slaves.' During their Haight Ashbury period, Parker contends, The Process also attempted to form a union with Anton LaVey, high priest and founder of the San Francisco-based Church of Satan. However, these efforts were unsuccessful. Through his own calculated Satanic-related media events, LaVey attracted the attention of such Hollywood bigshots as Sammy Davis, Jr. and sexpot Jayne Mansfield. Through these Hollywood connections, LaVey made inroads into the movie industry and was on the payroll of both *The Mephisto Waltz* and Roman Polanski's *Rosemary's Baby*" (Gorightly, 2013).

2. "In *Helter Skelter*, Vincent Bugliosi recounted how Manson had been bragging about a relationship with The Process, until one day he was paid

a visit in jail by two brethren of the church, 'Father John' and 'Brother Matthew.' After their departure, Manson seems to have clammed up for good about The Process, and since then has made no further comments. Prior to the visit by these two mysterious Processean MIB's, Manson was asked by Bugliosi if he knew Robert DeGrimston, and his reply was to the effect, 'He and I are one and the same.' After their visit with Manson, the two Process members met with Bugliosi and assured him that Manson and DeGrimston had never met" (Gorightly, 2013).

3. An article in the British magazine *Fortean Times*, "A Saucerful of Secrets" wrote this about *Oz* magazine: "Oz was less keen on UFOs, editor Richard Neville being more interested in provoking the establishment through explorations of radical politics or sex than through modern myths. But when Neville took his eye off the ball for issue nine, leaving the work to poster artist Martin Sharp and designer John Goodchild, he was shocked at the result: 'To my embarrassment, it was devoted to flying saucers.' ... But were it not for the hippies' interest in flying saucers, nurtured by John Michell, it's doubtful that the continuing interest in such subjects would be part of our cultural landscape in the 21st century" (Roberts, 2007).

4. Litvinoff eventually fell foul of the Kray brothers and was the recipient of "the Chelsea grin": "the shocking sword punishment meted out to [him] whereby Ronnie pushed a sword into his mouth virtually splitting his face in two from ear to ear" (http://film.thedigitalfix.com/content/id/4856/the-krays-the-final-word.html). The Chelsea grin (worn by Heath Ledger's joker in *The Dark Knight*) is said to have originated in the Glasgow underworld, yet it was named after the district of London where Litvinoff lived, and where The Pheasantry is located. In another strange personal overlap, Jimmy Boyle, who was among the most notorious Glaswegian criminals of the 1960s, was my late brother's business associate and lover in the 1980s. My brother lived in Chelsea at the time he met Boyle (he later moved to Edinburgh and opened a charity workshop with him). Boyle reputedly worked with the Krays and was under their protection when he fled the law to London in 1966. He was arrested in 1967.

5. The Jersey child abuse investigation 2008 is an investigation into historic child abuse in Jersey that started in the spring of 2007. Formerly, a social worker, Simon Bellwood had made a complaint about a "Dickensian" system where children as young as eleven were routinely locked up for twenty-four hours or more in solitary confinement in a secure unit where he worked. The wider investigation into child abuse over several decades became public in November that year. "The investigation

involves the abuse of boys and girls aged between 11 and 15, since the 1960s [and] involves several government institutions and organisations in Jersey, with the Haute de la Garenne home and Jersey Sea Cadets the main focus of the inquiry. A police spokeswoman said more than 140 potential victims or witnesses had contacted a helpline since the investigations began" (*BBC News*, 2008).

6. "Thank you for your postcard. I very nearly went to Jersey myself, as I have never been there, and hear from so many people that it is quite delightful" (Barrett, 2009).

7. "According to Teale, the Krays had paid informers at every level inside the force. They'd meet detectives in a hotel in Jersey, where carrier bags of banknotes would change hands. Furthermore, 'If the Krays did a job with someone who then didn't give them the lion's share of the readies, a couple of weeks afterwards the former partner would find himself arrested'. There was even an Establishment connection and cover-up. Though the bisexual Conservative peer Robert Boothby had a relationship with Ronnie, attending gay orgies with him, the authorities didn't want Boothby investigated in case his affair with Harold Macmillan's wife came to light" (Lewis, 2012).

8. Associate clinical professor in psychology at Harvard Medical School at the Beth Israel-Deaconess Medical Center, senior author of *Memory, Trauma Treatment and the Law*.

9. "Spending 'over 60 hours interviewing and testing Mr. Sirhan,' reading everything on the case, including FBI files, interviewing witnesses, administering myriad psychological tests, questionnaires, scales etc., Dr. Brown, 'under penalty of perjury,' arrived at a startling conclusion; that 'Mr. Sirhan did not act under his own volition and knowledge or intention at the time of the assassination and is not responsible for actions coerced and/or carried out by others, and further that the system of mind control which was imposed upon him has also made it impossible for him to recall under hypnosis or consciously, many critical details of actions and events leading up to and at the time of the shooting in the pantry of the Ambassador hotel'" (Morales, 2012).

10. Ty Brown in his "Whitley Strieber and the Paradigm of Doom" series from 2007, noted that "... in July of 1968, the People's Front for the Liberation of Palestine hijacked an Israeli passenger plane in Rome, Italy and diverted it to Algiers. Many of the Israelis on board were held hostage for five weeks as a bargaining chip for the release of some Palestinian prisoners." Brown admits it's a stretch but still worth putting on the table. As is the fact that Sirhan Sirhan is Palestinian.

11. "He has traveled through many parts of the world, working in fields as diverse as intelligence and filmmaking" (from the author's bio notes for *The Hunger*, first edition).

12. Other references from *The Life & Teachings of Carlos Castaneda*, by William Patrick Patterson, Arete, 2008, pp. 115–117. In the first book in the Castaneda series, *The Teachings of Don Juan*, Castaneda's nagual tells him, "I killed a man with a single blow of my arm."

Chapter XII

1. Keith's Harman anecdote source is Lee & Shlain, 1992.

Chapter XIII

1. "I read *Sorcerer's Apprentice* with absolute fascination. Like millions of others, I had always wondered what was behind the Castaneda myth. My own life once gave me the choice of going down the guru path, a choice I rejected because, to me, it's morally wrong for one person to claim closer knowledge of deity than any other. It's always a lie, and the fearsome consequences of that lie in the life of the unfortunate creature who takes the guru path, as well as his followers, is exposed here with breathtaking candor. *Sorcerer's Apprentice* is an extremely powerful book and fair warning both to those who would presume to claim special favor in the spirit, as well as those drawn by their own needs to such people. Amy Wallace warns us with her honesty and her careful attention to crucial emotional details, that guru-worship is a disease. For those who have wondered whether or not Castaneda's various guides were real in some objective sense, reading this book will clear up the mysteries that need solving. But it is also a compassionate book, deeply so, because compassion inevitably flows from honesty of this high an order. It is a triumph of Amy Wallace's heart to have written this, and I thank her for the wisdom and enrichment of spirit that reading it has given me." (From publicity for the book.)

Chapter XIV

1. "J. Gordon Melton's monumental Encyclopedia of American Religions reports the histories and doctrines of thirteen flying saucer cults: Mark-Age, Brotherhood of the Seven Rays, Star Light Fellowship,

Universariun Foundation, Ministry of Universal Wisdom, White Star, Understanding Incorporated, The Aetherius Society, Solar Light Center, Unarius, Cosmic Star Temple, Cosmic Circle of Friendship, and Last Day Messengers. These groups mix together various supernatural notions from many other traditions, but a common thread is the idea that the Earth is but a small part of a vast inhabited galaxy. Some, like The Aetherius Society, contend that our planet is the pawn in an unseen interstellar war, and if such a cult became influential our society might invest in cosmic defenses which incidentally would develop the planets as bastions. Others feel we must perfect ourselves in order to qualify for membership in the Galactic Federation of enlightened species, and if such a cult became influential our society might invest much in the attempt to contact the galactic government. These flying saucer cults are all quite insignificant, but one like them could well rise to prominence in a future decade. We need several really aggressive, attractive space religions, meeting the emotional needs of different segments of our population, driving traditional religions and retrograde cults from the field" (Collins & Collins, 2006).

2. On page 59, Strieber says to the Master of the Key, "You mentioned monsters in the world of the dead." This is one of the things that didn't make it into the first edition, and it's doubly strange because despite Strieber's question, the phrase "monsters in the world of the dead" doesn't appear anywhere else in the text.

Chapter XVII

1. There are many different version of Wells's tract, only some of which refer to a world religion. This quote is culled from two different versions, *The Open Conspiracy: Blue Print for a World Revolution* (1928) and "What Are We to Do with Our Lives?" (1930). The final version appeared in 1933 under the original title.

2. On one occasion, Clarke said of pedophilia: "I think most of the damage comes from the fuss made by hysterical parents afterwards. If the kids don't mind, fair enough … There are two different definitions [of pedophilia], anyone who interferes with young boys who are not old enough to know their own minds and that's my definition. It varies for me" (Coleman, 2013).

3. "Sensational stories generated by human-piloted flights meant publicity for NASA, larger audiences for the media networks, and positive

projections of America's power in the Cold War world. Many of the themes that had structured both popular science fiction and popular western tales echoed in the Media age's presentation of the space race: danger, heroism, competition, suspense, and problems overcome through ingenuity. Yet the dramas that played out at Cape Canaveral and Houston, as exciting as fiction, had the added attraction of being 'real.' The spectacularity of the space race helped sustain the older print-pictorial media, pioneered a compelling early version of 'reality TV,' and proved attractive to filmmakers and space center visitors. And this fast-changing and competitive media environment, in turn, boosted the visual spectacularity of the Space Age" (Rosenberg, 2008).

4. "The enormous prestige that the Americans gained around the world from the successful program soon after frittered away as the gloomy national malaise of the '70s set in. The flood of socio-political problems during and after the Vietnam involvement turned the public away from 'large' space budgets. The conventional wisdom of the '70s claimed that, instead of billions of dollars for 'a few moon rocks,' the money should be allocated for social purposes. The one-sided space race had indeed ended" (William Brown and Herman Kahn, "Long-Term Prospects For Developments In Space," p. 126).

5. "[W]hen Senator Edward Kennedy first attached the 'Star Wars' label to Reagan's vision in comments made on the floor of the Senate the day after the speech, it was to accuse the President of 'misleading Red Scare tactics and reckless Star Wars schemes.' Kennedy's comments were meant to point out the fantastic nature of Reagan's missile defense program and the real dangers of his escalation of the arms race into space. Yet, despite these critical intentions, the 'Star Wars' label was so evocative and ambivalent that it was immediately embraced by some of Reagan's supporters, and henceforth the program, which did not acquire its official and rather uninspiring title Strategic Defense Initiative (SDI) until the spring of 1984, was universally known as 'Star Wars'" (Kramer, 1999).

Chapter XVIII

1. See Andrew Boyd's *Blasphemous Rumors: Is Satanic Ritual Abuse Fact or Fantasy?—An Investigation.*

REFERENCES

Albarelli, H. P., Jr. (2005). An utterly fascinating book. Review of Peter Levenda's *Sinister Forces*. Amazon, July 22. See http://konformist.com/archives/2005/07-2005/sinisterforces.txt

Bainbridge, W. S. (1991). Social construction from within: Satan's process. In: J. T. Richardson, J. Best, & D. G. Bromley (Eds.), *The Satanism Scare* (pp. 297–300). New York: Hawthorne/Aldine de Gruyter.

Bainbridge, W. S. (2005). Utopian communities. In: B. R. Taylor (Ed.), *Encyclopedia of Religion and Nature* (pp. 1686–1688). London: A & C Black.

Boyd, A. (1991). *Blasphemous Rumors: Is Satanic Ritual Abuse Fact or Fantasy?—An Investigation*. London: Collins Fount Paperbacks.

Brown, N. O. (1985). *Life Against Death: The Psychoanalytical Meaning of History*. Middletown, CT: Wesleyan University Press.

Campbell, J., & Moyers, B. (1988). *The Power of Myth*. New York: First Anchor, 1991.

Castaneda, C. (1981). *The Eagle's Gift*. New York: Washington Square Press.

Castaneda, C. (1984). *The Fire from Within*. New York: Washington Square Press.

Castaneda, C. (1993). *The Art of Dreaming*. New York: HarperCollins.

Chesterton, G. K. (1924). Column. *Illustrated London News*, April 19.

Conroy, E. (1990). *Report on Communion*. New York: Avon.

Dick, P. K. (1994). *The Selected Letters of Philip K. Dick: 1972–1973*. Novato, CA: Underwood-Miller.

Ferguson, M. (1980). *The Aquarian Conspiracy: Personal and Social Transformation in the 1980s*. Los Angeles, CA: J. P. Tarcher.

Freud, S. (1921). *A General Introduction to Psychoanalysis*. New York: Boni & Liveright.

Freud, S. (1961). *The Standard Edition of the Complete Psychological Works, Volume 21*. J. Strachey, A. Freud, & C. L. Rothgeb (Eds.). London: Hogarth.

Hansen, G. (2000). Margin note in *Saucer Smear, 47*(10), December 1.

Harman, W. (1974). The social implications of psychic research. In: J. White (Ed.), *Psychic Research: Challenge to Science* (pp. 640–669). New York: G. P. Putnam's Sons.

Jaynes, J. (2000). *The Origin of Consciousness in the Breakdown of the Bicameral Mind*. Boston, MA: Houghton Mifflin Harcourt.

Jung, C. G. (1933). *Modern Man in Search of a Soul*. W. S. Dell & C. F. Baynes (Trans.). New York: Harcourt Brace.

Jung, C. G. (2015). *Aspects of the Masculine*. Hove, UK: Routledge.

Kalsched, D. (1996). *The Inner World of Trauma: Archetypal Defenses of the Personal Spirit*. Hove, UK: Routledge.

Keith, J. (1997). *Mind Control, World Control*. Kempton, IL: Adventures Unlimited Press.

Kripal, J. (2015). The traumatic secret: Bataille and the comparative erotics of mystical literature. In: J. Biles, & K. Brintnall (Eds.), *Negative Ecstasies: Georges Bataille and the Study of Religion* (pp. 153–169). New York: Fordham.

Kurzweil, R. (2005). *The Singularity Is Near: When Humans Transcend Biology*. New York: Viking.

Kushner, D. (2009). When man and machine merge. *Rolling Stone, 1072*: 56–61.

Lee, M. A., & Shlain, B. (1992). *Acid Dreams: The Complete Social History of LSD: The CIA, the Sixties, and Beyond*. New York: Grove.

Levenda, P. (2006). *Sinister Forces, Book Three: The Manson Secret*. Walterville, OR: Trine Day.

Levenda, P. (2016a). *The Lovecraft Code*. Lake Worth, FL: Ibis Press.

Lewis, R. (2002). *Anthony Burgess*. London: Faber & Faber.

Markley, O. W., & Harman, W. (1982). *Changing Images of Man*. Oxford: Pergamon.

McGowan, D. (2004). *Programmed to Kill: The Politics of Serial Murder*. Lincoln, NE: iUniverse.

Miller, A. (2012). *Healing the Unimaginable: Treating Ritual Abuse and Mind Control*. London: Karnac.

Mitchell, E. (1974). From outer space to inner space. In: J. White (Ed.), *Psychic Research: Challenge to Science* (pp. 25–50). New York: G. P. Putnam's Sons.

Mogenson, G. (2005). *A Most Accursed Religion: When a Trauma Becomes God.* Thompson, CT: Spring.

Nietzsche, F. (2003). *Beyond Good and Evil.* London: Penguin.

Ollie, J. (2013). 78,000 people apply for one-way trip to Mars. *Time,* May 9.

Peters, F. (1971). *Gurdjieff Remembered.* New York: Samuel Weiser.

Picknett, L., & Prince, C. (1999). *The Stargate Conspiracy.* New York: Little, Brown.

Proud, L. (2009). *Dark Intrusions: An Investigation into the Paranormal Nature of Sleep Paralysis Experiences.* San Antonio, TX: Anomalist.

Ring, K. (1992). *The Omega Project: Near-Death Experiences, UFO Encounters, and Mind at Large.* New York: William Morrow.

Roberts, A. (2007). A saucerful of secrets. *Fortean Times,* October 19.

Sanders, E. (2002). *The Family.* Boston, MA: Da Capo Press.

"Simon" (1977). *The Necronomicon.* New York: Avon.

Stevenson, R. L. (2006). *Strange Case of Dr Jekyll and Mr Hyde and Other Tales.* Oxford: Oxford University Press.

Strieber, W. (1987). *Communion: A True Story.* Sag Harbor, NY: Beech Tree.

Strieber, W. (1987). *Communion: A True Story.* Later edition with new introduction. New York: HarperCollins, 2008.

Strieber, W. (1988). *Transformation.* New York: Avon.

Strieber, W. (1996). *Breakthrough: The Next Step.* New York: HarperCollins.

Strieber, W. (1997). *The Secret School.* New York: HarperCollins.

Strieber, W. (2011a). *Solving the Communion Enigma.* New York: Tarcher/Penguin.

Strieber, W. (2011b). *The Key: A True Encounter.* New York: Tarcher/Penguin.

Strieber, W., & Kripalk J. (2016). *The Super Natural: A New Vision of the Unexplained.* New York: Tarcher/Penguin.

Taylor, C. (2014). *How Star Wars Conquered the Universe.* New York: Basic Books.

Tiemersma, D. (1989). *Body Schema and Body Image: An Interdisciplinary and Philosophical Study.* Amsterdam, the Netherlands: Swets & Zeitlinger.

Wallace, A. (2003). *Sorcerer's Apprentice: My Life with Carlos Castaneda.* Berkeley, CA: Frog.

White, F. (1998). *The Overview Effect: Space Exploration and Human Evolution.* Reston, VA: AIAA.

Websites

All last accessed January 19, 2017.

Above Top Secret (2016). I'm Tom DeLonge, Co-Author of *Sekret Machines: Chasing Shadows,* Ask Me Anything. *Above Top Secret,* April 11, 2016. www.abovetopsecret.com/forum/thread1113008/pg1

Ace Reporter (2003). Origins and Essence of the Study. *Ace Reporter*, vol. 1, no. 1, April 2003. www.cenpaticointegratedcareaz.com/content/dam/ centene/cenpaticoaz/Documents/ACE-Scores-Article.pdf

Bainbridge, W. S. (2002). The Spaceflight Revolution Revisited. www. astrosociology.com/library/pdf/the%20spaceflight%20revolution%20 revisited.pdf

Bainbridge, W. S. (2009). Religion for a Galactic Civilization 2.0. *Institute for Ethics and Emerging Technologies,* August 20, 2009. www.ieet.org/index. php/IEET/more/bainbridge20090820/

Barrett, D. (2009). Letters shed new light on Kray twins scandal. *Daily Telegraph,* July 26, 2009. http://www.telegraph.co.uk/news/uknews/law-and-order/5907125/Letters-shed-new-light-on-Kray-twins-scandal. html

BBC Home (2003). 1968: Krays held on suspicion of murder. *BBC Home,* October 2003. http://news.bbc.co.uk/onthisday/hi/dates/stories/ may/8/newsid_2518000/2518695.stm

BBC News (2008). Child's body found at care home. *BBC News,* February 23, 2008. http://news.bbc.co.uk/2/hi/europe/jersey/7260625.stm

BelleNews (2013). Marianne Faithfull and Mick Jagger story. *BelleNews,* January 5, 2013. www.bellenews.com/2013/01/05/entertainment/ marianne-faithfull-and-mick-jagger-story/#ixzz2QN393a2a

Blackmore, L., & Curtis, K. (1988). "Communion with Whitley Strieber." *Terror Australis* No. 2: www.scribd.com/doc/23213635/Communion-With-Whitley-Strieber

Boyle, A. (2014). Mars One Puts Out the Call for Red Planet Experiments. *NBC News,* June 30, 2014. http://www.nbcnews.com/science/space/ mars-one-puts-out-call-red-planet-experiments-ads-n143956

Boyle, A. (2016). Mars One says its first crew won't land on Red Planet until 2032—but will they ever? *Geek Wire,* December 7, 2016. http://www. geekwire.com/2016/mars-one-says-first-crew-wont-land-red-planet-2032-will-ever/

Brainsturbator (2007). Scientists on Acid: The Story Behind "Changing Images of Man." http://www.brainsturbator.com/, July 12, 2007. http://www.brainsturbator.com/posts/187/scientists-on-acid-the-story-behind-changing-images-of-man

Brown, T. (2007). 10,000 Heroes—SRI and the Manufacturing of the New Age. March 19, 2007. https://auticulture.files.wordpress. com/2017/01/10000-heroes-sri-new-age.pdf

Brown, W. M., & Kahn, H. (1977). Long-Term Prospects For Developments In Space (A Scenario Approach). Hudson Institute (for NASA), October 30 1977. https://ntrs.nasa.gov/archive/nasa/casi.ntrs.nasa. gov/19780004167.pdf

Cannon, M. (1990). *The Controllers: A New Hypothesis of Alien Abduction.* *Constitution Society.* http://www.constitution.org/abus/controll.htm

Carberry, C., & Zucker, R. (2016). Is there a business case for Mars? *The Space Review*, October 10, 2016. http://www.thespacereview.com/article/3080/1

Coleman, L. (2013). Prince Charles, Arthur C. Clarke and the paedophile connection. *The Coleman Experience*, April 2013. https://thecolemanexperience.wordpress.com/2013/04/27/prince-charles-arthur-c-clarke-and-the-paedophile-connection/

Collins, P., & Collins, P. D. (2006). MJ-12: The Technocratic Thread. *Conspiracy Archive: Secret Societies, Cryptocracy and Deep Politics*, June 2014. www.conspiracyarchive.com/Commentary/MJ-12_Technocratic.htm

CriticaLink (1998). Lacan: The Mirror Stage—Overview. *CriticaLink.* Department of English, University of Hawaii, Manoa. www.english.hawaii.edu/criticalink/lacan/index.html

Daily Telegraph (2011). Jimmy Savile Obit. *Daily Telegraph*, October 29, 2011. www.telegraph.co.uk/news/obituaries/8857428/Sir-Jimmy-Savile.html

David, L. (2001). Uploading Life: Send Your Personality to Space. *Accelerating Intelligence*, June 28, 2001. www.kurzweilai.net/uploading-life-send-your-personality-to-space

De Grimston, R. (2016). Process Church Documents: The Holy Writ of The Process Church of the Final Judgment by Robert De Grimston. http://fliphtml5.com/gfou/otdg/basic/101-150

DeMause, L. (1994). Why Cults Terrorize and Kill Children. *Journal of Psychohistory*, 21(4), 1994. https://ritualabuse.us/ritualabuse/articles/why-cults-terrorize-and-kill-children-lloyd-demause-the-journal-of-psychohistory/

DeMause, L. (1995). The Social Alter (transcript of speech). http://primal-page.com/psyalter.htm

Disch, T. M. (1987). "The Village Alien." *The Nation*, March 14, 1987. www.press.umich.edu/pdf/9780472068968-27.pdf#page=1&zoom=auto,0,674

Educate Yourself (2005). The Story of the CIA's "Finders" Abduction Operation: The CIA Traffics in Drugs, Child Ritual Sexual Abuse, and Global Murder. *Educate Yourself*, July 2005. www.educate-yourself.org/cn/ciadrugsabusemurder.shtml

Esther, S. (2010). The Process Church and Dominatrix Founder–Mary Ann Maclean. www.powersexxxx.com/gpage4.html

Fahey, T. B. (1991). The Original Captain Trips. (Originally published by *High Times*, November 1991.) http://www.fargonebooks.com/high.html

Feral House (2013). The Process Church Timeline. http://feralhouse.com/wp/wp-content/uploads/2010/10/LSFD_timeline.pdf

Fertility Factor (2009). Rectal Electroejaculation. *Fertility Factor*, 2009. www.fertilityfactor.com/infertility_ree.html

Flatley, J. L. (2013). The cult of Cthulhu: real prayer for a fake tentacle: The strange story behind the real-life followers of H. P. Lovecraft's "Necronomicon." *The Verge*, November 12, 2013. www.theverge.com/2013/11/12/4849860/the-cult-of-cthulhu-real-prayer-for-a-fake-tentacle

Gilmore, P. H. (2013). NECRONOMICON: Some Facts about a Fiction. *Church of Satan*, December 2013. www.churchofsatan.com/necronomicon-facts-about-fiction.php

Gorightly, A. (2013). The Process Church of the Final Judgment and the Manson Family: The Robert F. Kennedy Connection. *Paranoia*, January 2013. www.paranoiamagazine.com/2013/01/the-process-church-of-the-final-judgment-and-the-manson-family-2/

Gray, D., & Watt, P. (2013). Giving Victims a Voice: A joint MPS and NSPCC report into allegations of sexual abuse made against Jimmy Savile under Operation Yewtree. www.nspcc.org.uk/globalassets/documents/research-reports/yewtree-report-giving-victims-voice-jimmy-savile.pdf

Hastings, C. (2006). Revealed: how the BBC used MI5 to vet thousands of staff. *Daily Telegraph*, July 2, 2006. www.telegraph.co.uk/news/uknews/1522875/Revealed-how-the-BBC-used-MI5-to-vet-thousands-of-staff.html

Keep, E. (2015). Mars One Finalist Explains Exactly How It's Ripping Off Supporters. *Medium*, March 16, 2015. https://medium.com/matter/mars-one-insider-quits-dangerously-flawed-project-2dfef95217d3#.arvsvvh10

Kramer, P. (1999). Ronald Reagan and *Star Wars*. *History Today, 49*(3), March 1999. www.historytoday.com/peter-kramer/ronald-reagan-and-star-wars#sthash.2f1ZnOfK.dpuf

Laycock, J. (2012). Carnal Knowledge: The Epistemology of Sexual Trauma in Witches' Sabbaths, Satanic Ritual Abuse, and Alien Abduction Narratives. *Preternature: Critical and Historical Studies on the Preternatural, 1*(1), 2012, pp. 100–129. Penn State University Press. https://auticulture.files.wordpress.com/2017/01/1-1-laycock.pdf

Levenda, P. (2016b). Election 2016: You May Not Be Interested in Parapolitics. *Secret Sun*. Comments section. November 7, 2016. http://secretsun.blogspot.ca/2016/11/election-2016-you-may-not-be-interested.html?showComment=1478537668416#c867526432209322943

Lewis, R. (2012). "We've just murdered your dad–but cheer up, here's a puppy." *MailOnline*, June 7, 2012. http://www.dailymail.co.uk/home/books/article-2155989/Weve-just-murdered-dad--cheer-heres-puppy-BRINGING-DOWN-THE-KRAYS-BY-BOBBY-TEALE.html#ixzz2PcdPzeZg

Mac Tonnies (2005). *Post-Human Blues*, July 29, 2005. http://posthuman-blues.blogspot.ca/2005/07/whitley-strieber-has-written-his-most.html

Mars-One (2015). 705 potential Mars settlers remain in Mars One's astro-naut selection process. *Mars-One*. May 5, 2014. http://www.mars-one.com/news/press-releases/705-potential-mars-settlers-remain-in-mars-ones-astronaut-selection-process

Martian Colonist (2015). How Were Mars One Candidates Selected? *YouTube*, March 20, 2015. https://www.youtube.com/watch?v=4pVBUKQ2sT0

Mindless Ones (2011). The League of Extraordinary Gentlemen Century 1969: the annocommentations part II. *Mindless Ones*, July 28, 2011. http://mindlessones.com/2011/07/28/the-league-of-extraordinary-gentlemen-century-1969-the-annocommentations-part-ii/

Mitchell, E. (2009). The Overview Effect and the future: About the Author. *The Overview Institute*, June 24, 2009. http://www.overviewinstitute.org/blog/item/the-overview-effect-and-the-future

Mitchell, E. (2014). The Intersection of Science and Religion. *Great Mystery*, 2014. http://greatmystery.org/Faculty/EdgarMitchell.html

Morales, F. (2012). The Assassination of RFK: A Time for Justice! *Global Research*, June 16, 2012. http://www.globalresearch.ca/the-assassination-of-rfk-a-time-for-justice/31450

NBC (1977). The Children and the CIA—partial report. Section Three: The Children and the CIA. Kevin Crosby, *YouTube*. www.youtube.com/watch?v=QbaKn6qIOOM

Ottawa Citizen (1998). UFOs: It's a Cover-Up. *Ottawa Citizen*, October 11, 1998. http://www.ufoupdateslist.com/1998/oct/m12-010.shtml

Overview Institute, The (2012). Declaration of Vision and Principles. *The Overview Institute*, 2012. http://www.overviewinstitute.org/about-us/declaration-of-vision-and-principles

Parkin, D. (2002). YTV's boardroom appointments to strengthen regional role. *Yorkshire Post*, October 14, 2002. www.yorkshirepost.co.uk/news/ytv-s-boardroom-appointments-to-strengthen-regional-role-1-2437966

Popham, P. (1998). The mysterious Sri Lankan world of Arthur C. Clarke. *The Independent*, February 2, 1998. www.independent.co.uk/news/the-mysterious-sri-lankan-world-of-arthur-c-clarke-1142640.html

Proud, L. (2012). Aliens, Predictions & the Secret School: Decoding the Work of Whitley Strieber. *New Dawn*. www.newdawnmagazine.com/articles/aliens-predictions-the-secret-school-decoding-the-work-of-whitley-strieber

Rosenberg, E. S. (2008). Far Out: the Space Age in American Culture. In: Dick, S. J. (Ed.), *Remembering the Space Age*. NASA, Office of External Relations, History Division. www.nss.org/resources/library/spacepolicy/Remembering_the_Space_Age.pdf

Sky News (2013). Jimmy Savile: Ex-Policeman "Acted for Star." *Sky News*, February 20, 2013. http://news.sky.com/story/jimmy-savile-ex-policeman-acted-for-star-10454018

Spotlight on Abuse (2002). Tim Tate on the making of the Franklin Scandal documentary Conspiracy of Silence. *Spotlight on Abuse*, May 2, 2002. spotlightonabuse.wordpress.com/2013/05/02/tim-tate-on-the-making-of-the-franklin-scandal-documentary-conspiracy-of-silence/

Strieber, W. (2000). More Childhood Memories and Another Encounter. *Unknown Country*, March 18, 2000. www.unknowncountry.com/journal/more-childhood-memories-and-another-encounter

Strieber, W. (2001). Christmas Joy: Mankind is Awakening. *Unknown Country*, December 14 2001. www.unknowncountry.com/journal/christmas-joy-mankind-awakening

Strieber, W. (2003a). The Boy in the Box. *Unknown Country*, March 14, 2003. www.unknowncountry.com/journal/boy-box

Strieber, W. (2003b). Dancing in the Mirrors. *Unknown Country*, September 21, 2003. www.unknowncountry.com/journal/dancing-mirrors#ixzz2OKzs76Z6

Strieber, W. (2004a). Whitley Strieber's 1986 Hypnosis Sessions 1 and 2. *Unknown Country*, January 1, 2004. www.unknowncountry.com/whitleysroom/whitley-striebers-1986-hypnosis-sessions

Strieber, W. (2004b). CIA mind control with Donald Bain. *Unknown Country*, June 5, 2005. www.unknowncountry.com/dreamland/cia-mind-control-donald-bain

Strieber, W. (2006b). Unpublished Close Encounters: Part 2. *Unknown Country*, February 25, 2006 www.unknowncountry.com/whitleysroom/unpublished-close-encounters-part-2

Strieber, W. (2007a). *Unknown Country* Message Board, February 10, 2007. www.unknowncountry.com/board/messages/58/24904.html?1171148896

Strieber, W. (2007b). The Mystery of the Drones. *Unknown Country*, June 8, 2007. www.unknowncountry.com/journal/mystery-drones#ixzz2O3DzdpFp

Strieber, W. (2010). Intelligence Community Child Abuse Pt. 1, *Unknown Country*, January 9, 2010. www.unknowncountry.com/dreamland/intelligence-community-child-abuse-pt-1

Strieber, W. (2013). Pain, a Short Story by Whitley Strieber. *Unknown Country*, March 11, 2013. www.unknowncountry.com/whitleysroom/pain-short-story-whitley-strieber

Strieber, W. (2016). Unidentified Scholarly Subject. *Texas Monthly*, February 2016. Comments section. www.texasmonthly.com/the-culture/unidentified-scholarly-subject/#comment-2493898946

The Gateway Experience (2011). Robert Monroe and The Explorers. *The Gateway Experience*. www.thegatewayexperience.com/explorers-of-hemi-sync/

Thomson, G. (2005). Symbiosis/Symbiotic Relation. *International Dictionary of Psychoanalysis*. www.encyclopedia.com/psychology/dictionaries-thesauruses-pictures-and-press-releases/symbiosissymbiotic-relation

Ulam, S. (1958). Tribute to John von Neumann. *Bulletin of the American Mathematical Society*, 64(3). https://docs.google.com/file/d/0B-5-JeCa2Z7hbWcxTGsyU09HSTg/edit?pli=1

Vice (2016). Hillary Clinton's Campaign Manager Says "Legitimate Questions" about UFOs Should Be Answered. *Vice*, March 4, 2016. www.vice.com/en_us/article/hillary-clintons-campaign-manager-wants-to-answer-peoples-legitimate-questions-about-ufos-vgtrn

Wall, M. (2015). Mars One Colony Project Delays Manned Red Planet Mission to 2026. *SPACE.com*, March 21, 2015. https://www.yahoo.com/news/mars-one-colony-project-delays-manned-red-planet-153657202.html?ref=gs

Wells, J. (2005). Before the apex stone is fitted. *Rigorous Intuition*, October 9, 2005. http://rigorousintuition.blogspot.ca/2005/10/before-apex-stone-is-fitted.html

Wikileaks (2016a). Apollo Astronaut, Dr. Edgar Mitchell's, Request for Meeting to discuss Disclosure. *Wikileaks*. https://wikileaks.org/podesta-emails/emailid/41124

Wikileaks (2016b). Re: Apollo Astronaut, Dr. Edgar Mitchell's, Request for Meeting to discuss Disclosure. *Wikileaks*. https://wikileaks.org/podesta-emails/emailid/15052

Wikileaks (2016c). email for John Podesta (Eryn) from Edgar Mitchell re Skype. *Wikileaks*. https://wikileaks.org/podesta-emails/emailid/44097

Wikileaks (2016d). email for John Podesta c/o Eryn re Space Treaty (attached). *Wikileaks*. https://wikileaks.org/podesta-emails/emailid/1802

Wikileaks (2016e). Fwd: Important. *Wikileaks*. https://wikileaks.org/podesta-emails/emailid/4804

Wikileaks (2016f). General McCasland. *Wikileaks*. https://wikileaks.org/podesta-emails/emailid/3099

Wikileaks (2016g). Re: Interesting news. *Wikileaks*. https://wikileaks.org/podesta-emails/emailid/50448

Wikileaks (2016h). Re: A good read ... *Wikileaks*. https://wikileaks.org/podesta-emails/emailid/51537

Wikileaks (2016i). VICE News. *Wikileaks*. https://wikileaks.org/podesta-emails/emailid/57684

INDEX

in infant-to-mother relationship, 88
interference of, 191–194
machinery of God, 173
in Mars Anomalies Research
Society, 67–68
memories of abuse, 4–5
in metaphysical dread of
damnation, 178
mind-as-weapon, 228
missing time, 81
motivator, 186
pain, 73
personal recapitulation series, 236
philosophy out of transcendental
power of pain, 78
Pomegranates as symbol, 81
radiant being, a, 178–179
1986 recording of hypnosis
session, 81
rectal probe, 59, 68–69
reenactment of trauma, 34
reenactments of trauma, 19
out of secret school, 54
Secret School, The, 53–55, 60
shattering the mirror of
expectation, 29, 35
short story "Pain", 55
Solving the Communion
Enigma, 36
somatic symptoms, 33
Super Natural, The, 63
technological support provider, 186
Transformation, 53, 55, 58, 80, 83, 91,
101, 109, 119
UFOs as "prison guards", 173
Unknown Country, 5, 36, 79, 135,
154, 235
visitors preparing human for
elsewhere, 157
Wolfen, 89
wounded soul, 77
as writer, 62
writings turned into basis for new
religion, 173
sublimation, 16
suicide, 12, 31–32, 108, 158, 261

Super Natural, The, 63, 82, 247
experiences become "stories", 251
inconsistencies, 249–250
Kripal's "traumatic secret", 250
path between belief and dismissal,
248
at regular intervals to turn
materialist paradigm upside
down, 248
rejection for prophetic voice, 249
self-protective strategies, 251
surrendering autonomy to another, 91
symbiotic psychosis, 47
symbol for the new mythology, 149

Taylor, C., 219–220
technology interfering with sexual
organs, 69
Tiemersma, D., 47, 262
transcendental experiences, 255
transcendental man as alien
intelligence, 184
Transformation, 53, 55, 58, 80, 83,
91, 101, 109, 119
Transhumanism, 167, 176 *see also*:
Bainbridge; galactic religion;
machine intelligence;
old seers
being between lives, 178
capitalism, 170
Earth as death trap, 173
escape before catastrophe and
Christian Rapture, 172, 174
to fix human error, 188
healing of the original split, 171
ideas embed in consciousness
actuate as reality, 168
need of space travel, 174
New Freemasonry, 169–170
religious engineering, 167, 171, 177
scientistic cults, 170
second attention, the, 175
sect-cult distinction, 169
soul's descent into body, 173
souls made into intelligent
machines, 173, 176

ABOUT THE AUTHOR

Jasun Horsley is the author of several books, including *Paper Tiger* and *Dark Oasis*. *Prisoner of Infinity* is the second in a loose "cultural engineering" trilogy, with *Seen and Not Seen* (2015) and *The Vice of Kings*, forthcoming from Aeon Books. He hosts a regular podcast, *The Liminalist*, at his website, Auticulture.